0066350

DATE DUE	
JUN. 3 O 1993	

BRODART.   Cat. No. 23-221

ENGLISH COUNTRY FURNITURE

ENGLISH COUNTRY FURNITURE

THE NATIONAL & REGIONAL VERNACULAR 1500-1900

DAVID KNELL

CROSS RIVER PRESS
A division of Abbeville Press, Inc.
NEW YORK

First published in the United States of America in 1992
by Cross River Press, a division of Abbeville Press, Inc.,
488 Madison Avenue, NY 10022.

First published in Great Britain in 1992 by
Random Century House, 20 Vauxhall Bridge Road, London, England.

ISBN 1-55859-399-3

CONTENTS

ACKNOWLEDGEMENTS

M Y INTEREST IN OLD FURNITURE DEVELOPED WHILE growing up in Canada and it was naturally influenced by the largely vernacular traditions of that country. Thus, the significance and subtle charms of everyday furniture were instilled in me at an early stage. It has always seemed strange to me that the immensely rich vernacular heritage of England, particularly that postdating 1700, has received so little serious attention over the years; the subject appeared to lack even a recent general introduction.

The opportunity to fill that gap resulted in a project which has been at the same time both challenging and satisfying. The history of English vernacular furniture over more than four centuries is a vast territory that still remains largely uncharted or, where previously explored, very often an old minefield of inaccuracies and uncorroborated assumptions. This present investigation is itself unlikely to be entirely free of similar faults and it is in the nature of a brief general survey to be prone to sweeping generalisations. But where it has negotiated the terrain successfully, much of the credit must go to travellers other than myself and it is with pleasure that I am able to record my gratitude here. In mentioning their names, however, I wish to avoid any danger of implying that they necessarily either share the views or concur with the attributions expressed in this book; the responsibility for errors is certainly mine alone.

My initial thanks are to Jacqueline Fearn, who suggested that I write a book in the first place, and to my fellow members of the Regional Furniture Society, a scholarly organisation which is annually establishing new frontiers and to whose informative publications I owe a large debt. In addition to those and other articles or catalogues, the student of English vernacular furniture is fortunate in having been recently provided with invaluable studies in book form: notably, Victor Chinnery's magnificent *Oak Furniture. The British Tradition* and, within the last two years, Dr Bernard (Bill) Cotton's definitive *The English Regional Chair* and Christopher Gilbert's *English Vernacular Furniture 1750–1900*, a mine of literary and pictorial evidence. I warmly appreciate the generous advice and/or loan of photographs kindly supplied by James Ayres, Victor Chinnery, Dr Bill and Gerry Cotton, Christopher Gilbert, Nancy Goyne Evans, Mary Greensted, Malcolm Lawson-Paul and Gabriel Olive. Without their various contributions this book would have been much the poorer.

Inevitably, the material needed to illustrate this project adequately must come from a large variety of sources — museums, libraries, galleries, auction houses, antique dealers and private individuals. I never ceased to be amazed and moved by the enthusiastic and generous response to my enquiries from all of them. It is a particular pleasure to record my gratitude to Dr Margaret Rule and the team at The Mary Rose Trust for going far out of their way to help even when under enormous pressure from other commitments; to Nicholas Day at Haddon Hall; to Chloë Bennett at the Ipswich Museum; to John Creasey at the Museum of English Rural Life; to Elizabeth Schmidt at Agecroft Hall; to Jon Roberts at the Weald & Downland Open Air Museum; to Jessica Rutherford at the Royal Pavilion, Brighton; to R.H. Laver of Brasenose College, Oxford; to Patrick Baird of the Birmingham Reference Library; and to Sarah Medlam at the Bowes Museum.

A large proportion of the photographs used are the result of a magnificent response from Sotheby's of London, Sussex and Chester; I am especially indebted to Lindsay Monkhouse and Samantha Georgeson. I am also extremely grateful for the kind contributions from Christie's, Bonham's, Phillips and many other auction houses. The help provided so unselfishly by dealers and private individuals was vital to success in this project and, while I apologise for not having space to name them all here, I must express my particular thanks to Paul Hopwell, Robert Young, Michael Wakelin, Helen Linfield, Derek Green, P.J.W. Keil, Tobias Jellinek, Michael Golding, Oswald Simpson, Paul Cater, David Seligmann, Colin Springett, Robert Pilbeam, Rosemary Stewart-Jones, John Humphry, Derek Thrower, Vicki Emery, Mark Chapman, Rod Wilson, Clare Wilson, Suzie Ryder, Elizabeth Hand and Doris Rayment. I very much appreciate the loan of a valuable photograph by Mrs E. Barnsley.

I am deeply grateful to Andrew Mardell, who took a large number of the photographs, often at short notice and under very inconvenient circumstances, and to my editors, Euan Cameron and Lucilla Watson, for their invaluable criticism and patience.

Finally, my heartfelt thanks are due to my mother, who first nurtured my developing passion for history, and to my wife, Andrea, for her unflagging enthusiasm and encouragement; without her support this project would not have been possible.

David Knell

PREFACE

ESPITE THE TITLE 'ENGLISH COUNTRY FURNITURE', many of the pieces described and illustrated in this book were neither made in the countryside nor intended primarily for rural use. Their inclusion here is not a mistake; the error, rather, lies in the misleading umbrella term that is popularly used to describe the vast majority of everyday furniture used by ordinary people in the past, regardless of whether it was actually of rural or urban origin.

The better and more expensive classes of furniture have for long been designated as 'fine' or 'town' furniture, anything remotely inferior being dismissed as 'country'. It may be assumed that the reasoning behind the latter term is either that 'country' is employed as a synonym for 'provincial' – on the basis that inferior pieces could not possibly have been made in London (quite erroneous, of course, since not every Londoner lived in luxury) – or that 'country' is used merely in a derogatory sense. At any rate, to take the description literally and assume that urban furniture-makers produced only fine furniture for the rich while all other furniture, including that made for the large majority of townsfolk (who were certainly not rich), was produced exclusively in small village workshops out in the countryside is patently ludicrous.

During the heyday of the urban trade guilds and companies, rigid standards of workmanship were normally strictly enforced within their domain. Town furniture was therefore likely to be superior to those pieces made in rural areas outside the scope of such regulation. Nevertheless, not all towns had such organisations, while in others they were weak, and even in those towns which had strong companies, they were professional bodies and had little influence over the standards of 'homemade' furniture which was not ostensibly produced for retail purposes. It must be appreciated too that a company's primary concern was with workmanship; within that criterion a craftsman was free to make his furniture opulent, and exclusive to the rich, or to a minimum standard to bring it within the reach of the less well-off. It is evident that, at least by the late 17th century, urban furniture was made in different grades, its quality governed by the market at which it was aimed.

By 1700, the power even of the London companies had begun to decline; certainly, a great deal of somewhat inferior furniture must have been produced in or around the capital during the 18th and 19th centuries (see **Figure 88**). Very often, the most readily apparent distinction between the lower grades of town furniture and the better class of country-made pieces during that time would have lain more in the subtle quality of the timber than that of the workmanship; urban makers were more likely to have a wider range of imported and choice native timbers at their disposal.

There is such a thing as real country furniture made by rural craftsmen, of course. Before the 19th century over three quarters of the English population lived in rural areas; much of the furniture used in those areas was made locally and could therefore be correctly described as 'country'. Even after 1800 the manufacture of some items, such as Windsor chairs, although catering largely for an urban market, was for convenience often deliberately based in woodland locations. There were also distinctive types of furniture which were far more likely to be found in rural areas than in a metropolis. Nevertheless, in the absence of proven provenance, it is virtually impossible to distinguish many of those pieces made in villages from those pieces of the same class made in towns and cities. Urban furniture produced for the lower market was often every bit as crude, sometimes equally conservative and, in small towns at least, just as likely to be fashioned from local native timber. In view of that, any attempt to discriminate fastidiously between essentially identical items of furniture purely on the basis of whether their origin was strictly urban or rural would be pedantic for our purposes and, ultimately, beside the point.

The choice of a term which embraces the everyday furniture of ordinary people, as opposed to expensive 'fine' articles, has obviously presented somewhat of a problem over recent years. In the 18th century, such pieces were logically known as 'common' furniture. This apt, though rather uncompromising, term found little favour in the present century, however, and various substitutes were employed. Terms such as 'cottage', 'farmhouse' or 'provincial' are not really satisfactory as overall generic labels since, like 'country', they all imply too restricted a use or too narrow a geographical distribution. As the class of furniture that we are seeking to name was found in almost every kind of building, and equally in rural and urban environments, including London, the only accurate term will be one that concentrates on its unifying characteristics. The label most favoured in academic circles nowadays is 'vernacular' – an adjective borrowed from architecture and implying a relatively unsophisticated product of ordinary people, normally of a regionally traditional design frequently made of native materials, and usually with connotations of general, utilitarian use. In its widest sense, 'vernacular furniture' is the furniture 'of the people', as opposed to that of a privileged few.

'Vernacular' is certainly accurate but it has yet to achieve popular usage – which is why it has been relegated to the subtitle. I have reluctantly succumbed to the description most readily understood by most people and used 'country furniture' as the main title. Perhaps I can justify it on the grounds that it is, after all, the *vernacular* expression for *vernacular* furniture. I offer my apologies to those academically inclined people who shudder at its inaccuracy and can only hope, with them, that in time 'vernacular' will be more widely recognised. (To avoid monotonous repetition of the word 'vernacular', I have also occasionally employed such adjectives as 'country' or 'cottage' in the text but, in the cases where they are not to be taken literally, they appear within inverted commas.)

I should perhaps add that this book is by no means specifically restricted to *regional* furniture. Since they often overlap, there is some danger of mistaking 'regional' and 'vernacular' as synonymous; they are not. The term 'regional' can be applied to any furniture, vernacular or 'fine', displaying characteristics which are identifiable with, and often peculiar to, a particular locality. Even the most costly specimens of 'fine' furniture produced for grand houses are occasionally 'regional'. On the other hand, while many pieces of 'vernacular' furniture *are* the identifiable products of a specifically regional tradition, there also exist numerous examples which are certainly not – these being of a standard, even cosmopolitan, design which was never confined to any one area.

In the following chapters, I have endeavoured to show a reasonably balanced, comprehensive picture of everyday furniture through the ages. I have not confined illustrated pieces to those with specifically regional characteristics; to do so would entirely invalidate my aim by necessarily causing the omission of many widely used but locally unspecific items.

Nevertheless, I have attempted to impose one geographical restriction on the items discussed within this book – a national one. As far as possible, I have tried to limit entry to furniture that is English, either by manufacture or, at least, by long residence. If I have inadvertently included the occasional Welsh, Scottish or Irish piece then I regret my error. I can only plead that in the case of shared borders, at any rate, there was always a great interchange of ideas and design and that, in many instances, it is impossible, in the absence of documentary provenance, to be absolutely certain of national origin.

INTRODUCTION

I T IS PERFECTLY UNDERSTANDABLE THAT THE MOST DESCRIBED, ILLUSTRATED and documented pieces of English antique furniture should be those of the highest quality, on which the greatest skills, invention and expense have been lavished. Such a selective analysis of what was in fact only a small proportion of the furniture made over the centuries has, however, distorted the average account of its history; the pieces which actually constituted the large majority of furniture in the past, if included at all, are relegated to a tiny section at the back, almost as an afterthought, under the dismissive heading of 'country furniture'.

Such a biased viewpoint serves only to promote the impression that in the past people either lived in stately manors furnished by Chippendale and Hepplewhite or eked out a miserable existence in almost bare hovels. While everyone has some idea of what the grand halls and drawing rooms of aristocratic mansions looked like before modern times, the popular conception of an average domestic interior during the same period tends to be either vague or non-existent. It is in an endeavour to redress the balance and accord ordinary furniture the attention it properly deserves that this book has been written.

The English obsession with 'quality' has dominated written accounts of national history until fairly recently. While the details of royal and noble lives were explored in the greatest depth, the story of how most people lived and worked was virtually ignored. This situation is gradually beginning to change; English social history has now become popular and, it is to be hoped, its furniture will likewise be the object of increasing interest. It is certainly not before time. Many other countries, such as the United States, have for long treated their native vernacular furniture with respect and studied it at some length. They have built up a wealth of knowledge that would take English furniture historians a long time to equal.

Vernacular furniture is often impossible to date with any precision and it has sometimes been said that dating it is unimportant anyway since it is its craftsmanship and appearance that should be judged. Such an attitude is rather sidestepping a central issue. Taken to its natural conclusion, there would be no superiority of an antique over a good reproduction and no point in writing this history. Both craftsmanship and appearance can be reproduced; it is historical value which is unique to an old object and it is that which gives it special significance. An antique artefact demands an intellectual appreciation above the mere admiration of its physical attributes. It is vitally important at least to make an attempt at dating old furniture and thus arrive at some idea of the vanished social context in which it was created and first used.

The task of gathering information on the dates, costs, sources, styles and uses of past vernacular furniture is by no means an easy one. The various cabinetmakers' pattern books produced during the 18th century were naturally aimed at the lucrative fashionable market and are of great help to the student of furniture made for richer homes; with few exceptions, they provide little information on plain furniture for ordinary households. Of course, much can be learned from old paintings and illustrations, particularly those depicting genre scenes, which incidentally include items of furniture. There are also occasional, more or less casual, references to vernacular furniture in books primarily devoted to other subjects but it is seldom analysed in any detail.

By the 19th century the situation improves considerably. John Claudius Loudon (1783–1843) published his *Encyclopaedia of Cottage, Farm and Villa Architecture and Furniture* in 1833. In a chapter devoted to 'Furniture for Cottage Dwellings' he discussed various types of everyday furniture that he advocated as suitable for poorer people. Although he was a landscape gardener by profession rather than a cabinetmaker, his critical observations of contemporary furniture and the rational definitions of nomenclature interspersed in his text have proved invaluable to modern furniture historians. Loudon was a Scot born and bred, not arriving in London until he was twenty, but his terminology was that of the English capital. While probably by no means uniform throughout the nation, since even as late as the 19th century regional dialects varied considerably, it clarifies verbal usage which, in some cases, has now been almost lost.

Useful information can also be garnered from such sources as the various cost books produced from the mid-18th century onwards, which list expenses for specific furniture-making tasks, and from 19th-century trade catalogues of larger manufacturers and retailers, as well as advertisements, wills, inventories, trade directories, census returns and so on. Eventually, the results of this research will provide a clearer picture of how ordinary furniture fitted in to the daily lives of its users, both at home and at work.

The serious and objective study of old English furniture is a comparatively recent phenomenon. Until well into the 19th century, early furniture would be considered worthy of attention by most people only if it had some association, real or imagined, with an historic person or event or if it was 'quaint' and 'picturesque' enough to fit in with a mythical, romantic notion of the medieval or Elizabethan era. The sketch of 1832 depicting the somewhat battered remains of a medieval chest (Figure 1) is possibly representative of the latter viewpoint though, in this case, the chest has been accurately recorded and the artist may have been motivated by genuine antiquarian interest. Whatever the artist's own motivation, the chest's ruinous state would certainly h. been more attractive to contemporary popular taste, obsessed as it w. with the emotive aspects of ruined architecture such as chapels and castles, than if it had been pristine. It must be said that the chest in this condition would also be attractive to the

Figure 1.
Pen and ink sketch, dated 1832.
There was a strong interest in medieval antiquities during the Romantic Age. The profusely carved 'clamped-front' chest depicted may possibly be from East Anglia and appears to date from about 1350–1450.

modern academic, though for a different reason, in that it is demonstrably 'honest', not having suffered the over-zealous attentions of an unsympathetic 'restorer'.

By the end of the Victorian period, the historic importance of early oak and the superlative quality of fine 18th-century furniture had become widely appreciated but the more mundane furniture of past times was generally either ignored by 'serious' connoisseurs or thought of merely as a poorer collector's substitute for the 'real thing', an irritating view that persists in some quarters to the present day. Nevertheless, there was growing popular demand for old vernacular furniture and Arthur Hayden's *Chats on Cottage and Farmhouse Furniture*, a pioneering work on the subject, was published in 1912. More recent research has, naturally, revealed several inaccuracies in his book but Hayden was thorough as far as contemporary knowledge would allow and gathered in book form information that had formerly been scattered in only a few magazine articles.

Even as early as the beginning of the present century, Hayden was concerned about the widespread dispersal of old vernacular furniture and called for a systematic collation of information on regional types: 'the study of local types affords considerable scope for critical study. It is essential that such pieces should be identified and classified before it is too late. Rapidly all cottage and farmhouse furniture is being scattered over all parts of England.'

In presenting a general book on English vernacular furniture without dividing it into regional sections, there is some danger of giving the impression that all the examples discussed and illustrated were uniformly distributed over the whole nation. As mentioned in the Preface, many types of furniture were common not only throughout England but also in many other parts of the world, yet there are also numerous instances where styles, and even basic kinds, were purely a local tradition. It is vital to appreciate that it was not until the widespread use of cheaper and more efficient transportation, communication and mass-produced goods late in the 19th century that England became the fairly homogeneous nation that it is today, although even now a large number of differences still exist between one area and another. Before the late 19th century, those differences were far more marked. Each area had a distinct dialect and way of life and, in many cases, distinct forms of local architecture, furniture and other everyday objects. These dissimilarities were created and defined by ethnic, geographic and economic factors rather than by political boundaries. Thus, such regional cultures often bear little relation to either county or even national borders; they may be contained within a small part of a single county or stretch over several. Since these regions were in some cases virtually self-contained, travelling from one to another must have been almost like visiting a foreign land.

It is natural then that strong regional traditions would not be hastily discarded in deference to latest fashions from London or elsewhere, particularly among the poorer people, who were generally closer to their local roots than the more affluent. Their reluctance to change was not necessarily due to ignorance of new patterns but rather to a tendency to cling to age-old customs. Although it is generally true that the regions most remote from large cities and those with a poorer economy were usually the slowest to adopt new styles, there are many instances of designs (Chippendale-style chairs, for example) persisting, for decades after their incipience, on the very doorstep of London and, possibly, in London itself.

Quite apart from instilled regional traditions, there is an innate conservatism in human nature which occasionally manifests itself in a reluctance to change merely for the sake of it.

Burdening all vernacular furniture with the misleading adjective 'country' has obscured the fact that much ordinary furniture was made in towns and cities. Many leading urban cabinetmakers produced a range of 'common' furniture aimed at the less affluent, in addition to their up-market products. The bureau in **Figure 2** is just such an example; it still bears the label of the firm that made it, pasted inside the top right-hand drawer, which reads 'G. Coxed and T. Woster at the White Swan, against the South-Gate in St. Paul's Church Yard, London'. Thomas Woster is recorded as having died in 1736,[1] and it is rare indeed for any English furniture of this period to retain a maker's label. The partnership of Coxed and Woster is known to have produced many pieces of very fine furniture; this bureau was one of their lesser, 'common', items in wainscot, or imported Continental oak. It is interesting to reflect that, had it not been for the label, many people would automatically dismiss this bureau as 'country made' merely because it is constructed from oak. In fact, 'wainscot' was not particularly cheap and truly rural makers might have found it quite difficult to obtain.

Inaccuracies apart, one of the chief dangers of using the term 'country' to describe vernacular furniture is that the word has become highly charged with emotive preconceptions of an idyllic rural past that never existed in reality. Instead of allowing old furniture to speak honestly for itself, there is a temptation to mould it to fit into that fantasy of storybook cottages in a Beatrix Potter village. It is vital, for example, to recognise an original paint finish as an integral component of a piece. This was as much a part of its total concept as any constructional member. It is, therefore, difficult to understand that, only a short time ago, people who would blanch at the idea of ripping off the stucco rendering on the John Nash terraces surrounding Regents Park in order to reveal the 'original' brickwork, would cheerfully strip the paint from vernacular furniture of the same vintage in order to expose the 'original' pine. The original paint finish is as much and as vital a part of the furniture it was applied to as the stucco is of the Regents Park terraces; its needless removal is vandalism. There is, of course, a world of difference between an original and a recent paint finish; but in many cases the former may still lie more or less intact under later paint and, with care, may be revealed by dry scraping, the skilful removal of individual layers of paint by scalpel rather than by solvents or heat.

There is always some difficulty in deciding how to arrange a book on antique furniture. There is much to be said in favour of dealing with furniture by functional type – storage, tables, seating and so on – and devoting a separate chapter to each. This method certainly works well when dealing with a relatively short period; however, the extremely long expanse of time, at least some four hundred years, covered in the present work makes such an arrangement seem unwise here. Furniture can be more closely connected by factors other than use. A 17th-century joined oak armchair, for instance, has more in common with other kinds of furniture from its own period (in terms of construction, timber, decoration and finish) than with a 19th-century 'smoker's bow' Windsor chair, with which it merely shares a similar function. A system of chronological divisions has therefore been adopted in order to present a reasonably cohesive picture of each stage in furniture history.

2

Figure 2.
BUREAU.
Oak. London, 1710–30.
Although made in London, this bureau has spent much of its existence in the village of Geddington, Northamptonshire, and may have been brought there when new. The double half-round mouldings between the drawers are repeated on the top surface and the perimeter of the cleated fall. There is often a moulding, as here, to mark the division between the desk section and the chest of drawers below it in this early period. The blank space between the lopers is filled by an interior well. The handles are modern.

Figure 2a.
(Detail of Figure 2.)
The maker's label of G. Coxed and T. Woster pasted inside a drawer is a rare survival. The handwritten '£2.2.-' (£2.10) at the top is probably the original price.

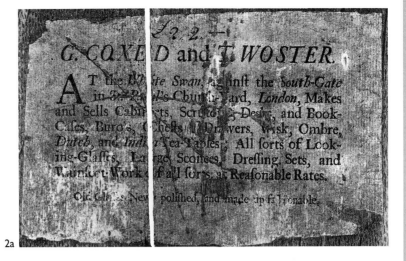

2a

Somewhat arbitrarily, though conveniently, each chapter is devoted roughly to a century. In practice, of course, furniture cannot be so neatly categorised. For example, early 18th-century furniture is often more closely related to late 17th-century pieces than it is to those dating from later in the 18th century, which in turn anticipate developments associated with the early 19th century. Nevertheless, a line has to be drawn somewhere, and within these chronological sections, pieces are further divided according to their function.

It would take nothing less than a work approaching the scale of a very large set of encyclopaedias to cover in detail the vast subject of English vernacular furniture over four hundred-odd years and this present book can only skim the surface. There is naturally a great deal that has been omitted. As far as possible, the following chapters describe and illustrate examples of the kind of furniture which would have been in popular, mainly domestic, use by people other than those in the upper classes. The account is necessarily inconsistent. Since very little true English cottage furniture survives from before the mid-18th century, most of the pieces shown in the early chapters belonged originally to people who were better off. After 1680, people of that same class were often furnishing their houses in walnut and, later, mahogany – at least, in the main reception rooms. For the most part, however, pieces made from 'fine' timber, either solid or veneered, have been excluded and, taking advantage of the increased survival of lesser pieces, this account concentrates more on furniture that would have been within reach of both the middle *and* the lower classes after 1750.

Some of the pieces illustrated are exceptionally attractive and desirable; many are very ordinary. Since the general object is to show representative specimens of different types in common use, the individual quality, or lack of it, of the examples chosen within that criterion is irrelevant. Several of the pieces illustrated have been altered slightly or repaired since they were made. While every effort has been made to ensure their authenticity, their use as a visual reference is paramount and total originality cannot be guaranteed in every case. Some pieces, particularly those in pine, have inevitably lost their original finish and in many cases handles have been replaced. Such imperfections, where noted, are mentioned in the captions. The captions also give timber, finish (if significant) and a range of dates

3

BORN
IN THIS
HOUSE
THE 9TH
OF MARCH
1762.

CUP·BOARD
OF THE LATE
W.COBBETT ESQ.
M.P.
FOR OLDHAM.

WHOSE GREAT
LIGHT
WAS
EXTINGUISHED
THE 18TH OF
JUNE
1835.

between which the item was likely to have been made. In several instances the date range covers a very long period indeed, a century or so. Such terms as 'circa' have been rejected since they are open to wide interpretation and frequently impose too narrow a restriction, particularly when applied to vernacular furniture, where styles and other factors were especially long-lived.

In many cases the furniture illustrated is accompanied by a regional attribution. Such information is intended to serve solely as an indication of the likely origin of the specific piece shown. In a number of instances the regional attribution is based purely on the individual provenance of an item; it therefore refers only to that piece and does not necessarily indicate the presence of any features exclusive to a particular area. Thus, another example, which is visually identical, may come from an entirely different part of the country. That said, the majority of regional indications given in the captions are indeed based on the conventional method of typological observation, in which certain characteristics appear to be peculiar to one district and in which comparative analysis can reveal shared trends. Although such a system can lead to firm conclusions, in the absence of corroborative proof an attribution must not be treated as an indisputable fact. The regional indications in many of the captions are offered only as probabilities, or occasionally even as mere suggestions; they deserve to be challenged rather than simply accepted. In the absence of a specifically regional attribution, the likely origin of some items has been somewhat inexactly expressed as 'North' or 'South'; with scant regard for geographical niceties but purely to serve as a rough guide for the purposes of this book, a broad and blurred border has been drawn from the Severn to The Wash.

Figure 3.
CUPBOARD.

Pine. 19th-century paint finish with commemorative inscriptions. Farnham area, Surrey, 1690–1730. A simple joined cupboard in pine which is unlikely to have survived had it not been part of the fittings of the birthplace of William Cobbett, the well-known author and reformer. Of ordinary farming stock, Cobbett was born at Farnham in 1763 (not 1762 as stated on the cupboard). His critical observations on contemporary furniture are mentioned on page 141. There are groove mouldings to the frames of the fixed side panels and the central door is affixed by butterfly hinges. There may originally have been a lower section on which the cupboard (4 feet long) rested.

1 CONSTRUCTION

L ONG AFTER STRETCHERS TO CONNECT LEGS AND PEGS TO STRENGTHEN mortise-and-tenon joints had been generally abandoned as old-fashioned and unnecessary on expensive furniture intended for fine interiors, they continued in use on 'country' furniture. This does not necessarily indicate a lack of skill or confidence on the part of the vernacular craftsman (the same maker might well be capable of producing fine pieces as well) but was, rather, a sensible anticipation of the use to which the article would be put. Furniture that was to be subjected to the constant wear and tear of everyday household life obviously needed to be more durable than a costly showpiece in a stately drawing room where the most traumatic moment in its life would be the occasional dusting by a maid or footman. Moreover, while the rich could afford to change their furniture as fashions changed, the majority of the population could not. Before the present century, most people had little money to spare for furniture. They bought what was strictly necessary and expected that most of it would not only last their lifetime but would be handed down from one generation to the next. To cater for this market, a craftsman would not only have to ensure that the furniture he made *was* durable but also that it *looked* durable, even to a layman.

Today we tend to think that all antique vernacular furniture was well made. Such was not the case, of course. It is simply that sturdily built examples have survived in reasonable numbers while, for obvious reasons, those of weaker construction have tended not to.

Since ordinary furniture had to be within the reach of people with very little purchasing power, it follows that its construction, although sturdy, should be simple and its material cheap and readily available. A variety of materials, including stone and metal, have been used in the construction of furniture at some stage in English history. 'Basketwork' furniture has been made since Roman times and chairs, hassocks, cradles (or bassinets) and hampers composed of rushes, straw, wicker or similar plentiful materials were common in vernacular interiors up to the present day.

Since this book deals with furniture whose principal constituent was solid wood, some account of the growth of trees and how they are converted into usable timber is called for.

TIMBER

England's generally rich soil and its comparatively mild and moist climate have provided its inhabitants with an abundance of trees ideal for use as timber. Throughout English history wood has been utilised for nearly every form of necessity – from houses and ships to cups and plates. Wood has always been an exceptionally useful material – easily fashioned and accessible to even the poorest labourer.

As a tree grows taller it also increases its girth by producing a new layer of wood under the bark. This layer is called sapwood and, in temperate climates such as that in England, it grows at different speeds according to the season. In spring, when growth is most rapid, the texture of the sapwood tends to be coarse, in summer it is fine, and in autumn and winter there is hardly any growth at all. These seasonal layers of sapwood are known as annual growth rings (concentric in cross-section). Each year, as a

Figure 4.
CORNER CUPBOARD.
Elm with burr elm panels and drawer fronts.
Lincolnshire, 1730–80.
Timber with such superb burr figuring as seen here was always highly esteemed. This cupboard was removed from a Lincolnshire farmhouse. The door panels are fielded and the two central drawers are lip-moulded. The half-round moulding below the cornice suggests a fairly early date and the whole rests on 'stump' feet – downward continuations of the stiles. The hinges and drawer knobs are later.

4

5a

5b

5c

Figure 5a.
Underside of an early 19th-century oak drop-leaf table. The irregular marks of a hand-saw or pit-saw can be seen on all the surfaces.

Figure 5b.
Underside of a 19th-century pine drawer, showing the regular, parallel marks of a mechanical frame saw.

Figure 5c.
Underside of a 19th-century pine drawer, showing the curved marks of a mechanical circular saw.

new layer grows over the previous one, the old sapwood gradually becomes part of the heartwood, or core of the tree. Sapwood is generally paler, softer and more vulnerable to woodworm than heartwood and, for that reason, is usually avoided in furniture construction.

Wood is partially composed of many tube-like fibres which run the length of the tree. It is partly these fibres and their disposition in the annual growth rings which constitute the grain visible on timber. The cross-section of a felled tree frequently reveals small channels radiating from the centre core and intersecting the annual growth rings. These channels, known as medullary rays, convey moisture from the sapwood to the inner core of the tree.

Perhaps the most exotic figuring on timber (and therefore the most highly prized in furniture) is that caused by burrs and pollards. A burr, or burl,[1] is an excrescent growth on a tree's surface that is usually the result of disease or injury. Pollarding a tree (lopping off the top of the trunk in order to encourage a thick growth of young shoots that are then trimmed annually) artificially produces a tumour similar to a burr. A cross-section of a burr or pollard reveals a convoluted pattern of tightly grained knots and whorls which can be spectacularly beautiful. This is most often associated with elm, maple, oak, walnut and yew. It is also occasionally possible to obtain timber with a burr effect from the root area of a tree.

The appearance and characteristics of a piece of timber depend largely on the way it has been taken from the original log. Some timbers (particularly oak) lend themselves to a technique known as riving. An iron wedge is forced into the log's grain and, with leverage, the log is split open. The process is repeated all round the log until rough planks are created. These riven planks will, of course, be uneven and of tapering thickness as they cleave from the log much like slices from a cake.

In England until the 19th century, the most common method of sawing logs into planks was by means of a long saw with a handle at each end, worked by two men. The log was placed either on a pair of trestles completely above the ground or with one end on a single trestle and the other resting on the earth. One sawyer stood on the log, the other below it, and between them they worked the long saw up and down lengthwise through the log. The English term for such a saw is a pit-saw, as it was common in this country, from at least the 15th century onwards, to dispense with trestles altogether and, instead, suspend the log on a frame over a pit, one man standing inside it.[2] A hand-sawn log is always described as pit-sawn in England, whether a pit was actually involved or not. Naturally, in this strenuous, manual sawing method the marks left by the saw on the timber are irregular – a distinctive pattern which can be useful when inspecting the unfinished surfaces of a piece of old furniture in order to assess the probable period of its manufacture. Modern saw marks are, of course, an indication of modern origin – at least for the particular part on which they appear.

Another method of sawing logs was in a mechanical sawmill. The log would be passed through several long saw blades mounted vertically and parallel in a frame, the space between each blade equalling the required thickness of the planks. The saw blades would be driven up and down by a crank powered by a watermill or windmill, and the marks left on the wood are regular and parallel. Although mechanical frame saws are known to have existed in Europe before 1300, they did not become common in England until the end of the 18th century. This was partly because of opposition from manual pit-sawyers who feared loss of employment. What may have been the earliest English sawmills were destroyed by sawyers in 1663.[3] A recorded instance of a sawmill in England in the 18th century is that of James Stanfield, who set one up in Yorkshire and was awarded a prize of £300 for it by the Royal Society for the Encouragement of Arts, Manufacture and Commerce in 1761.[4] It was powered by water and was based on existing mills in Norway and Sweden.

The curved marks left by a circular saw are often thought to be an indisputable sign of very late manufacture. In fact, mechanical circular saws existed in the 18th century. One was patented by Samuel Miller in 1777[5] and within twenty years primitive versions were being installed in or near naval dockyards. Their advantages were soon recognised and, by the early 19th century, circular saws were also in ordinary commercial use for furniture-making,[6] although it was not until the time of the Great Exhibition of 1851 that they were adopted on a really wide scale in England. A design for a band-saw was patented in 1808 by William Newberry of London[7] but, owing to difficulties in tensioning the steel, working machines were not in production until 1855. After 1803 some of the dockyard sawmills were powered by steam engine and, as the 19th century progressed, this source of power increasingly took over from watermills and windmills.

The most obvious method of converting a log into planks is simply to slice it into parallel layers from one side to the other. This is known as plain or straight sawing and the timber produced is called 'run of the mill', hence the expression. This certainly causes the minimum amount of waste but it is unlikely to reveal much interesting grain and only the centre planks are not liable to warp badly as they dry. In order to produce planks with attractive grain patterns (possibly showing medullary rays) and with a resistance to warping, the log can be quarter-sawn. By this technique, the log is first divided lengthwise into quarters and then planks are sawn from each quarter – usually following the natural radius of the tree. Boards created this way are also more weather-resistant. Logs can also be tangentially sawn – that is, a plank is sawn off each of four sides in rotation until the centre is reached. Again, this produces good grain patterns.

6

Figure 6.
CHAIR.
Ash. 1690–1740.
A vernacular chair in ash with pleasantly scrolled crest rail and prominent finials but only the very simplest of turnings for the front legs. A solid seat and a series of vertical slats represent cheaper substitutes for the caned components of earlier fashionable chairs.

CRICKET TABLE.
Walnut. 1760–1820.
The beaded moulding to the squared top section of the legs suggests a later date than the pad feet would seem to indicate. Solid walnut was used for vernacular pieces long after it had ceased to be a highly fashionable timber for 'fine' furniture.

WOOD GUIDE

The following descriptive list of the timbers most commonly employed in the construction of English vernacular furniture is given to assist in their identification. It must be stressed, however, that a description of various timbers, even if accompanied by colour photographs, can never be more than a very rough guide and is certainly no substitute for seeing and handling them. Grain patterns can vary enormously, even in timber cut from the same tree. Colour depends on age, degree and length of exposure to air and light, on surface finish (staining or waxing, for example) and on the patination of dirt, handling and so on. Many woods can look very similar (ash, oak and chestnut, for instance), particularly in a patinated state, and the different types of fruitwood are notoriously difficult to distinguish from each other.

Timbers are divided into two basic classes: the hardwoods (dicotyledons, with fairly broad, flat leaves and normally deciduous in temperate climates) and the softwoods (conifers, with needle-like leaves and usually evergreen). These terms are perhaps confusing in that they do not necessarily describe the relative hardness or softness of the timber.

Hardwoods

Alder (*Alnus glutinosa*). Pale when freshly cut, turning to orange-brown on exposure. No distinctive figure.

Apple (*Malus* spp.). Pale to medium pinkish-brown (sometimes speckled with tiny knots). Very fine and hard texture. Not quite as fine as pear.

Ash (*Fraxinus excelsior*). Greyish-white to medium brown. Conspicuous dark grain pattern. Its toughness and ability to be bent to shape by steaming make it an ideal timber for chair-making.

Beech (*Fagus sylvatica*). Pale to pinkish-brown. Normally straight grain which can be quite conspicuous on flat surfaces. The most recognisable characteristic is the flecking of medullary rays. Even texture ideal for turning and, like ash, it can be steam-bent. Particularly susceptible to woodworm.

Birch (*Betula* spp.) Pale yellow-brown. Soft but bends well when steamed.

Boxwood (*Buxus sempervirens*). Pale to deep yellow. Used for inlay and stringing.

Cherry (*Prunus* spp.). Pale pinkish-brown when freshly cut, turning to dark red-brown on prolonged exposure. The finest of the fruitwoods, it was often available in wide planks and bears a superficial resemblance to mahogany. The fine, even texture readily takes a high polish. The sapwood, when present, is a pale creamy colour.

Chestnut (*Castanea sativa*). Reddish-brown. Strong grain markings like those of oak but without the medullary ray figure and more susceptible to woodworm. It is also softer and weaker than oak.

Ebony (*Diospyros* spp.). Imported from India and the East Indies. Black. Used for inlays and stringing.

Elder (*Sambucus nigra*). White. No visible grain pattern.

Elm (*Ulmus* spp.). Pale to medium reddish-brown. Distinctive, conspicuous grain pattern with characteristic zig-zag markings. Available in wide planks but warps badly. Much used for the seats of Windsor chairs. Wych elm (*Ulmus glabra*) often has a slight greenish tint.

Holly (*Ilex aquifolium*). White to greyish-white. Used for inlays.

Hornbeam (*Carpinus betulus*). White. Fine texture.

Horse chestnut (*Aesculus hippocastanum*). Creamy white with a fine texture. Soft, weak wood, similar in character to poplar.

Laburnum (*Laburnum anagyroides*). Yellow-brown with dark streaks. Used for inlay and treen.

Lignum vitae (*Guaiacum officinale*). Imported from West Indies. Medium to dark brown heartwood streaked with pale sapwood. Extremely hard and very heavy. Much used for treen; it was originally believed to have great medicinal powers.

Lime (*Tilia* spp.). White to yellow-brown. Even texture ideal for carving.

Mahogany (*Swietenia* spp.). Occasionally brought to England as a curiosity from the late 16th century onwards but not imported in large quantities until the 1720s. Spanish mahogany (*Swietenia mahogani*) varies according to its place of origin. That from Jamaica and San Domingo tends to be very dark, heavy and straight-grained; that from Cuba is dark to reddish-brown and lighter in weight and often exhibits an attractive range of figuring. Honduras mahogany (*Swietenia macrophylla*), varieties of which are also known as baywood, is paler, lighter and softer than the Spanish type. Orange to reddish-brown and sometimes well-figured. Used from the late 18th century onwards.

Maple (*Acer campestris*). Creamy-white, sometimes with a yellow or red tint. Occasionally exhibits figures such as 'bird's eye' (many small knots), 'tiger' (darker stripes) or 'curly' (rippled).

Mulberry (*Morus* spp.). Golden brown with dark streaks.

Oak (*Quercus* spp.). Pale to dark brown. English oak tends to have a fine and closed grain and is frequently of crooked growth. Continental oak has a coarse, open texture with more obvious medullary rays and is normally of straight growth. Both types are fairly resistant to woodworm and decay. Continental oak was much admired for its straight growth and has been imported into England since the Middle Ages.

Pear (*Pyrus communis*). Pinkish-brown, sometimes with darker flecks. Finer texture than apple.

Plum (*Prunus* spp.). Pale cream when fresh turning to red-brown. Similar to cherry.

Poplar (*Populus* spp.). Whitish-yellow. Fine, even texture. Generally straight grain.

Rosewood (*Dalbergia* spp.). Imported from Central and South America and the East Indies. Brazilian rosewood is pale to purplish-brown with dark, almost black, streaks. East Indian rosewood is much darker but lacks such distinctive streaks. Much imitated in paint finishes on cheaper furniture.

Sycamore (*Acer pseudoplatanus*). This is a European variety of maple (the American 'sycamore' is a plane tree). Creamy-white with fine, even texture. Frequently flecked and sometimes having a striped or rippled figure.

Walnut (*Juglans* spp.). European walnut (*Juglans regia*) is pale to medium (or greyish) brown, usually with dark, even black, streaks. Very susceptible to woodworm. American Black walnut (*Juglans nigra*), also known as Red or Virginia walnut, was imported from an early date and by the mid-17th century was being grown in England. Red-brown and usually darker than the European variety, it is more resistant to woodworm.

Whitebeam (*Sorbus aria*). White to pale pinkish-brown. Fine, even texture. Closely related to rowan, or mountain ash, and both used for inlays.

Willow (*Salix* spp.). White. Fine texture with a mainly featureless grain. Much used for basketwork.

Softwoods

Cedar (*Cedrus* spp.). Imported as timber and ready-made furniture from Mediterranean areas. Pale reddish-brown. Fine, soft texture. Prized for aroma and resistance to decay. American timbers used as substitutes for true cedar include Spanish cedar (*Cedrela odorata*) and Virginia cedar (*Juniperus virginiana*), which were both imported from the 16th century onwards.

Cypress (*Cupressus* spp.). Pale yellow-brown. Fine texture. Faint cedar-like aroma.

European redwood (*Pinus sylvestris*). Also known as Scots pine. Reddish-brown heartwood. Well-marked growth rings and usually knotty. Mildly resinous.

Fir (*Abies* spp.). Creamy-white to pale brown. Usually straight-grained. Similar to spruce although not as lustrous.

Larch (*Larix* spp.). Pale to medium reddish-brown. Conspicuous growth rings and sometimes many small knots.

Pitch pine (*Pinus* spp.). Imported from south-eastern United States and West Indies. Yellow-brown to red-brown. Very conspicuous growth rings.

Spruce (*Picea abies*). Also known as whitewood. White with high lustre. Growth rings are not as conspicuous as those of European redwood. Also less resinous and lighter in weight.

Yellow pine (*Pinus strobus*). Imported from eastern North America. Introduced to England in 1705 and much planted by the first Viscount Weymouth at Longleat – hence its popular name 'Weymouth pine'.[8] In North America it is known as 'eastern white pine' ('yellow pine' there refers to another timber). Pale yellow to light brown, sometimes with slight pinkish tint. Fine, even texture. Growth rings are not obvious and grain is normally straight.

Yew (*Taxus baccata*). Dark reddish-brown with pale yellow sapwood. Irregular grain pattern, often with small knots and whorls. Burr figure is particularly attractive. Has great elasticity and is one of the few softwoods that can be steam-bent. Resistant to woodworm.

Two well-known groups of timber are known collectively by a single term. These are:

Fruitwood (hardwood)
Includes apple, cherry, pear and plum.

Pine or deal (softwood)
Strictly only timbers of the *Pinus* genus, but commonly extended to embrace many other members of the *Pinaceae* family, including European redwood, fir, larch, pitch pine, spruce and yellow pine. (Cedar is also of the *Pinaceae* family but not generally considered as 'pine' or 'deal'). The term 'deal' is derived from an old German word referring to a portion of sawn timber; it originated in the Middle Ages, when large quantities of ready-sawn pine planks were imported to England from the Continent.

Marblewood and plywood
Ways of supplementing or improving upon natural timber were also devised. One of the earliest composites is marblewood, a compressed mass of wood shavings and glue, used as a substitute for burrs and pollards.

The principle of gluing layers of wood together, alternating the direction of the grain, in order to gain strength and avoid warping, was employed in the 18th century. It was not, however, until the mid-19th century that plywood was produced on any scale, when it was being used by the Austrian, Michael Thonet, (who utilised a flat form for chair seats in the 1850s) and by the Americans, John Belter and John Mayo. By the late 19th century, a large plywood factory had been established by Christian Luther at Reval (or Tallinn) in Estonia. The earliest mass-produced plywood was three-ply and large quantities were imported into England.

Wainscot
As it has two different meanings, the term 'wainscot' is open to some confusion. The origin of the word itself is unclear, although various theories exist.[9] Suffice it to say that, by the 16th century, the term had acquired the two meanings that it has today: a) wall-panelling and b) oak (strictly speaking, Continental oak).

7

Figure 7.
ARMCHAIR.
Elm. Shropshire, 1760–1850.
Dug-out construction; an example of furniture at its crudest. A naturally hollow tree trunk has been roughly shaped and a seat and two armrests added. With a few cushions, it was probably not too uncomfortable and at least provided some protection from draughts.

METHODS OF CONSTRUCTION
Sawn timber was frequently made into furniture straight as it came. Only the more visible surfaces were subsequently smoothed, the original saw marks left untouched on those parts – such as backs and interiors – which were not likely to be seen. This was not always the case, however, since timber was sometimes smoothed prior to construction.

It is common, but quite wrong, to think of timber as being invariably smoothed with an adze in early times. Planes were in use from Roman days and many examples are depicted in medieval manuscripts. Both Roman and Saxon specimens have been excavated in England.[10] The first planing machine was patented by Samuel Bentham in 1791[11] and by the end of the 19th century such machines were common.

There are several methods of converting timber into furniture:

Dug-out
In early times, when even a basic knowledge of carpentry or joinery was fairly rare in England, the simplest way of creating 'case' furniture was to hollow out a log with tools (perhaps with the aid of fire), leaving the outer surfaces as the base and sides. This technique is extremely laborious (and wasteful of timber), of course, but requires no sophisticated skills.

Several dug-out chests have survived in English churches; they are roughly squared and the severed upper portion of the original log serves as a lid. They are iron-bound and were used for collecting alms or storing valuables. Rather than a sign of any lack of skill, their crude construction may sometimes have been the result of a need for security; their very weight made them unlikely to be stolen and their solid form may have

8

appeared much stronger than boarded or joined types. These chests usually give the appearance of having great age. Although many are indeed medieval, the type seems to have persisted even into the 17th century.[12] It is likely that these dug-out logs with their naturally domed lids gave rise to the term 'trunk' for any bound chest with a rounded top.

A few examples of dug-out chairs remain from the 17th to 19th centuries. Making a chair from a log is certainly much easier than making a chest since no ends are needed. It was simply a matter of finding a naturally hollow trunk, cutting it to shape and fitting a seat.

'Primitive'

Although any crude furniture may popularly be called 'primitive', the term is more properly reserved for pieces with a simple form of wedged construction – generally based on a central slab (a seat or table top) with whittled stake-like members wedged into it to create legs and uprights. The member is deeply notched at one end, the notched end is rammed through the appropriate hole in the slab and a wooden wedge hammered into the notch to hold the member firmly in place. The protruding wedged end of the member is then cut off flush with the slab surface. There is seldom any form of decoration or any need for nails or screws. Primitive furniture of this type (such as stools, forms and tables) must once have been extremely common over most of Europe and is often shown in medieval manuscripts. Its cost was negligible and it could be obtained or home-made by members of any social class.

These utilitarian pieces of furniture were usually intended for hard, daily use and the great advantage of simple, wedged construction was that legs and so on could easily be replaced by new ones when the originals

Figure 8.
FORM.
Pine seat, ash legs, remains of black over red paint finish on all surfaces. 1790–1850.
The legs are strengthened by pine blocks nailed to underside of the seat.

Left:
STOOL.
Burr elm seat, ash (?) legs, old brown paint on seat. 1800–80.
Both this stool and the form are of 'primitive' construction.

Right:
STOOL.
Elm seat, beech legs, dark stain. 1880–1930. Although similar at first glance to true 'primitive' furniture, this stool with turned legs was the relatively sophisticated merchandise of a large retailer and is stamped 'MAPLE & Co. Ld.' under the seat. This family firm was founded in London in 1841 and by 1903 employed over 3000 people in its Tottenham Court Road premises alone.[19] A great deal of the furniture sold there was bought from other businesses.

Figure 9.
ARMCHAIR.
Ash. 1675–1710.
Whereas triangular turned chairs from the 17th century are quite often encountered, stools of the same form, although frequently depicted in old illustrations, do not appear to have survived. The wooden seat is held in place by grooves on the rails.

broke or wore down. It is not uncommon, therefore, to find that the legs on an antique example are newer than the slab top; this natural evolution in the item's existence need not detract from its value.

By its very nature primitive furniture is extremely difficult to date with any precision. Articles made in the present century are probably identical to those made in the Middle Ages. However, their obvious lack of intrinsic value has caused a very low survival rate and it is unlikely that many specimens pre-dating the 18th century still exist; most are far more recent.

All forms of primitive furniture were provided with either three or four legs, three legs giving greater stability on an uneven floor. Chairs were created by inserting a series of spindles into the slab seat and uniting them at the top with a simple rail. These chairs represent a crude, though not necessarily early, version of the Windsor chair but, as Windsor chairs usually incorporate the refinement of turning and were normally the sophisticated product of a professional turner or chairmaker, they are more often classified separately.

Turned construction (turnery)

Perhaps the most obvious refinement to primitive furniture was the early use of a lathe as a more sophisticated means of reducing and trimming the long members than merely whittling them.

The turners' lathe, like the potter's wheel, is one of the oldest forms of machinery. In common with the products of a potter's wheel, articles turned on a lathe were described as 'thrown', *throw* (or *thrawan*) being an Old English equivalent of turn. The term has no connection with a potter casting clay onto the wheel, as might be supposed.

The simplest, and possibly earliest, form of lathe was a pole lathe. The piece of wood to be turned was mounted horizontally with a long cord wound once or twice around it. One end of the cord was knotted to the tip of a long, springy pole high above the turner's head and the other end was attached to a foot treadle. As the turner pressed the treadle, the wood spun in the lathe while he shaped it with a chisel; when the treadle was released the springy pole would pull the cord up again.

Although turning contributed much to the decoration of joined furniture, the range of furniture that could be made solely by a turner was necessarily limited, the most common items being stools and chairs.

Figure 10.
CHEST.
Elm. West Country, dated 1692.
Simple boarded chests such as this were made from the Middle Ages up to the 19th century. The carved decoration on this example includes stylised tulips and daisy-like flowers incongruously springing from the same stem, and the initials TB. The lock has been replaced.

Turned armchairs such as that shown in **Figure 9**, with three or four posts, certainly had medieval antecedents and the type was relatively common in the 17th century. However, the vast majority of surviving turned chairs are either of the rush-seated variety or the Windsor.

Boarded or plank construction (carpentry)

The quickest and easiest way of fixing the edges of two pieces of wood at right angles to one another is simply to pin them together with nails or pegs. Sometimes one edge is rabbeted (stepped back) to make a firmer join but no complex wood-cutting is called for. Both iron nails and wooden pegs were used from the Middle Ages onwards. This form of construction (at least as far as furniture is concerned) was the province of the carpenter. In the 17th century the more advanced technique of wood joinery was restricted by law in some places, (including London) to the joiners. Of course, the ruling was probably not always strictly adhered to (particularly away from large towns). In truly rural areas in the 18th century the trades were often combined, and Adam Smith observed in his *Wealth of Nations* of 1776 that 'A country carpenter deals in every sort of work that is made of wood . . . [he] is not only a carpenter, but a joiner, a cabinet-maker and even a carver'. Nevertheless, carpentry in furniture-making generally implies a form of simple plank construction and boarded furniture has never shared the same status as that which is joined.

The natural limitations of this technique have restricted boarded furniture to fairly box-like forms. There are also inherent problems in fixing wood across the grain. Timber shrinks across the grain, even after prolonged seasoning and, if this movement is inhibited by nails or pegs, the wood is forced to split. Nevertheless, the ease and lack of skill involved in creating furniture by simply nailing wood together has ensured that the method has never really ceased to be employed, especially for cheap or homemade items.

11

Figure 11.
Tenon, *showing the hole drilled for the peg. The corresponding hole in the mortise would have been further from the shoulder.*

12

Figure 12.
CHEST OF DRAWERS.
Oak. 1670–1720.
A piece calling for much time-consuming labour. There is a simple, vertically grooved dentil moulding along the front below the thin top and the geometrically moulded drawer fronts are divided by half-round mouldings applied to the carcase. The bun feet are modern additions; originally the stiles ran down to the floor like those at the back. The handles are also new.

CHAIR.
Oak. 1700–50.
An awkward, though charming, combination of 18th-century high fashion (crest rail and splat) with an archaic base form echoing that used in caned chairs.

Joined furniture was considerably more expensive than 'primitive', turned or boarded; neither of these pieces would have been found in a contemporary cottage.

Figure 13a.
Through dovetails.
(Corner of elm chest, circa 1810.)

13a

13b

Figure 13b.
Lapped dovetails on drawers.
The large dovetails of the early 18th-century drawer on the left contrast sharply with those of the right-hand drawer, which dates from the 19th century.

Joined construction (joinery)

Joinery is essentially the art of fixing timber together by cutting interlocking portions in the wood itself. An early form of joining was employed in the construction of the medieval 'clamped-front' chest (**Figure 21**) and the same principle was used for arks (**Figure 38**). The horizontal boards on the front and back of the chest are made with continuous tenons on their ends which slot into grooves on the inside edges of the four wide, vertical stiles, one stile at each corner of the chest and extended below the base to form feet. The chest ends are boards also held by grooves in the stiles.

The mortise-and-tenon joint is of great antiquity and was much used in English house-building during the Middle Ages. Its application to furniture in this country appears to have been somewhat limited, however, until its use on a large scale (primarily in the framework of panelling) during the 15th century. The joint is made by inserting a tongue, or tenon, (usually rectangular) made on the end of one piece of wood into a corresponding cavity, or mortise, excavated in the side of the other piece. Before strong glues were available the joint was held in place by one or two pegs inserted into holes drilled right through the mortise and tenon. The hole in the tenon was drilled slightly closer to the shoulder than the corresponding hole in the mortise so that, when the peg was driven home, the two pieces of wood were drawn tightly together.

These wooden pegs were known as trenails (literally 'tree nails') and were almost invariably fashioned from riven timber because split wood is so strong. These pegs (at least on genuine old furniture) were seldom perfectly circular in section and, in fact, they were often deliberately cut squarish in order to produce a better grip when hammered into the hole. On the exterior of old furniture, the ends of these pegs stand slightly proud of the surface – a point much overrated in the past as supposedly proving the age of a piece and based on the theory that as the surrounding wood shrinks over many years the peg is left standing out. The theory is correct (although pegs were not always cut off flush to begin with) but fakers have always found this 'evidence' extremely easy to reproduce and, anyway, the effect can occur quite naturally within an amazingly short space of time.[13] On interior surfaces – particularly under chair seats and table tops, which are seldom seen – the inside ends of the pegs were not normally cut off but left pointed.

When strong glue became commonplace in the early 18th century, the use of pegs to secure a mortise-and-tenon joint was gradually abandoned on most fashionable furniture. Pegs were, however, often retained for the construction of vernacular furniture (for reasons given at the beginning of this chapter) well into the 19th century.

One of the great advantages of joined work over that which is boarded is its ability to form frames for panels. Panelled furniture is considerably lighter than an equivalent piece created from boards and yet it is equally strong, if not stronger. Also, since a panel of wood is simply held in place by grooves on the frame and not fixed by nails or glue, the unrestricted timber can 'move' freely without cracking.

The constituent members of panelled furniture have been given specific names over the years and they should be mentioned here. Generally speaking, the main vertical members (the four corner posts on a chest, for instance) are *stiles*, into which the horizontal *rails* are tenoned. Shorter vertical members which tenon into rails at top and bottom are termed *muntins*.

Dovetailed construction (cabinetmaking)

The segregation of mortise-and-tenon joints under 'joinery' and dovetailed joints under 'cabinetmaking' may seem rather arbitrary as the distinction between joiners and cabinetmakers was not, in fact, always clear. Dovetailing is essentially a form of joinery; joiners used dovetails and cabinetmakers used mortise-and-tenon joints. Nevertheless, it is not the use of dovetails in minor items (like drawers and boxes) but their application in the construction of larger, flush case furniture, as opposed to panelled furniture, which really distinguishes the two trades. Flush case furniture (which was ideal for veneering) became fashionable by the end of the 17th century and it was this demand that caused many joiners to adopt the technique, discard their old title and assume the more prestigious one of 'cabinetmaker'. A cabinetmaker may be defined, then, as a craftsman who, in addition to possessing a thorough knowledge of ordinary joinery, is also skilled in the application of dovetails to fine cabinetwork. Competence in related skills, such as carving, inlaying and veneering, is implied as well.

A dovetail is basically a wedge-shaped tenon fitted into a mortise of corresponding shape. Like the normal mortise-and-tenon joint, it was used in medieval English house-building. Later, single dovetails were used for such things as joining the legs of a tripod table to the column.

Multiple dovetails are a series of dovetails cut on the ends of wide boards so that the boards interlock when joined at right angles. They were employed in England from at least the 16th century, although only rarely and, even then, mostly by immigrant craftsmen.[14] It was not until the second half of the 17th century that the use of multiple dovetails became widespread in this country.

In 'open' or 'through' dovetailing, the ends of the joining members show on both sides of the angle. In 'concealed' or 'lapped' dovetailing the cavities that receive the wedges are not cut right through, thus preserving one unmarked surface. Lapped dovetailing was ideal for the fronts of drawers where it was desirable to conceal the construction.

FINISH

The bare timber surfaces of a piece of furniture were given some form of finish both for practical and aesthetic reasons. Oil and beeswax (probably two of the earliest transparent finishes for furniture) and varnish (basically a suspension of gum or resin in a solvent which was used at least from the 17th century) gave some protection against damage and decay without unduly obscuring the timber. Varnish is often regarded as totally alien to vernacular furniture, particularly by those who cling to the belief that the centuries-old patina that they prize is purely the result of oil and beeswax. Though this may often be the case, varnish was in fact commonly used after 1700, even for relatively rustic furniture, either as an original finish or as a means of resuscitation. Indeed, there are probably few early items which have not been varnished at least once in their history. It is this old varnish (not to be confused with some of the later, less attractive products), now enhanced by generations of wax and friction polishing, that has frequently helped to create the finest examples of deep, glowing patination that modern collectors find so attractive.

Stain has been applied to vernacular furniture from an early date. A great deal of 18th and 19th-century furniture made from cheaper timber was originally stained to resemble that made from expensive woods like

14

Figure 14.
CHIFFONIER.

Pine, black over red-brown scumble finish imitating rosewood, brown over yellow scumble finish on back panel imitating maple or satinwood, white patterns with red details and yellow striping. 1825–45.

There was apparently no limit to the materials that painters attempted to simulate on pine furniture. Not only has fine timber (rosewood and maple or satinwood) been imitated for the main structure and marble (brown over yellow scumble) for the top surface; even the conventional pleated yellow silk behind brass latticework has been rendered entirely in paint on the wooden door panels — an astounding example of trompe l'œil. The white patterns with red details to the upper back and columns and the yellow striping on a 'rosewood' ground are copies of inlay and are highly reminiscent of finishes on contemporary American fancy chairs, although there is no reason to doubt that this piece is English. Chiffoniers were often placed as pier tables between windows and intended to serve as incidental bookcases or as small, or 'morning', sideboards to hold light refreshments.

Figure 15.

BOX.

Pine, brown over yellow scumble finish with dark striping, green painted interior. 1850–1910. This well-made box is dovetailed and the painter has attempted to convey the impression that it is constructed of oak with mitred joints. The 'medullary rays' on the front 'panel' are fairly convincing at first sight. Even metal trunks were often painted in this way at the time, though it is rather unlikely that the deception would have fooled anyone for long; it was really intended merely as a decorative finish.

15

16

Figure 16.

Boxed set of steel combs.

19th-century.

Different sizes and grades were used for a variety of graining effects.

mahogany. Occasionally it was necessary to stain only part of an article. On a chest of drawers made for the lower end of the market, for instance, the front and top might be veneered in mahogany while the pine sides were merely stained to match. Such stain was often only a tint in the first coat of varnish and will leave little trace if a piece has been refinished.

The black, or almost black, stain so often found on 17th-century oak furniture is not, of course, original. This unattractive finish was applied by the Victorians and Edwardians, who felt that early furniture should be dark and insisted on making it conform to their preconceptions. Fortunately, fashion has changed and sometimes this stain has mostly worn off to reveal the authentic brown.

Furniture has been painted from the earliest times and the use of paint to finish vernacular furniture has continued to the present day. In particular, furniture constructed of 'inferior' timber, such as pine, or fashioned from several different woods, was often considered suitable for painting in order to conceal the fact. Indeed, until the 1960s, pine was usually heavily disguised by stain or paint as a matter of course – most exceptions to the rule being either items intended for kitchen use or those general utilitarian pieces which, because of their basically ephemeral nature, were not considered worthy of any treatment. Naturally, few early examples of the latter category have survived. However, paint was not always used merely to conceal the underlying wood but would in many cases have been considered a desirable decorative finish in its own right. At various periods, it even enjoyed a considerable vogue on expensive furniture.

Painted furniture may be divided into three broad categories: monochrome, polychrome and simulation.[15] A monochrome finish was applied basically as protection but also lent brightness to what were often dimly lit cottage and farmhouse interiors. Polychrome finishes, which form perhaps the most exciting category, can elevate a rather humdrum piece to the prized realms of folk art. Usually the colour scheme accentuates constructional or architectural features but the occasional use of geometric or floral designs can be even more attractive, especially when the work is initialled and dated.

The most common finish, along with monochrome, is simulation. Furniture made from cheaper timber was often painted in such a manner as to give the impression that it was constructed of more expensive wood. This was normally achieved by scumbling, the manipulation of layers of different-coloured paint; a woodgrain effect was produced by drawing a comb, brush or feather through a dark glaze laid over a lighter ground before the glaze had dried – thus revealing streaks of the ground. With a skilled hand the effect could be startlingly realistic; pine could be made to look like oak, and oak to look like mahogany. Frequently the painter gave full vent to his imagination and produced a finish which bore little or no resemblance to any real wood. Materials other than wood could be simulated in the same way. A marble effect was particularly suitable for table-tops and fire surrounds. Expensive tortoiseshell could also be simulated quite easily. Fantastic finishes, not based on any real material, could be invented and used purely for decorative effect.

As a result of the recent craze for stripping paint from furniture in order to expose the timber, a piece of 'country' furniture with its original paint has now almost become the exception rather than the norm, so that it is difficult for us today to appreciate fully the enchanting range of beautiful tones and colours that must have been common in past vernacular interiors. Paint, even when protected by a coat of varnish, is a thin and therefore naturally fragile membrane that becomes damaged or disfigured all too easily. What we may now consider a pleasantly time-worn condition was

Figure 17.
Advertisement for a wholesale ironmonger appearing in the Wrightson and Webb *Directory of Birmingham, 1835.*
While nails, screws and hooks are mentioned, this firm obviously specialised in hinges for use both in houses and in furniture. Several types much associated with earlier centuries, such as H and HL hinges (bottom) or butterfly hinges (near top right), are illustrated. 'Cut nails' were standard by this time although they were still forged by hand in more remote areas. In the last line, Thornton is appealing to foreign buyers; British hardware was exported all over the world.

17

Figure 18.

Inside surface of a drawer front. (Bureau circa 1800.)

Note the circular brass nuts on the threaded posts of the drawer handle. That the handle is original is suggested by the absence of holes for other fittings and by the patinated condition and pale yellow colour of the brass. Nevertheless, actual proof of originality depends on more than these superficial criteria. Salvaged handles or top-quality reproduction handles may have been fixed using the old post holes. A very convincing patina can be produced artificially with chemicals and, despite a widely held belief to the contrary, the colour of modern brass is not necessarily any different from that of old. The best reproduction handles are made of an alloy of precisely the correct colour, provided with traditional circular nuts and well-finished. A truly conclusive opinion must then be based on a really thorough inspection: the post threads must be examined for signs of modern manufacturing techniques; the wood surface underneath the front plate must be observed for indications of previous 'bruising', and so on. Too often handles are confidently pronounced 'original' on flimsy evidence.

18

in the past regarded as ugly and shabby. The article would be discarded or repainted. What remains of early paint finishes today should be treasured and preserved as an integral part of the piece.

HARDWARE

The metal fittings used in early furniture were usually provided by blacksmiths if made of iron, or brassfounders if made of brass. By the late 17th century, the production of furniture hardware of either metal had grown into specialised trades. Brass was, however, very seldom used for furniture fittings before about 1660 and, even after that time, its comparatively high cost normally restricted its use to more costly furniture; the cheapest grades of vernacular furniture continued to be fitted with iron. By the late 18th century virtually all furniture-makers could obtain most items they needed from large ironmongers or hardware suppliers.

The first nail-cutting machines were introduced at the end of the 18th century, the first English machine being patented by Thomas Clifford in 1790.[16] Up until then all nails were either forged or cut by hand. Not all hand-forged nails had the well-known, large heads which were faceted by hammering and are known as 'rose heads'. Often, hand-forged nails – particularly those known as 'finishing nails' – had small heads or no heads at all. However, hand-forged nails are almost always square or rectangular in section and taper on all sides to a sharp point. Machine-cut square or rectangular nails generally taper only on two sides (which usually show tiny burrs made by the cutter) and have square, blunt points. The modern wire nail, consisting of a cylindrical shank with a sharp point at one end and a flat head at the other, had also come into use by 1890.

By 1720, screws were in fairly general use on furniture, though because of their high cost they were employed only where absolutely necessary. These early hand-made screws had irregular threads and, contrary to popular belief, normally tapered to a sharp point. In 1760 Job and William Wyatt patented a machine for the mass-production of screws;[17] machine-made screws were naturally much cheaper and rapidly superseded the hand-made variety within a decade or two, although the latter continued to

19

be produced in more remote areas until the end of the century. It was these early machine-made screws (commonly but erroneously presumed by modern collectors to have been made entirely by hand) that usually had no points; they also tended to have less taper than hand-made screws but retained the same style of flat head, which had a narrow, V-section slot often cut off-centre. It was not until around 1850 that machine-made screws were commonly fashioned with a full taper and with gimlet points – thus reviving the design of their 18th-century hand-made counterparts. By this time too, machinery had greatly improved; the slots were more exactly centred and the threads had become perfectly regular and fairly standardised.[18]

Larger items of hardware, such as locks, handles, escutcheons and hinges, are dealt with as they occur in the captions to the furniture shown in the following chapters. It cannot be stressed enough that metal hardware (even if undoubtedly original) cannot be treated as a reliable means of dating vernacular furniture without considering all other factors. Original hardware may indicate the earliest date possible for a piece of furniture but not necessarily the latest. It is only natural that furniture makers, particularly in remoter areas, should sometimes hoard fittings (perhaps taken from a much earlier piece) and may not have found a need for them until several years or even decades later. Potentially useful hardware was seldom discarded and could be used or re-used generations after its manufacture.

Figure 19.
SMALL BOX.
Pine, covered in brass-studded leather. 1650–1720. The product of a coffermaker. There are fragments of the original block-printed lining paper inside. Both the lock and the hinges were probably supplied by a whitesmith, a craftsman specialising mainly in tin and tinned finishes; this layer of tin has mostly worn off the lock but that on the butterfly hinges is still brightly polished. Such a finish has seldom remained intact over the years; its survival in this case is explained by the fact that for much of its existence this box was under a later covering of black buckram.

2 MEDIEVAL &
SIXTEENTH CENTURY

THIS CHAPTER IS NECESSARILY SHORT, ITS BREVITY DICTATED NOT ONLY BY the need to devote more space to later periods but also by the simple fact that very few examples of humbler vernacular furniture predating about 1600 survive. Indeed, very little remains of *true* cottage furniture even from before the mid-18th century. Not that furniture itself was a rare commodity. By the end of the 16th century, the population of England was possibly over 4 million and even fairly humble cottages had at least one or two pieces of furniture but, in most cases, they were probably simple in the extreme and their lack of intrinsic merit has long since resulted in their demise. Over the course of four hundred years, it is natural that generally only the best examples of furniture should have survived, anything inferior having fallen victim to rough usage and been discarded. A very few items (usually either protected by institutional use, like the bedstead in **Figure 37**, or from archaeological sources, such as articles from the *Mary Rose*) are the exceptions. It must be appreciated too that, contrary to popular belief, furniture of this early period was not invariably made of oak. Oak is reasonably resistant to decay, but a great deal of furniture in all ages, and particularly in poorer homes, was fashioned from other plentiful native timbers such as elm, beech, chestnut and the fruitwoods. None of these woods has nearly the same durability as oak and they are far more susceptible to woodworm.

Even fine furniture earlier than the 17th century is relatively scarce today. Before fairly modern times, old objects were valued mostly by only a small number of antiquarians, and then often merely for their associations with famous people rather than as historical artefacts in their own right. To the vast majority of people, old furniture was simply old-fashioned and to be replaced as soon as possible by something new. The survival of the few pieces of early furniture that still exist is thus generally more accidental than contrived.

The scarcity of surviving early furniture has given rise to the modern impression that in the Middle Ages even great castles were extremely sparsely furnished, while peasants in their hovels sat on mud floors and slept on a pile of straw in one corner. In many cases, such an impression may not be far removed from the truth. Certainly, the owners of castles and

Figure 20.
Woodcut frontispiece to the Contra Tenor section of The Whole Psalmes in Foure Partes, *printed by John Day, London, 1563.*
While his wife and most of his children are relegated to a form or stools, the man is seated on a 16th-century version of the four-post turned chairs mentioned on page 119. The seat, here covered with a bulky cushion, may have been made of wood, leather or rushes. Judging by their clothes, the members of this household seem quite prosperous (although the little boy holding a hobbyhorse is barefooted) and it looks as if an addition to the family is fairly imminent. Note the wooden latticework in the window opening.

20

fortified manor houses in more remote and vulnerable positions would be likely to limit their furniture to strictly utilitarian pieces which could be easily dismantled and removed or were expendable in the event of an attack. Wealth was more sensibly displayed in smaller items, such as tapestries, clothes and plate, which were easily portable. The living conditions of the lowest medieval peasants were universally abysmal and possessions of any kind were meagre. Yet life varied considerably in different regions of England and it is reasonable to suppose that many larger houses in richer and more settled locations were, in fact, furnished quite well. By the 15th century, documentary evidence gives a fairly comfortable picture of living standards in the houses of yeomen and burgesses (the highest classes of peasantry) and even somewhat poorer homes must generally have been provided with at least one rough table, a few crude stools or forms, a food hutch or cupboard, a bedstead of sorts (for the slightly better-off) and perhaps a chest or box for storage. In addition, many simple dwellings would have had some form of built-in furniture, such as shelves, benches and alcoves.

The economic and social structure of 15th and 16th-century England was undergoing a massive change and some headway was made in undermining the old, rigid medieval hierarchy. One contributory factor in the gradual improvement of the lot of the general peasantry was, ironically, the decimating effect of the plagues of the 14th century, the most notorious being the Black Death of 1348–49 (called the 'Great Mortality' at the time) which alone killed off nearly half the population. The resulting shortage of labour led to a greater appreciation of the surviving workers, and their bargaining position was consequently strengthened.

Many members of the yeoman class had thrived from an early date in some areas, often being fairly wealthy freehold farmers, and quite substantial houses formerly belonging to them have survived from the 13th century. By the early 15th century, in a prosperous county like Kent, some yeomen were building large houses such as Bayleaf, the interior of which is illustrated in Plate XII. In 1968 this house was removed from its original location (threatened by a reservoir) and later re-erected at the Weald and Downland Open Air Museum at Singleton, West Sussex, where it has been restored to its probable appearance shortly after the addition of a new bay in the early 16th century.[1] Bayleaf has been furnished as it may have been in about 1540, using modern reconstructions meticulously based on period evidence of the sort of articles used in a home of this status. The photograph shows the high open hall, the main communal room. It will be noted that at this time the hearth was placed in roughly the centre of the floor, chimneys not being usual in ordinary houses until later in the century. The fire's smoke found its way out through openings in the roof and, no doubt, combustion was aided by the draught from the window, which was not glazed but merely covered by shutters when necessary. Similar houses were built by prosperous traders and craftsmen in towns and it has been estimated that there may have been over 100,000 hall-houses of one type or another in England at the end of the Middle Ages.[2]

Contemporary with the reconstructed interior of Bayleaf are actual artefacts recovered from the submerged wreck of the *Mary Rose*, the 700-ton flagship of the English fleet, which sank at Spithead, off Portsmouth, on 19 July 1545 as a result of poor manoeuvring during a skirmish with the French. The ship lay under the sea for over four hundred years until the remains were salvaged in 1982.[3] The wreck and its site have been thoroughly excavated and the numerous items recovered have shed unexpected light on aspects of daily life in the first half of the 16th century. Of particular interest are various items of furniture, a few of which are illustrated in this chapter. While iron fittings, such as nails, hinges and locks, have corroded away leaving only residual traces, the wooden fabric of these pieces is in a remarkable state of preservation – due to the oxygen-starved conditions obtaining under the seabed where it lay buried. Although forming part of the furnishings or of the personal possessions on board a ship of war, many of the pieces (e.g. **Figure 22**) must have been identical to types found in contemporary domestic situations on shore.

The *Mary Rose* has played the part of a 16th-century time-capsule. One great advantage that the retrieved artefacts have over similar articles surviving naturally on land is that we can be absolutely certain of their authenticity in every respect; none has ever been subsequently improved, repaired or tampered with in any way. Items of utilitarian plainness or pieces constructed of more perishable timber, which would normally have stood little or no chance of survival, have been preserved.

An enlightening insight into the way that English life had changed by the end of the 16th century is given by the famous topographer William Harrison (1534–93) in his *Description of England* of 1577. Of houses, he notes the common substitution of glass ('come to be so plentifull') for the older latticework of wicker or oak used in windows, and the increasing use of chimneys even in ordinary houses, so that the fireplace would now be set against a wall rather than in the centre of the room. Thus there was no longer the need for a hall open to the roof. Harrison remarks that furniture (in the wider sense of the word) of a costly kind, which had formerly been the sole province of the rich, was now available

> *even unto the inferiour artificers and manie farmers, who have learned also to garnish their cupbords with plate, their joined beds with tapisterie and silke hangings, and their tables with carpets and fine napery, whereby the wealth of our countrie doth infinitlie appeare . . . and whilest I behold how that in a time wherein all things are growen to most excessive prices, we doo yet find the means to obtain and achieve such furniture as heretofore hath been impossible.*

Harrison's specific use of the word 'joined' to describe beds had more significance than may be immediately apparent to modern ears. Furniture of joined construction was far more expensive than the basic 'primitive', turned and boarded varieties. For 'artificers' and 'farmers' to be able to afford joined furniture was indeed a prestigious advance in their position.

The distinction between social classes (or, at least, wealth) not only by the decoration of their furniture but the technique by which it was made was not to change again until multiple dovetailing for cabinetmade furniture came into increasing use in the later 17th century. Of course, as in any fashion, ownership of furniture made by distinct methods was not defined purely or necessarily by class but also by such factors as regional influence and personal preference. Nevertheless, it is true to say that joined furniture was confined mainly to those who were reasonably better off, until well into the 17th century at least.

Originally a derogatory term coined by 16th-century Italian scholars to describe what they regarded as the debased architecture of the entire Middle Ages, the adjective 'Gothic' was later restricted to the most dominant style which developed during and after the 12th century – one typified particularly by the pointed arch. Although essentially architectural and possessing religious connotations, the Gothic style was by no means confined either to architecture or to clerical applications. The forms were frequently adapted as decoration to furniture, both ecclesiastical and secular, during the late Middle Ages, a characteristic expression being the imitation of tracery, 'blind' (Figures 1 and 23) and 'open' (Figures 28 and 29).

The Classically inspired Renaissance style had reached England by the early 16th century and soon began to manifest itself in native applied arts. The components and motifs of Classical architecture came to dominate the decoration of both public and domestic furniture after 1550 and gradually ousted the last remnants of Gothic ornament from fashion, although at least some medieval elements occasionally persisted at a vernacular level for a very long time (quite apart from the conscious revivals of Gothic motifs during the 18th and 19th centuries). The new Classical style was no doubt much encouraged not only by foreign craftsmen working in England but also by the various Continental pattern-books published throughout the 16th century that disseminated such perennial designs as fluting, gadrooning, lunettes and the guilloche.[4] In the uninformed climate of 16th-century England, Classical elements were often applied in an almost haphazard fashion with little relation to their prototypal origins and it was not until the following century that correct architectural practice began to be more widely adhered to in its modified use on furniture.

STORAGE

The terms 'chest' and 'coffer' are often used interchangeably by modern dealers and collectors. However, Randle Holme (1627–99), an heraldic artist living in Chester, makes a sharp and clear distinction in his *Academy of Armory* (written in 1648–49 and published in 1688): a chest had 'a streight, and flat cover', whereas a coffer had 'a circular lid, or cover'. The word 'chest' comes to us via Latin from the Greek *kiste* (a box); 'coffer' is ultimately derived from the Greek *kophinos* (a basket), perhaps implying a lighter construction. Certainly, the term 'coffer' is properly associated with comparatively light, portable trunks, usually covered with studded leather or cloth, primarily used for storing valuables, and generally having a domed lid. It was one of the products of the 'coffermaker', a manufacturer specialising in leather-covered goods. There is some evidence to suggest that in the past the word 'coffer' was often extended to describe, specifically, boarded chests, as opposed to those which were joined and panelled.[5] For the purposes of this book, however, we will abide by Holme's definition and term all flat-lidded wooden boxes intended to stand on the floor 'chests'.

The need for some form of container to hold possessions must have been basic to all but the most primitive home even in the Middle Ages. Chests, then as now, were marvellously versatile; they could also occasionally serve as a table, seat or bed. Chests of one type of construction or another comprise by far the largest proportion of surviving examples of ordinary furniture from the medieval period. Other items, such as cupboards, chairs, stools, tables and bedsteads (all of which, judging by written and pictorial evidence, were plentiful at the time), are now either extremely rare or, in the case of some varieties, have vanished altogether. The disproportionate survival of chests appears to be due largely to their common use as receptacles for records, alms and other valuables in public repositories, such as churches, which provided a comparatively safe and stable environment. Their preservation in a church does not invariably imply an ecclesiastical origin. It was a custom in the Middle Ages for richer people to deposit a chest of valuables in a church for safe keeping (for instance, until an heir came of age), removing the contents when the time came and leaving the chest behind as a token of thanks. Many old domestic chests were also given or bequeathed to churches in later times.

Whatever the history of the piece in **Figure 21**, it is a fine example of a 'clamped-front' chest and, if of secular origin, would have come from a prosperous household. In common with a great deal of better medieval furniture, this chest was originally painted in bright, vibrant colours;[6] traces of red, blue and yellow can still be found in the crevices of the carved decoration. The paint appears to have accentuated the carving, the three roundels being picked out in red and yellow, the triple incised lines in red and blue, and so on. Unfortunately, any colour on the flat surfaces has

Figure 21a.
(Detail of Figure 21.)
The hinge is formed by a pin inserted through a batten on the lid and covered by a kite-shaped iron plate on the rear stile.

Figure 21.
CHEST.
Oak, traces of red, yellow and blue paint finish.
South-East, 1250–1350.
The motif of three carved roundels is characteristic of chests from South-East England. On this example at Chichester Cathedral, Sussex, the front and lid of the chest are bordered by triple incised lines. One of the pair of carved spandrel brackets, with residual red and yellow paint, has survived but an applied framework on the ends has left only traces. The lock and front part of the lid are later replacements.

21

disappeared entirely, or is at least invisible to the naked eye; it would be interesting to know whether this was merely monochrome or patterned in some way.

'Clamped-front' chests seem to have been first made in England around the beginning of the 13th century[7] and the method of construction is discussed briefly on page 25. On the chest from Chichester shown in **Figure 21** there are signs that an applied framework was originally attached to each canted end – a common embellishment on this type of piece, although it serves no functional purpose. A further example of the clamped-front form is the medieval chest depicted in the sketch of 1832 (**Figure 1**), where the front has been finely carved in imitation of Gothic tracery. The 'clamped-front' method survived well into the 17th century in the construction of arks or hutches[8] – basically grain or dough bins (**Figure 38**). They are generally of riven oak and this, coupled with their archaic structure, gives them the appearance of a much greater age than in fact many of them are likely to have.

Predating the introduction of clamped-front chests were the simpler, and naturally cheaper, chests of boarded construction. It is beyond doubt that this variety formed the vast majority of chests used in ordinary homes during the Middle Ages and for some time after. In their most basic form, these were constructed from six boards, five of them being nailed or pegged together to create a box and the sixth one hinged on top to form the lid. In order to preserve the chest and its contents from the effects of damp or vermin, the ends were often carried down below the main body of the chest to raise it off the ground (**Figures 22–24**). To enhance its appearance, spandrels, or shaped wooden brackets, were sometimes attached at the front (**Figure 22**). These vulnerable pieces have frequently been lost or have even been deliberately removed by unenlightened restorers in the mistaken belief that they are 'bracket feet' and must therefore be 18th-century

Figure 22.
CHEST.
Oak, left-hand spandrel in elm. 1510–45.
One of several chests of this type recovered from the Mary Rose. The lid overlaps the ends only by a fraction. There is a 'till' inside and clear marks caused by the iron lock, hasp and strap hinges remain. The use of elm for just one spandrel may indicate that this chest was originally painted. When found, the chest was empty except for seven gold and nine silver coins.

22

23

Figure 23.
CHEST.
Oak, traces of old paint finish. 1500–60.
The flamboyance of Gothic tracery has been simply expressed in outlines on the front of this boarded chest and filled by carved sunflowers, with cavities in the pointed arches. The slab ends are solid rather than having V-shaped cut-outs to form feet, as in the preceding and following examples. The lid and lock are later replacements and there were probably large spandrel brackets under the front board originally.

additions. The decorative treatment of the two boarded chests shown in Figures 23 and 24 provide an interesting comparison, the former expressing the final stages of medieval Gothic flamboyance and the latter having adopted the Classical theme of the Renaissance.

While larger possessions would be stored in a chest, smaller boxes were naturally essential in a well-furnished house to contain the numerous small, incidental items necessary to everyday life. Most people could neither read nor write during the Middle Ages but by the end of the 16th century literacy was gradually becoming more widespread and occasionally a middle-class home would be provided with a desk – a small, portable box with a sloping lid – in which to keep documents, letters, papers, pens

Figure 24.
CHEST.
Oak. 1580–1675.
In complete contrast to the Gothic medievalism of the previous example, the decoration of this later chest exploits the Classically inspired motifs of the Renaissance. Two rows of fluting dramatically cover nearly the entire surface of the front board, leaving only narrow borders and a small blank space for the lock. Each concave channel is further enhanced by a series of vertically punched small circles.

24

Figure 25.
CHEST.
Walnut, pine and poplar. 1510–45.
When discovered in the barber-surgeon's cabin on the Mary Rose, this chest still contained various items of his medical equipment. The early use of walnut in a fairly utilitarian piece of furniture is interesting and, coupled with the sophisticated dovetailed construction, perhaps reflects the important status of its owner and the value of its contents. Multiple dovetails are unusual for English furniture at this period, and it is possible that the chest was purchased abroad. The triangular blocks at each end are pierced to take rope handles. The hinges and lock are missing.

and ink. Such desks would rest on the user's lap or be placed on a convenient table when required, and were frequently fitted inside with shelves and drawers. The sloping lid was useful for resting a book or paper on while reading or writing and had the added advantage that the lid could be raised slightly to gain access to the interior without disturbing everything on it.

The desk shown in **Figure 27** exhibits several decorative features which had established themselves as part of the ornamental repertoire of makers in many areas of England by 1600. The lid and base edges are moulded with a relatively sophisticated combination of convex and concave profiles. The side edges of both lid and front are finished with a series of small gouged notches, a common form of decoration on boarded furniture which helps to protect the vulnerable end grain. The lid and front are also enhanced by bands of parquetry, a mosaic of shaped pieces of different-coloured woods let into a shallow recess in the main carcase. Parquetry is essentially a complex form of inlay, used from the mid-16th century, in which the carcase wood is not utilised as part of the pattern but merely frames it. The use of parquetry banding appears to have been fairly national at this period; while it is particularly common on furniture from the north of England, it is by no means unknown on that from the south as well and sometimes occurs on 16th and 17th-century fixed woodwork in the southern counties. Within the parquetry band on the front of this desk is an inner border of stamped fleurets, created by the repeated use of a metal punch similar to that used on leatherwork, such as bookbinding. Varieties of simple punched decoration frequently embellished plain surfaces, or were used in conjunction with carving (often interstitially), on both boarded and joined furniture over a very long period. A late example of its use may be seen on the box dated 1813 in **Figure 215**, where a series of zigzag punchmarks creates a diaper border round the inscription.

In the Middle Ages, the word 'cup' often implied a vessel of precious metal (a meaning it retains when applied to modern prizes or trophies); thus, at that time, the word 'cup board' indicated a board, or tiered set of

26

Figure 26.
CHEST.
Oak. 1510–45.
Found on the main deck of the Mary Rose among several other chests, this example (partially obscured in this photograph by the mountings in a museum display) may have belonged to a master gunner as, among personal possessions, it contained a gunner's linstock and a priming wire. The merchant's mark within a shield appearing below the lock cavity is possibly that of a clothworker, however, and the fact that it is inverted may indicate that the front board of this chest has been re-used from an earlier piece of furniture. The hinges and lock are missing.

Figure 27.
DESK.
Oak. Dated 1600.
Bands of parquetry border the mould-edged lid and the punch-decorated fluting on the front. The space left on the lower front is inscribed with the original owner's initials 'E [or F?] H' and the date '1600'. The inscription is partially filled with the remains of a black mastic composition. The lock is later and there are various repairs to the base.

27

boards, on which plate (or, in poorer homes, its pewter or treen equivalent) was stored and displayed. It was not until the mid-16th century that the term 'cupboard' was increasingly used to describe shelves which were enclosed within a compartment with a hinged door or doors and began to replace earlier terms (like 'aumbry') for such pieces. Most medieval and 16th century cupboards (using the word in its later sense) were of plain, nailed board construction and were either hung on the wall

Figure 28
FOOD CUPBOARD.
Oak. 1500–40.
One of several similar cupboards, or aumbries, at Haddon Hall, Bakewell, Derbyshire. The house was unoccupied from 1703 until 1912 and most of the cupboards were acquired during the refurbishment shortly after. The ends of this boarded example have been carried down to form feet and the boards flanking the front door have been correspondingly curved at the base. The present pine door and its hinges are later; judging by old hinge marks, there were originally two doors and the top one at least would have been pierced as in the following example. Bought in 1913 from a house near Newbury, Berkshire. (See also Figure 30.)

28

29

Figure 29.
FOOD CUPBOARD.
Oak. 1500–40.
This food cupboard almost certainly started life as the upper half of a taller, free-standing piece like the previous example. It retains its original door, which was possibly the upper one of two. The boarded construction is pinned by oak pegs and encloses two shelves. The large pierced openings in imitation of Gothic tracery provided ventilation and were originally backed by cloth to keep out pests. Those openings in the boards flanking the door are divided by carved motifs almost identical to those on the preceding cupboard. This specimen is said to have come from Ivychurch Priory (dissolved early in 1536 and now ruined) at Alderbury, near Salisbury, Wiltshire.

The hinges are later and the lock is missing.

(as depicted in early paintings) or provided with feet to stand on the floor.

All early food cupboards, both those dating from the 16th century (Figures 28–30) or the 17th century varieties, have come to be associated with 'livery' (the practice in better houses of dispensing the night's ration of food, drink and candles to the household) or with 'dole' (the free provision of food and other necessities to the poor). Early inventories frequently refer to the presence of livery cupboards in bedchambers and these would, no doubt, have been used to store the received livery overnight.[9] Tables and shelves were also used for the dispensation of livery; in fact, it is likely that any convenient form of furniture would have been employed. Unless there is evidence to the contrary (as in Figure 61), it is often impossible to be certain whether the intended function of a piece of furniture was specific or general.

TABLES

The word 'table' basically signifies a flat surface, a meaning which persists in such fields as geography and architecture. When applied to furniture, it originally referred only to the flat top; not until the 17th century was its meaning extended to refer to the entire piece of furniture, including supports. In medieval halls the customary large dining table consisted of a board or boards (the actual 'table') which rested on, but was not fixed to, two or more trestles (see the modern reconstruction of a 16th-century version, covered by a table cloth, in Plate XII). Being collapsible, such tables were eminently suitable for use in a room where space was required for a variety of functions apart from dining.

These early tables were normally narrow, as it was a common custom at that time for diners to sit only behind the table, with their backs against the wall, leaving the front easily accessible to those serving them. The centre of the hall was dominated by the open hearth. When chimneys became common at the end of the 16th century and hearths were moved to fireplaces at the side of a room, dining tables could now be situated more centrally if desired.[10] By this period, table-tops fixed to joined frames with four or more legs tied by stretchers had begun to oust the trestle table from fashionable domestic use.

30

Figure 30.
FOOD CUPBOARD.
Oak. 1500–40.
Another cupboard bought in 1913 to refurnish Haddon Hall (see Figure 28). This example retains the arrangement of two doors although both are replacements and it lacks the shaped base extension which originally formed its feet. Much plainer than the two previous pieces, it has no decorative carving and the openings are restricted to a series of triple-arched arcades very similar to the windows of some contemporary secular buildings. The previous owner acquired this piece in 1893 from a builder in Wantage, Berkshire. The hinges are replacements.

Figure 31.

TABLE WITH COMPARTMENT.

Oak. Possibly East Midlands, 1540–70.
Although dining tables, whether 'primitive', trestle-type or joined, were usually purpose-built, other functions of a table were often served by chests during the Middle Ages and later. This piece seems to come somewhere in between; while essentially a joined chest, the (originally) loose top and markedly high legs suggest that its primary use was as a table. Certainly, it was an expensive item of fine furniture when new and displays panel decoration typical on articles of its class at this period. The carved design of the three panels on the front is known as parchemin; that of the end panels (here horizontal, as opposed to the normal vertical) as linenfold. The bottom rail is shaped in an ogee arch, in this case with carved leaf ornamentation. The lock and hinges are later and the top, back and base have been replaced.

31

Figure 32.

CENTRE TABLE.

Oak. 1520–1600.

Made at a time when trestles were still a common form of support, this small table (3½ feet long) is an early example of the open box-frame type which eventually succeeded trestles and it has a curious hybrid character. The matching battens with shaped ends under the top and at the base are reminiscent of the upper and lower members on certain kinds of trestle; here the members have been incongruously combined with a box-frame where they are unnecessary. Those at the base serve no functional purpose at all; those under the top hold it in place, the top end rails being only thin apron-pieces grooved into the stiles in the same manner as panels.

While these battens may demonstrate a reluctance on the part of the joiner to abandon entirely a traditional method at this early date, they may equally represent merely a personal or regional style preference, and it is not suggested that an individual artefact such as this, taken out of context, is actually transitional. Distinct furniture types often developed independently, and the temptation of slotting single survivals neatly into 'missing link' categories should be avoided.

The ogee-arched profile of the rails is a recurring treatment on furniture up to the present day (cf. Figures 111, 156, 267 et al.).

The table illustrated in **Figure 31**, which would certainly have belonged to a person of some wealth, is included here primarily as an example of joined case furniture showing typical panel decoration of the period. It would be dangerous to be dogmatic as to whether this piece is really a table or a chest. However, despite the present fittings of hinges and lock, the top was originally loose and this type of furniture has sometimes been identified as a 'counter table', on which monetary calculations were made by using tokens (also known as counters or jettons) on a chequered background[11] – similar in principle to an abacus. The compartment beneath

32

was possibly used as a receptacle for money, tokens and so on when the top was slid back. Of course, there is no hard evidence that this piece was definitely made for that purpose (indeed, any flat surface could fulfil the role of 'counter table') and it may have been simply a table with a storage facility. Similar tables exist with fixed tops and a cupboard underneath.

The most common form of table in cottages would have been of 'primitive' construction, being merely a table-sized version of the type of stool shown in **Figure 33**, with a rectangular or circular top and either three or four legs.

SEATING

Stools and forms, either 'primitive' with three or four wedged legs (**Figure 33**) or boarded (**Figure 34**), are frequently depicted in medieval illustrations and were by far the most common type of seating in the period under discussion. Both 'primitive' stools and those of boarded construction probably remained the usual seating in cottage interiors long after joined versions had replaced them in richer households and they have continued to be made in much the same way up to the present day (two 19th-century examples are shown in **Figures 318 and 320**).

The modern reconstruction of a type of turned stool often depicted in early paintings where they are occasionally shown serving as convenient small tables can be seen in the foreground of Plate XII. In the pictorial sources, this type of three-legged stool is sometimes shown with one post extended above the seat and topped by a horizontal, usually bowed, crest rail, making a stool with a back, or backstool. Such a backstool is mentioned in the 1592 edition of William Warner's *Albion's England* as 'a stoole halfe backed with a houpe' in the setting of a humble cottage.[12] A turned backstool with four posts, or what we would now call a 'single' chair (i.e. without arms), is shown in the 16th-century woodcut reproduced in **Figure 20**.[13] (Single chairs were certainly not a Jacobean innovation, as some earlier writers have stated.) English references to backstools occur as early as the first half of the 15th century[14]; the term was by no means restricted to

33

Figure 33.
STOOL.
Elm. 1510–45.
An extremely rare 16th-century survival of a 'primitive' furniture type that must have been universally common throughout the Middle Ages and up to the present day. The preservation of this example is due solely to its having been buried with the Mary Rose for over 400 hundred years.

Figure 34.
STOOL.
Elm. 1510–45.
A plain, boarded stool from the Mary Rose, similar in principle to contemporary chests of nailed plank construction. The ends are rebated at the top to receive the side members and the outside bottom edges of both the ends and the side members are finished in a simple curved chamfer.

The fresh appearance of a piece from an archaeological source, its sharp edges and clean surfaces unmarked by the centuries of handling and polishing usual on artefacts surviving under normal circumstances, can be quite startling and provides a clear impression of how such early furniture looked when still new.

34

35

Figure 35.
STOOL.
Oak. 1500–1630.

A more sophisticated stool than those in Figures 33 and 34. The understructure on this example is not nailed or pegged together; instead, the side members are slotted into the ends. The buttress-like shaping of the ends and the pierced side member convey a hint of Gothic design; almost identical stools appear in late medieval illustrations, but most surviving examples are probably somewhat later than their archaic appearance would suggest. Purchased in Bury St. Edmunds, Suffolk, before the 1920s. The rear side member is missing.

turned furniture but was used as a synonym for 'single chair' of almost any form of construction at least right up to the end of the 18th century.

The chair, particularly the armchair, has long been regarded as a symbol of rank. Even today in the House of Commons, it is only the Speaker who is accorded the privilege of a chair; everyone else is seated on benches. This modern example, along with many others in colleges and elsewhere, is a survival of the general social custom prevailing in past times. Even in a small house, the head of the family, and perhaps his wife, might sit upon chairs at the dining table while the children and other lesser members of the household either sat on stools and forms or stood. The term 'chairman' is still used as a prestigious title for the leader at meetings.

OTHER TYPES

The form of bedding at this period might best be described by quoting again from William Harrison's *Description of England* of 1577. Here he records the reminiscences of old men living in his village:

> . . . *our fathers (yea) and we ourselves (also) have lien full oft upon straw pallets, covered onelie with a sheet, under coverlets made of dagswain or hopharlots (I use their owne termes), and a good round log under their heads in steed of a bolster, or pillow. If it were so that our fathers or the good man of the house, had within seven yeares after his mariage purchased a matteres or flockebed, and thereto a sacke of chaffe to rest his head upon, he thought himself to be as well lodged as the lord of the towne, that peradventure laye seldome in a bed of downe or whole fethers; so well were they contented, and with such base kind of furniture: which also is not verie much amended as yet in some parts of Bedfordshire, and elsewhere further off from our southerne parts. Pillowes (said they) were thought meet onelie for women in childbed. As for servants, if they hade anie sheet above them, it was well, for seldome had they anie under their bodies, to keepe them from the pricking straws that ran oft through the canvas of the pallet, and rased their hardened hides.*

36

Figure 36.
ASH BOX.
Elm. 1530–45.

Found on the Mary Rose and used for carrying hot ashes from the galley fire. A utilitarian piece of carpenter's work in elm which would have perished long ago under normal circumstances. The holes are for a rope handle.

37

Figure 37.
BEDSTEAD.

Oak. Probably Oxfordshire, 1570–1617.
Whereas truckle beds were normally equipped with
either a folding headboard or none at all, the
headboard in this case is fixed. The large wheels are
mounted within slots at the base of the four posts.
This example is believed to have been one of a set made
locally for the grammar school at Thame, Oxford-
shire, when it opened in 1570 and is associated with
John Hampden, the 17th-century statesman, who
was educated there. It was certainly made before
1617, if the date appearing among various inscrip-
tions on it is authentic. Apparently, the bedstead
remained at the school until 1877 and, although its
connection with Hampden may be apocryphal, it is a
rare survival of utilitarian furniture from such an
early period.

Presumably the old men whom Harrison quotes were reminiscing about conditions that had existed in the early 16th century or before but, as Harrison notes, the situation had changed little in many parts of the country by the time that he was writing, and for the very poor it was not to change for a long time to come. Nevertheless, Harrison goes on to say that a farmer living in his own day (and in his own area, at least) would expect to own 'three or foure featherbeds'. Many of these farmers would also possess at least one fine tester bedstead in which to use such expensive bedding.

At this time it was common for servants to sleep in the same room as their master or mistress, very often on a truckle bed, a low bedstead equipped with wheels which was normally stored under the main bedstead when not in use and rolled out at night. Truckle beds must also have frequently served for the children of a household, and the space-saving convenience of such furniture ensured its continued manufacture well into the 19th century. The example shown in **Figure 37** has the unusual feature of a fixed headboard and was presumably not designed for storage under a normal bedstead, an abnormality perhaps explained by its intended use in an institution rather than in a domestic setting. It possibly represents the type described by Randle Holme: 'being made higher with an head, so that they may be set in a chamber corner, or under a cant roofe, they are called a field Bed or cant Bed'.

38

Figure 38.
ARK.

Oak. 1550–1680
Most often called 'arks' in the North and 'hutches' in
the South of England, grain bins of this type represent
a late survival of traditional construction. Having
shaped feet and shaped ends to the lid, this example is
more decorative than most. Although now provided
with lock and hinges, the arched lid was originally
removable so that it could be inverted and used as a
kneading trough. The unevenness of riven oak is
particularly noticeable on the right-hand front leg.

3 SEVENTEENTH CENTURY

T HE ENORMOUS POLITICAL UPHEAVALS OF THE 17TH CENTURY NATURALLY had a powerful effect on the national economy. For most of the century it was volatile and frequently suffered from an adverse balance of trade and prolonged inflation. Nevertheless, for many people rising costs were more than matched by rising income; they prospered and their standard of living improved considerably.

Gregory King, a statistician writing at the end of the 17th century, divided the population of England into two halves. One half, according to King, increased the nation's wealth. This section consisted of yeomen upward through the social scale. The other half, he asserted, diminished it.[1] These were the poorer classes and we may conclude that most of them possessed very little. Whatever the validity of King's economic hypothesis, it is clear that the growing improvement in living standards was by no means universal.

To those in the middle of the social scale – the lower gentry, the yeomanry and the wealthier tradesmen – the 17th century offered great opportunities for advancement. Their lot was a comparatively pleasant one and it is their furniture which forms the vast bulk of surviving ordinary pieces from that time. The houses of people from this sector were quite comfortable. The open hall was mainly a thing of the past. There was now at least one fireplace with a chimney, a continuous upper storey for bedrooms, which intercommunicated (eventually there would be a central landing which allowed greater privacy), and the windows were glazed. By the end of the century, a good standard of terraced housing was becoming common in London.

The 17th century was marked by a dramatic revolution in the furniture belonging to the wealthier classes; by the final decades, the craft of the joiner had become eclipsed by that of the cabinetmaker. New fashions for more refined furniture, derived mainly from the Continent, arrived in England in the second half of the 17th century and permeated the upper levels of society. Among other innovations (including completely new types of furniture), walnut and other woods firmly supplanted oak as the most fashionable timber, and flush, dovetailed case furniture displaying fine veneers became the rage. This vogue flourished in the decades after the restoration of the monarchy in 1660 and was possibly influenced to some extent by the example of the fashion-conscious king, Charles II, who much admired the tastes of France and Holland. Certainly, the destruction of a large part of London (and its furniture) in the Great Fire of 1666 must have provided a stimulus by creating fresh demand for the latest sophisticated furniture on the part of the people who could afford it. Much of this influence was ultimately (and often directly) derived from the Orient but remained for the most part in a very adulterated and barely recognisable interpretation until the beginning of the following century.

Before the 17th century, joined furniture had been far too expensive for most of the population. Now, when many more people could afford pieces of that genre, furniture fashion had moved on and left them behind again. The new cabinetmakers' furniture was still more refined, still more expensive and quite distinct from the old joined type, not only because of the increased use of walnut and veneers but, perhaps more importantly, the use of dovetailed construction as a method of creating flush surfaces and of concealing the form of manufacture. The difference between the veneered, dovetailed furniture of the rich and the joined kind of the less well-off was as readily apparent as the old disparity between the joined and boarded varieties had been.[2] Although many cabinetmakers also supplied a cheaper range of their wares in solid oak rather than fully veneered, it was still comparatively expensive and dovetailed case furniture was not to become fairly common for most social classes until well into the 18th century.

Of course, not even the rich unanimously elected to switch to the new cabinetmakers' furniture overnight. Some wealthy people probably preferred the old-fashioned joined furniture and saw no reason to change. Certainly, the revolution in expensive furnishings had little immediate effect on the ordinary population; the furniture of the vast majority of people continued to be made basically along the old lines, with slight and occasional concessions to high fashion. The purchasers of cheaper furniture liked, naturally enough, to keep up with fashions but did not welcome the expense; thus the joiner catering for this market would imitate certain features of fine furniture while usually retaining the old basic design and construction. Stylish features of fashionable furniture were adapted to decorate traditional and regional forms. It is this varied and sometimes personal interpretation of fashionable motifs and styles, rather than a slavish copying of set patterns, that gives vernacular furniture so much of its vitality and individuality.

Change in traditional furniture, however small, was not universal nor was it evenly distributed throughout England at the same time. As will be seen in Chapter 4, which deals with the 18th century, age-old types, complete with carving of medieval or Renaissance inspiration, continued to be made in some areas – particularly those furthest from London – until a very late date. The traditional styles of certain regions were especially well-entrenched.

As with the pieces described in Chapter 2, it must be appreciated that most 17th-century furniture that has survived tends to represent the better sort. Because of their flimsy construction or their lack of more obvious aesthetic appeal, the cruder forms of cottage furniture that must have been so common in that period have for the most part not endured the long passage of time. Today they constitute a tiny minority of surviving 17th-century pieces. Also, whereas in large, richer houses old furniture could be banished to the attic or to servants' quarters, in a cottage space was always at a premium and a piece for which there was no longer a use, or which had been replaced, could not be kept. Thus the bulk of simple items must have ended their days as firewood. In fact, the true cottage of the 17th century was itself often ephemeral – a few timbers, mud walls and a thatch roof. The majority of houses built before 1650 that still stand today and that we may call 'cottages' were actually the homes of people who would have been thought fairly high on the social scale at the time.

STORAGE

Chests continued to be the most common means of storage for almost anything other than food until their supremacy began to be challenged by chests of drawers and clothes presses, even in less wealthy homes, after about 1680. Joined chests had been made since at least the early 16th century but, always being considerably more expensive than their plain, boarded counterparts, they seem to have been something of a status symbol until their popularity waned during the 18th century. It must be remembered that most people could afford only simple carpentry work and attempts were sometimes made to simulate panelling on boarded chests in order to give the impression that they were of superior construction (**Figure 42**). There also exist hybrid forms in which, for instance, only the front is properly panelled and the remainder simply boarded. Such chests must be regarded as having been made by an economical combination of means rather than as being a transitional form.

One of the most inconvenient aspects of storing articles in a chest is the fact that its entire contents have to be disturbed in order to reach an item at the bottom. A partial solution was to fit a small lidded compartment, or till, inside at one end near the top but this only solved the problem for very small items. (Incidentally, these tills were not intended purely for keeping sweet-smelling herbs, as is often claimed. It would have been more practical to pierce the side or lid of the compartment for that purpose.) The real solution was the provision of one or more unlidded boxes which could be withdrawn from the front of the chest without disturbing everything else. These boxes were, naturally enough, called drawers as they had to be

Figure 39.
CHEST.
Oak. Dorset, 1590–1620.
A joined chest from a wealthy household, this piece is remarkable for the exceptionally late use of linenfold-inspired panel decoration. It came from Wolfeton House, Charminster, Dorset, (contents dispersed in 1964) and probably dates from around 1600, when the house was extensively remodelled. The original bun feet are turned out of the bottom ends of the stiles.

39

Figure 40.
CHEST.
Oak. West Country, dated 1642.
A simple boarded chest with front and back boards overlapping the ends. The front bears an almost indecipherable date above a pair of coiled sea serpents. The saw-cuts forming the V-shaped cut-outs on the ends are deliberately continued higher on the external surface, being neatly chamfered as a decorative feature, and this appears to be a regional peculiarity. The lid has notched ends matching those on the front board, rather than the more refined ovolo moulding of the previous piece.

Figure 41.
CHEST.
Oak. Possibly West Country, 1630–80.
A theme of arched leaf decoration on the top rail, stiles and muntins frames the three panels with punch-decorated diamonds and stylised flowers on this fine joined chest. It is quite common for the number of panels on framed lids to be inconsistent with that of the front. The lock is on the inside of the top rail — a more sophisticated arrangement which was in occasional use by the mid-16th century.

drawn out from their cavities in the main carcase. Early examples of drawers survive from the late 15th century and, by the middle of the 17th century, it was becoming quite common to find them in tables, inside desks and cupboards and in the base of chests. The chest of drawers proper (i.e. a chest not enclosed by doors and not having a lidded compartment on top)

Figure 42.
CHEST.
Oak. 1640–1720.
A cheaper, boarded version of the type of joined chest shown in Figure 41. It even simulates the carved rail, stiles and muntin to give the same effect as panelling, although here the band of carving along the top of the front is a series of lunettes. In this instance, a notched front board is allied to a lid with an ovolo-moulded edge.
Diamonds on a horizontal axis, the two central motifs on this piece, are technically known as 'lozenges'.

42

Figure 43.
CHEST.
Oak. Dated 1670.
A riot of carved decoration, with vertical dentilation to the muntins, covers the front of this joined chest, and the top rail is devoted to commemorative lettering. While early chests are often initialled and dated, this inscription is unusually full: 'THOMAS HILL AND ELIZABETH HILL WAS MARYED THE TWELVET DAY OF IVNE 1670'. The lid is probably later.

had made its first appearance by 1650. It seems to have evolved partially from the chest with only one or two drawers in its base and partially from the cupboards fitted with drawers that had been in existence for some time.

Since early chests of drawers, by virtue of their novel, joined and relatively complex nature, were restricted mainly to richer households in the 17th and early 18th centuries, their decoration can naturally be expected to reflect their status as 'fine' furniture. Examples predating 1700 which possess a plainness comparable to some contemporary boarded chests are therefore rarely found. Perhaps the most familiar form of decoration associated with chests of drawers and many other items of better furniture of this period are applied, mitred mouldings, normally arranged to form a geometric pattern, and the frequent use of supplementary split turnings (i.e. a turned spindle cut vertically down its centre to create two flat-backed pieces) applied to stiles and muntins. The fashion for such applied ornament had originated in the classical inspirations of the

43

Figure 44.
CHEST WITH DRAWERS.
Oak. Dated 1669.
The carvers of both this and the previous chest were evidently afflicted with horror vacui ; every conceivable space on the front of this piece is ornamented, with much use of foliated scrolls on the rails, stiles and muntins. The initials 'EC' and the date have been squeezed into the spandrels of the two outer panels. The only hardware (apart from locks) is a pair of staple hinges to the lid and small metal rings on the fronts of the two drawers.

44

16th century and found fresh impetus with the strong influence of Continental trends (particularly Dutch) after the mid-17th century (see, for example, **Figures 12, left,** and **46**). The visual impact of this technique was sometimes emphasised by the use of contrasting colours (**Figure 46**), a dramatic effect that has all too often been dulled or altogether extinguished by the passage of time.

The large number of lidded, boarded boxes surviving from the 17th and 18th centuries acquired the misleading name of 'bible boxes' during Victorian times, as if a bible was the only item stored in boxes. While many of these early receptacles may well have occasionally contained a bible, among other things, it is hardly logical to presume that that was invariably their sole purpose. Boxes were naturally used, then as now, to hold the

Figure 45.
CHEST OF DRAWERS.
Oak. South, dated (16)76.
The moulding-bordered drawer-fronts are divided by half-round mouldings to the carcase. The two top drawers are inlaid with 'W 7' and '6 A' and the heart decorating the bottom drawer is a particularly pleasing feature. The turned 'feet' were probably much longer originally, becoming square-sectioned again further down and forming legs that were tied by stretchers, making a 'chest on frame' (cf. Figure 101). The knobs are modern.

45

Figure 46.
CHEST OF DRAWERS.
Oak, with red stained insets on the drawer fronts.
Probably South, 1670–1720.
This chest of three drawers displays the geometric pattern of mitred mouldings applied to drawer fronts so often encountered on examples of this period. This monochrome photograph does scant justice to the various colours on this piece, which were probably almost garish when it was new. The mouldings are in light oak, contrasting with the darker stained oak of the carcase, and the eight small pale areas bordered by mouldings on each drawer front are red. Applied half-spindles would originally have decorated the stiles. This piece has acquired an amazing assortment of key escutcheons, none of which appear to be original to the chest. The handles are also replacements.

46

47

Figure 47.
BOX.
Oak. 1630–1710.
The front is carved with a band of stopped fluting, with a punched fleuret in each channel, which ends rather abruptly at the right-hand edge, the carver not having allowed himself sufficient space to finish the design properly. The ends of the lid are notched. The internal lock is intact.

SMALL GATELEG TABLE.
Oak. South, 1675–1720.
A low occasional table with a single leaf and a drawer. The drawer runs on a central bearer which is tenoned into the rail below the drawer front and simply nailed to the underframe at the other end. The columns have a ring-turning near the base. The drawer knob has been replaced.

innumerable miscellaneous items of everyday life for which boxes are usually intended – clothing accessories, sewing equipment, books and so on.

These boxes were usually fitted with a lock and must often have been used as containers for valuable documents and letters. The box in **Figure 47** is shown resting on a low table, where it could be used as an occasional desk, the top forming a convenient writing and reading surface. Literacy was slowly becoming more widespread towards the close of the 17th century, even among the less well-off, and newspapers proliferated. Encouraged by a more efficient postal service, letter-writing was rapidly gaining in popularity, becoming less the sole prerogative of scholars and wealthy people. The large number of purpose-built writing boxes or desks with sloped lids dating from this time (**Figure 51**) are a reflection of the steadily increasing growth of literacy among the middle classes in general.

The type of furniture illustrated in **Figure 53** has been the subject of endless controversy among furniture historians. Earlier this century, it would have been called a 'court cupboard', a term that is now felt correctly to apply to a tiered set of unenclosed shelves. Among several contemporary alternatives, the label 'press cupboard' is nowadays usually preferred to describe the kind of item shown here.[3] In the 17th century, the word 'cupboard' was still ambiguous, being used either for an open set of shelves or for an enclosed cupboard in the modern sense but with connotations of the storage of 'cups' (or plate). The word 'press', on the other hand, consistently meant an enclosed cupboard for any purpose. So, although the term 'press cupboard' may sound like a tautology to modern ears, in the 17th century one word would have qualified the other.

In old inventories press cupboards are frequently mentioned as standing in the hall or parlour and were probably used mainly for the storage of

Figure 48.
BOX ON STAND.
Oak. Box dated 1682.
Decorated with a central moulding and notched front edges, the boarded box rests on a joined stand which is possibly not original but roughly contemporary. The front of the box bears the inscription 'EG 1682' in metal studs and is branded twice with the initials 'IW' — these probably being the initials of a later owner (not the maker) added during an inventory. The original lock is missing.

Figure 49.
BOX.
Oak. West Country, 1640–1730.
An example of a type of furniture which was given the misleading and irritating name 'bible box' during the 19th century. This example, decorated with relatively crude gouge-carved lozenges and punched circles, has the unusual feature of two secret drawers below an interior till.

Figure 50.
BOX.
Oak. Dated 1648.
A superb example of 'chip-carving', a method of
overall decoration on boarded furniture employed from
the Middle Ages onwards. When used on small boxes
such as this, the carving may have been amateur and
the item thus decorated intended as a love token.

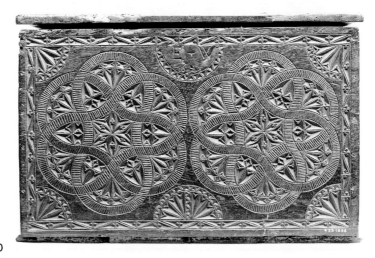

50

items such as pewter, crockery, cutlery and other objects associated with dining. Some areas of England (the Lake District, in particular) are notable for the frequency with which furniture was actually built in to the interiors of houses – including beds and wall cupboards. Press cupboards were often employed as room dividers, forming part of the interior partition walls, and occasionally have separate compartments, the front ones opening into the main parlour and others accessible only from the rear – in the adjoining room.

The late 17th-century press cupboards illustrated in **Figures 52 and 54** have small bulbous pendants on the front two corners of the overhanging top. These are the vestiges of what on earlier cupboards would usually have been complete pillars connecting the top overhang to the shelf below, decorative components of the design which must greatly have emphasised the impressive impact of a large item of furniture intended very much for show as well as for use. Press cupboards were in their day among the most prestigious pieces of furniture in an ordinary house, perhaps second only to

51a

Figure 51a.
(Detail of Figure 51.)
All-oak drawer from the interior of the desk. Note the
large hand-forged nails and the original wooden knob.

Figure 51.
DESK.
Oak. South Yorkshire, 1680–1710.
This desk combines an archaic carved decoration of
rambling thistles (not necessarily indicative of Scottish
origin) and small stylised roses with the fashion for
applied geometric mouldings. The flat ground of the
carving is matted to form a contrast. The lid, with
notched ends and affixed by butterfly hinges, conceals
an interior fitted with a shelf, above which are three
divided spaces for drawers, one of which remains. The
lock has been replaced and one section of the front
moulding is missing.

51

52

Figure 52.
PRESS CUPBOARD.
Oak. South Lancashire, dated 1682.
This piece, initialled and dated on the frieze, has the arrangement common on press cupboards whereby the doors swing on pin hinges integral to the inner frame member. The stylised dragons carved on four of the door panels are a recurring motif on furniture from this region[4].
The cornice is a modern addition; it is likely that there was originally no cornice at all. The knobs have been replaced.

53

Figure 53.
PRESS CUPBOARD.
Oak. Dated 1671.
A plain example, relying on the baluster pillars at each end of the upper stage for an impressive visual impact; carving is restricted to bands of crude foliated scrolls flanking the inscription 'TR IH + 1671' on the frieze. The only other decoration is provided by narrow bands of punch-enhanced zigzags, occasionally bordered by a series of gouges, on rails and muntins, and the obligatory channel mouldings. As usual, the upper and lower sections can be separated. There are signs that the lower cupboard doors, enclosing a single shelf, had butterfly hinges at one time. The cornice is later.

54

Figure 54.

PRESS CUPBOARD.

Oak. Pennines, dated 1695.

The carved date, accompanying the initials 'RMA' on the frieze, has an ornate numeral '1' – an idiosyncrasy common in the North of England (cf. Figure 52). The central panel of the upper section is deeply carved with a stylised thistle within a border of applied mitred mouldings; the door panels flanking it have paired foliated scrolls while the upper panels of the lower doors are embellished with a guilloche. The muntins are incised with vertical zigzags and punched with fleurets. This piece may originally have had a lower stage. The knobs and lower door hinges are later.

tester bedsteads, and this importance is indicated by the frequency with which one finds carved initials and dates on them. The initials are often those of a married couple, the letters sometimes arranged in pairs (as on the clothes press in **Figure 60**) or occasionally in a standard triangular formation (as in **Figure 52**), with the central letter slightly higher or, more rarely, lower than the two flanking it. In this latter example – $A^P E$ – the P is likely to be the first letter of the shared surname while A and E would be the initials of the husband's and wife's Christian names respectively. Such inscriptions were either commissioned before the piece was made or inserted on a ready-made item, a blank space having been deliberately left in the carved decoration for that purpose. Bare initials and dates must remain somewhat enigmatic in the absence of further information; they may or may not commemorate the actual year of marriage. It is rare that a carved inscription is as full and as enlightening as that on the 17th-century chest shown in **Figure 43**.

Figure 55.
LOW DRESSER.
Oak. 1680–1720.

The four cushion-moulded drawers are divided by hipped mouldings which are repeated on the front corners of the carcase and at the base of the baluster legs. Stretchers are kept to a minimum — a common feature of open-based low dressers, which frequently had no stretchers at all even at this early period. The shaped apron on this example foreshadows what was to become a recurring form of decoration on later dressers of this type (cf. Figures 111 and 220, et al.). The brass key escutcheons are original.

55

The presentation and dishing of food before it was taken to the dining table was an important ritual in the past and the varying types of furniture on which it was performed were known as 'dressers' since the way in which the meals were finally prepared, or 'dressed', was an essential part of that ritual. The almost regimental fashion in which meals were displayed was amusingly commented on by John Earle, a future Bishop of Salisbury, when in 1628 he asserted that the cook's

> best faculty is at the dresser, where he seems to have great skill in the tactics, ranging his dishes in order military, and placing with great discretion in the forefront meats more strong and hardy and the more cold and cowardly in the rear, as quaking tarts, and quivering custards, and such milk-sop dishes.[5]

As with the ceremony of livery, any convenient side table or surface could fulfil the function of dresser, although in rich households during the Middle Ages the *dressoir* (an Anglo-French term from which 'dresser' appears to be largely derived) or *buffet* was likely to be a grand piece of

Figure 56.
LOW DRESSER.
Oak. 1675–1720.

Turned front legs have been superseded by a flat variety whose profile echoes the peg-topped baluster of the late 17th century and is slightly reminiscent of the splats on later chairs. Such profile-shaping also occurred occasionally on other types of furniture and on architectural woodwork, such as staircases, of this period. The two rear legs are likewise of flattened section. There was probably a moulding along the base of the carcase originally.

56

57

Figure 57.
LOW DRESSER.
Oak. 1680–1720.

An enclosed form of low dresser, with three cushion-moulded upper drawers separated by a single moulding from two similar central drawers flanked by cupboard doors in the lower part. The high quality of this piece is indicated by the well-formed dovetails and thin round-topped sides of each drawer. The brassware is later.

furniture in keeping with the pre-eminence of the dining ritual, often with a high back or canopy and sometimes several tiers – a status symbol in which the display of food was usually of secondary importance to that of the gold and silver plate which contained it.

By the beginning of the 17th century the grand dresser had developed mainly into the court cupboard (a situation reflected in Randle Cotgrave's 1611 definition of *dressoir* as 'a cupboard, a court cupboard (without box or drawer) only to set plate upon'[6]) and, to some extent, the press cupboard. Although the term 'dresser' was probably still applied, at least temporarily, to any piece on which meals were displayed, it was commonly used as a description of the utilitarian 'dressing board' in a kitchen or scullery on which food was prepared prior to serving – a basic surface with perhaps a few crude shelves above it. The functional 'kitchen dresser' was fairly common over most of England by that time and its essential purpose has continued in ordinary kitchen and scullery settings (of both rich and poor houses) up to the present day. Its lack of ornamentation and its construction from cheap timber, such as elm or pine, reflect its utilitarian status and it is natural that few examples of the pure kitchen dresser have survived from an early date.

It is likely that the dressers shown here (**Figures 55–58**) were intended more as elegant pieces of furniture for the dining rooms of richer households on which to administer the final touches and suitably display the meals initially prepared on their inferior counterpart in the kitchen. As

Figure 58.
LOW DRESSER.
Oak. 1680–1730.
The practice of enclosing the entire front of a piece within a moulded frame is seen on later corner cupboards from the North-West (see Figure 127), although this may not be an indication of regional origin here. The small drawer, flanked by two double-fronted drawers, is set above a central fixed panel between two cupboards. The knobs are later.

58

such, they represent a species of 'formal dresser' (akin to the sideboard)[7] which evolved as much, if not more, from fine table furniture used for serving (e.g. the court cupboard) as from the purely functional kitchen dresser and were probably employed as prestigious showpieces displaying the wealth of the household; they were fairly expensive items of furniture, restricted to the middle classes and above. At this early period, they were usually of 'low dresser' type (without a superstructure of shelves) and took the form of long side tables with drawers (**Figures 55 and 56**), or were fully enclosed with a combination of drawers and cupboards (**Figures 57 and 58**). The expression 'dresser base' is occasionally used for such pieces but is rather misleading as it implies that they originally had a superstructure. Although many may have had shelves fixed to the wall above them, the concept of the true 'high dresser', having a set of shelves more or less

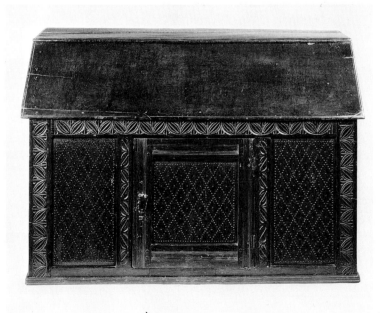

Figure 59.
FOOD CUPBOARD.
Oak. West Country, 1660–1700.
Although this piece looks a little like a grain bin at first glance, the sloped front of the top is not a lid but is fixed; entry is via the door in the front. Despite the large size of this hutch (nearly 4 feet long), it was quite possibly intended to hang on a wall. The front panels are pierced with scores of tiny holes in a diaper pattern and the sides are also pierced for ventilation. The hinges are later. (cf. F. Gordon Roe, English Cottage Furniture, figure 34.)

59

Figure 60.
CLOTHES PRESS.
Oak. North, dated 1694.
Apart from the top rail, which is carved and displays the marriage format 'RW:MW' above the date, this cupboard relies on embellished channel mouldings for its main decoration. The doors hang on decorated iron H-hinges and storage space extends continuously from the chest-like base to the main part behind the doors. The top right-hand hinge has been replaced, the legs have been shortened and various repairs made.

61

60

Figure 61.
HANGING FOOD CUPBOARD.
Oak. 1640–80.
Wall cupboards identical to this one, with rows of spindles for ventilation, were used either in domestic interiors as general food or livery cupboards, or in a public place (such as a church) as dole cupboards. The inscribed initials 'IHS' (a monogram for Jesus), together with a cross, on the top rail suggest the latter use for this example; donations of food would have been left in it for collection by the poor of the parish.

permanently attached to its top surface, does not appear to have been revived from the medieval *dressoir* and re-applied to 'formal dressers' on a large scale until the 18th century in England.[8]

It is crucial to recognise the distinction between the 'formal dresser' and the 'kitchen dresser' in the 17th century; since few early examples of the latter are extant, it has often been assumed that the former was the sole and definitive type of the age. This consideration is particularly important to dating the introduction of a shelved superstructure (the 'high dresser') – often thought to be an 18th-century innovation. Such a date may well apply in general to post-medieval English 'formal dressers'; 'kitchen dressers', on the other hand, are recorded with shelves at least as early as the first half of the 17th century and it is just possible that in some instances these formed a superstructure rather than being separately attached to the wall like the shelves in a pantry.

The combination of space-saving economy and functional versatility that wall cupboards provided ensured their widespread use in both rich and poor homes to keep anything from books and tools to food, supplementing

Figure 62.
HANGING CUPBOARD.
Oak. Dated 1650.
It is possible that this cupboard was once built in to a recess, although it is nevertheless complete, with original back, top, base and sides. There is no pierced ventilation and the front is decorated with incised patterns, including four sets of initials and a fleur-de-lis, and simple punched dots. The door has shrunk a little over the years and a modern fillet of wood has been added to compensate. The top hinge is original.

62

the grander pieces of storage furniture. Even households which could not afford a costly press cupboard must usually have owned a simple, boarded wall cupboard, such as that in **Figure 62**, which could serve as a container for dining articles and/or dry food. When intended mainly for the storage of perishable food, such boarded cupboards would be pierced for ventilation, as in the later example shown as **Figure 129**. Ventilation in superior joined food cupboards was provided by rows of spindles (**Figure 61**) or pierced panels of wood (**Figure 59**) or tin. While some free-standing food cupboards survive from this period, they were normally hung high on a wall to discourage attacks by vermin. For the same reason, some food cupboards would even be suspended from the ceiling by means of ropes and pulleys.

It was during this period that a specialised form of cupboard for storing clothes became increasingly common in ordinary houses. In most homes, clothes were merely hung wherever convenient overnight or stored in a chest for longer periods. Although some houses were provided with built-in closets, it was not until the 17th century that large free-standing cupboards for clothes came into really widespread domestic use. Such a cupboard simply had a series of pegs fixed inside on which garments could be hung and was known as a 'clothes press'. The medieval word 'wardrobe' would continue to imply a room rather than a piece of furniture until late in the 18th century. (Many clothes presses which apparently date from this period have actually been made up from 17th-century wall-panelling comparatively recently. It is always wise to examine examples closely.)

TABLES

The Victorians were obsessed with clerical origins for early furniture, regarding ecclesiastical life as a cultural oasis in the Middle Ages. They had no hesitation in using monastic terminology even for items made long after

63

Figure 63.
LONG TABLE.
Oak. 1680–1730.

The top is formed from three wide planks joined by a pair of end cleats, strips of wood running at right angles to them, which neatly finish and protect the end grain of the boards. The frieze is carved on the side not shown. Spandrels decorate the underframe and a later drawer has been added to one end at some time. The damaged base of the right-hand leg reveals the end of a stretcher tenon. The feet have been reduced.

the dissolution of the monasteries between 1536 and 1540. The anachronism was ignored and thus it was that any large, old oak table used for dining acquired the label 'refectory table' during the 19th century. Of course, most of these tables have no connection with any kind of refectory, whether monastic or secular, and were simply domestic dining tables.

Early versions of joined dining tables with four or more legs connected by stretchers are frequently narrow, with the frieze often decorated on one side only; the explanation normally given for this is either that they were used merely as large side tables or that the diners sat only behind them with their backs against the wall, in medieval fashion, leaving the decorated side

Figure 64.
GATELEG TABLE.
Oak. North Midlands, 1680–1720.

This table, although fairly small, is provided with a drawer at each end. Gateleg tables were often covered with a tablecloth when in use, hence the plain tops (carving on the surface is never original). Attention was focused on the turning of the legs — here in a repeated reel form on either side of paired balusters. The handle is later and the leaf ends have been restored. 64

Figure 65.
GATELEG TABLE.
Oak. 1690–1730.
The leg turning suggests a fairly late date for this example with a single drawer. The handle is a replacement.
An interesting feature of this piece is the obvious re-use of timber from another item, as shown by the carved lunette decoration on the inside of one of the stretchers, which the joiner did not take the trouble to plane off. The carving may be up to a hundred years earlier than the table of which it now forms part. Good seasoned timber seldom went to waste and evidence of re-used wood occurs many times on antique furniture. There is certainly no reason to suspect fakery unless other factors suggest it.

exposed. It is also apparent that dining tables were frequently intended to stand near walls provided with fixed benches. Seldom being seen, the inward-facing side was left plain. The side facing the room, to which movable forms or stools were drawn up, was fully visible and therefore more eligible for ornamentation (Figure 63).

During the 17th century, the tradition of dining in a large communal room or hall was gradually dying out in richer houses. With the increasing subdivision of houses into smaller rooms for privacy, it became the fashion to dine on a lesser scale in one room set aside for that purpose. Thus it is that better examples of large dining tables surviving from late in the century tend to be either from less fashionable regions remote from London or, occasionally, from true refectories in institutions. The use of large dining tables, of basically utilitarian form, persisted in humbler households, particularly farmhouses of course, into the 19th century.

The practicality of having a dining table (or, indeed, a table for any purpose) which took up little space when not in use yet which could be enlarged when necessary by means of folding leaves hinged to the fixed top, was recognised from an early date, and the principle was employed in the 16th century. By the mid-17th century this idea had evolved into what is now known as a gateleg table (a common contemporary term was simply 'oval table', to distinguish it from the large, rectangular, fixed type). The leaves of a gateleg table are supported in the horizontal position by joined open structures (or gates) which fold back against the sides when the leaves are no longer required. Figures 64 and 65 are common representatives of the type.

Not all gateleg tables are oval; rectangular ones are fairly common, and would be more common still had not many of them since been cut down to an oval shape (which is far more saleable today). Gateleg tables with octagonal tops are also encountered fairly often. The gateleg technique was employed for tables in a range of sizes, from those with single-piece tops and gates that folded completely flat, more conventional small versions for occasional use (Figure 66) and varieties with a single leaf (Figure 47) to very large dining tables provided with four gates – two each side – some of which are capable of accommodating sixteen or more people.

Figure 66.
SMALL GATELEG TABLE.
Oak and elm. 1685–1710.
A convenient size for occasional use rather than for dining. The plain gates of this table pivot between the top and a shaped flat base; turning is reserved for the supports at each end. The top and leaves are simply butt-jointed. The feet have been re-tipped. (cf. Victor Chinnery, Oak Furniture. The British Tradition, figure 3:221.)

Figure 67.

SIDE TABLE.

Oak. Possibly East Anglia, 1660–1720.

A long side table with a channel-moulded frieze, standing on ball-and-fillet turned legs tied by heavy (and well-worn) stretchers. The open drawer clearly shows its construction; the front is merely nailed (rather than dovetailed) on to the thick sides, which have horizontal channels cut into them to allow the drawer to be suspended on strips inside the carcase. The three-board top, flanked by narrower edging boards which are mitred to the end cleats, has been marked at some time to allow shove-halfpenny to be played on its surface. This later adaptation presumably has some connection with the table's reputed provenance from an inn at Exning, near Newmarket, Suffolk. The handles have been replaced.

The table in **Figure 64**, with its leaves down, clearly shows the usual tongue-and-groove joint between the fixed top and the leaf. A continuous tongue runs along the inside edge of the leaf, fitting into a corresponding groove on the edge of the table-top when the leaf is raised. Some tables have no joint at all (or, more correctly, a flush-edged butt joint) in this position but are not necessarily older – just cruder. The rule joint, whereby a convex moulded edge to the top neatly fits a concave moulded edge on the leaf (see **Figure 141a**), although used in the 17th century, did not come into general use until the early 18th century.

Side tables are so named because their place is at the side of a room, against the wall; their backs are consequently left unfinished. Tables intended to stand against a wall assumed a variety of forms and decoration according to their function – from fine serving and display pieces in main rooms to workaday dressing boards in kitchens. However, the term 'side table' is most readily associated today with the small joined table, generally having a drawer or two under a fixed top, which became especially popular during the latter half of the 17th century (**Figure 69**).

68

Figure 68.
CRICKET TABLE.
Oak. 1630–80.

Setting a circular table-top on a three-legged frame ensured stability on uneven floors; here the legs are also splayed for extra stability. It is perhaps surprising that three legs did not become more common for joined stools as well. The stout central tapered columns of the legs are embellished with squat ball-turnings to top and base; both frieze and stretchers are channel-moulded.

69

Figure 69.
SIDE TABLE.
Oak. 1675–1710.

A good-quality example with a double-fronted single drawer, with applied mouldings, below an ovolo-moulded top with a generous overhang. The ball-and-fillet turned legs and pierced spandrels enhance its overall appearance. As is frequently the case with early side tables, the drawer does not have a lock, thus obviating the need for a rail above the drawer front to contain a mortise.

SEATING

It is perhaps appropriate that a discussion of 17th-century seat furniture should begin with an item that has become so popularly associated with the period – the 'joint' stool (Figure 70). The word 'joint' is no more than a retention of the 17th-century spelling of 'joined', and is really no more applicable to stools than it is to any other piece of joined furniture. All furniture of mortise-and-tenon construction is joined.[9] The label does serve, however, to distinguish this type from stools of boarded or of 'primitive' construction, which were made at the same time. Less desirable is the continued use of the term 'coffin stool', merely because joined stools were often employed in the past to support a coffin. While some stools were no doubt specifically made for that purpose (and many others commandeered from their original use), the vast majority of 17th-century joined stools were emphatically not intended to support coffins; they were made to seat living people.

In the first half of the 17th century, stools far outnumbered chairs. It was only after 1650 that the position slowly began to be reversed. As previously mentioned, most people other than perhaps the master of the house, and occasionally his wife, either sat on stools and forms or simply stood at mealtime. Settles had existed since the Middle Ages but stools, of one kind or another, were by far the most common type of seating in the average domestic interior.

In genuine joined stools of the 17th century, the legs splay outwards from the long sides but seldom from the ends. The stretchers are flush with the legs, and the seat, generally finished with a moulded edge, overhangs the frame. The seat was fixed to the frame by pegs. The oft-repeated warning that on genuine stools the seats were always pegged only into the rails and never into the tops of the legs is not valid; perfectly authentic stools occasionally had their seats fixed by the latter method.[10] Although it is poor woodworking practice to rely on the end grain of the legs to hold the pegs, different standards of workmanship existed, then as now. Occasionally, joined stools incorporate a box or drawer under the seat, or

70

Figure 70.
STOOL.
Oak. 1630–90.

A fairly typical example of a joined stool of the period. The ovolo-moulded seat is pegged to a frame with channel-moulded rails and plain column legs enlivened only by a ring-turning near the top. The inner ends of the stretcher pegs can be clearly seen on the furthest leg. These stools are normally found singly, or occasionally in pairs, today; few larger sets remain intact although sets of six or more were common at the time.

Figure 71.
STOOL.
Oak. 1630–75.

Replacing the original seat, the present top, leaves and folding brackets were added to this mid-17th-century stool about twenty to eighty years after it was made in order to use it as a small table. Conversions of this kind frequently extended the lifespan of an otherwise outmoded piece of furniture, although examples of 'stool tables' originally constructed in this way are known. (c.f. Victor Chinnery, Oak Furniture. The British Tradition, figure 3:116.) 71

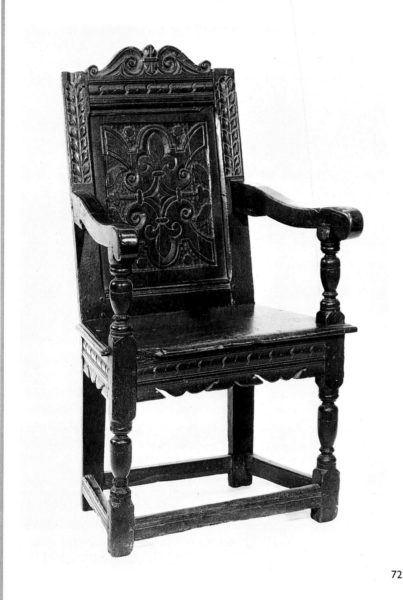

Figure 72.
ARMCHAIR.
Oak. West Country, 1620–60.
A fine piece made in the heyday of joined armchairs of this solid type. The back panel is competently carved with a medieval design, two arms of a cross fleurée ending in fleurs-de-lis, enhanced by Renaissance scrolls on a ground matted by punched fleurets. The scrolled crest and arched leaf decoration of the frame are essentially Classical. Profile-cutting of the underside of seat rails was a common device during the 17th century.

72

have hinged leaves supported by sliding lopers or folding brackets (**Figure 71**) which allow the stool to be used as a convenient small table. There exist full-scale tables of this latter form where the brackets are solid rather than joined; a type well-known in the United States as a 'butterfly table'.

Stools have been referred to as 'crickets', or sometimes 'crackets', particularly in the north, at least since the 17th century. At that time, the term appears to have mostly been used to describe very low stools (of varying forms of construction) which served for such uses as children's stools, footstools and, apparently (from contemporary references), as platforms to stand on when making a speech.[11] It is probably from simple, three-legged versions of this stool that the later term 'cricket table' is derived (see pages 173–176).

The word 'buffet' (pronounced as it is spelt, with the 't' sounded) seems to have most frequently described a common, three-legged stool in the 15th century.[12] By the 17th century it was also used as a synonym for the joined variety in some areas. The term was employed over most of England, for one type or another, at that time, but has lingered in the north to the

Figure 73.
ARMCHAIR.
Oak. South Yorkshire, dated 1680.
In this robust chair, the large crest rail, with three plain lobes between profiled scrolls, overlaps the uprights and is finished with shaped earpieces below the ends. The original owner's name, with a date, is inscribed in full: 'THOMAS KYRKE 1680'. The panel (lower frame moulding missing) bears a diamond with petalled lobes and the usual punched detailing. Ball-and-fillet arm supports contrast with simple 'egg' turning to the front legs.
By this time, the solid joined armchair had been superseded in highly fashionable furniture by caning and fixed upholstery.

73

74

Figure 74.
ARMCHAIR.
Oak. 1620–80.
A simpler example than the previous piece. Here the back panel comes right down to the seat; its carved decoration consists solely of a band of stopped fluting and the arched crest rail is crudely embellished with punched fleurets and semicircles. The pyramid-topped uprights are simply moulded to match the seat rails. Both crest rail and front seat rail are branded 'IG' – probably an inventory mark. The feet are missing and later triangular blocks have been added to reinforce the intersection between seat rail and upright.

present day.[13] Randle Holme (see page 34) stated that the joined variety was termed a 'Buffit stool' in most places in Cheshire, and also indicated that a joined chair was termed a 'Buffit chaire'.

Holme mentioned other types of chair which were common in this period, including turned chairs (with or without arms) and canopied basketwork chairs ('principally used by sick and infirm people' or pregnant women), and illustrated a 'settle chaire' having a curved back and sides of vertical planks which he described as 'being so weighty that it cannot be moved from place to place, but still abideth in it[s] owne station, haveing a kind of box or cubbert in the seate of it'. The great majority of chairs surviving from Holme's day are of joined construction and the typical armchair of this genre has popularly come to be called a wainscot chair. In the 17th century, the word 'wainscot' meant either oak (especially that imported from the Continent) or wall-panelling. Joined armchairs of this period are usually made from oak and, certainly, they normally incorporate a panel or two, but such criteria may equally apply to many single chairs (chairs without arms) (see **Figures 79 and 84**) or, indeed, to any oak or

75

76

panelled furniture. In 16th-century wills references are made to 'wainscot beddes' and 'waynscott tables'. The normal contemporary name for the piece represented in **Figures 72–74** was simply 'armchair'. Large, impressive armchairs of this type were descendants of earlier throne-like chairs with base and sides enclosed by panels. They were very much symbols of rank and status, lending a great air of authority to the occupant, an intention emphasised particularly by the prominent and sometimes ostentatiously elaborate cresting seen on many examples. Such symbolic seating represented the owner's confidence in, or assertion of, his position in a society where class was fairly rigidly defined.

By the middle of the 17th century, joined chairs without arms (backstools, single chairs or side chairs) had become common. Up until the 19th century side chairs were precisely that; they stood in rows around the sides of the room with their backs against the walls, being moved to the table only when required. The rear surfaces of early chairs, then, were seldom decorated in any way as they were not usually seen. This old practice has continued in chair-making up to the present day, even though the backs are more likely to be visible in modern room arrangements, where chairs are ranged around the dining table.

The most popular kind of joined single chair in southern England was a simple joined frame with the seat and back upholstered – backed with canvas webbing, padded with hay or straw and covered with leather which

Figure 75.
CHAIR.
Oak. South Yorkshire/North Derbyshire, 1650–90.
The theme of an arcaded back was derived from Renaissance Italy[14] and appears on 17th-century chairs from as far afield as Holland and Spain. On this chair from northern England, it is enhanced by small turned buttons and allied to uprights ornamented with split turnings and scrolled finials. The leather cushion is later.

Figure 76.
CHAIR.
Oak upholstered in leather. South, 1660–1710.
A type of backstool popular in the South; leather upholstery was extended to contemporary armchairs and settles of similar basic form. The simple ball turning, seen here on the front legs and stretcher, was particularly common in the genre. Earlier examples of this chair type had higher seats and lower front stretchers. The feet are missing.

Figure 77.
CHAIR.
Oak. South Yorkshire/North Derbyshire,
1660–1700.
The two crescent-shaped slats typical of chairs from this region often bear the carved representation of the head of a bearded man in the centre, as here. This motif also occasionally appears on other contemporary furniture types and has often been identified with Charles I. The 'martyr-king' had a large cult following in the second half of the 17th century and the region from which these chairs come had been predominantly royalist during the Civil War. However, anonymous human faces, often bearded, are a recurring theme on everyday artefacts of the period and it is difficult to find conclusive proof of a specific person being intended. The feet and lower stretchers have been restored.

77

78

Figure 78.
CHAIR.
Oak. North Midlands, 1680–1720.
A simpler version of its regional type, this chair echoes the scrolled finials of the previous piece but decoration has been kept to a minimum; a plain crest rail and a turned central rail (cf. the regionally related table legs in Figure 64) have been substituted for skilful carving and the turning of the front legs has been restricted to a simple reel variety. Note the low position of the front stretcher on this example. The left-hand finial is damaged.

was fixed to the frame by large brass or iron nails (**Figure 76**). This style of leather-upholstered chair has long been popularly described as 'Cromwellian'. The term may be based on their simplicity (an attribute much associated with the Commonwealth period) but it has little basis in fact since the type had first appeared a great deal earlier and most surviving examples were made somewhat later and even well into the 18th century. Plainness was by no means a Puritan monopoly. Upholstery was comparatively unusual for ordinary chairs in the north of England. Instead, a variety of distinctive regional types with carved decoration developed (**Figures 75, 77 and 79**).

Generally speaking, the seat height of joined single chairs was reduced as the 17th century progressed to allow them to be used for dining at gateleg tables. By the end of the century, it also became more customary to position the front stretcher higher from the floor, on a level with the two

79

highest side stretchers (e.g. **Figure 77**). However, there are too many exceptions (e.g. **Figure 78**) for such a large generalisation to be an infallible guide when dating these chairs. Craftsmen were individuals who cannot be expected to have rigidly abided by hard and fast rules.

Both armchairs and single chairs of heavy construction with solid seats were gradually superseded in fashionable circles during the second half of the 17th century by lighter cane-backed and cane-seated chairs of a style that appears to have been directly influenced by Dutch or Flemish types, although being ultimately of East Indian inspiration.[15] These chairs generally had walnut or ebonised beech frames and, often, elaborately carved and pierced crest rails and front stretchers, which sometimes bore the motif of a royal crown held by a pair of cherubs. This latter expression of royalist support was not necessarily contemporary with the Restoration of 1660; the same motif appears on the spandrels of clock dials as late as the

Figure 79.
PAIR OF CHAIRS.
Oak. South Lancashire, 1680–1720.
The pyramid finials to the back posts are a regional feature. The stylised grapes, flower and oak leaves, seen on the arched crest rail and panel, are also recurring motifs on chairs from this area. Here, the seats come over the frame instead of being inset as on the previous three chairs. The front stretchers are ball-and-fillet turned.

Figure 81.
ARMCHAIR.
Oak. Cheshire/South Lancashire/North Der-
byshire, 1680–1725.

Unlike those from Yorkshire, armchairs and back-stools from this region often match and the single version of this armchair type is frequently encountered (see Figure 80). Apart from the arms (with a pronounced downward sweep on this piece), the distinguishing characteristics of the armchair form are greater width and single stretchers solely round the base. The arm supports and front legs of this example are simple columns with a central ring-turning.

80

81

Figure 80.
CHAIR.
Oak. Cheshire/South Lancashire/North Der-
byshire, 1690–1720.

The late 17th-century fashion for high backs is apparent on this piece. Both the scrolled finials and the crescent-shaped slat are reminiscent of those on the chair in Figure 77, although here there is a complete absence of carving and the moulded seat overlaps the frame. A common type, this example is one of a set of five.

1720s and was merely a stock patriotic design. On a humbler or more utilitarian level, the fashionable caned chair was translated into an inferior form (Figure 82) or, on a still less authentic plane, its basic style was adapted to earlier traditions; here the caned back was replaced by solid panels (Figure 84 and the settle in Figure 188) or a series of vertical slats (Figures 6, left, and 83). The latter permutation also echoed the fine chairs with carved vertical members to their backs which had become popular very late in the 17th century.

In the 1680s a fashion for chairs with very high backs had come in, becoming extreme in the 1690s, especially on the expensive caned varieties, and this was often extended to more vernacular types (Figures 80, 83 and 84). The passion for such chairs gradually diminished in the early 18th century when people found that the backs readily became loose – an inherent weakness of the design. This was particularly a fault with flimsy

82

82a

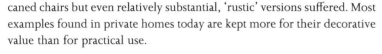

Figure 82a.
(Detail of Figure 82.)
A thickly patinated surface (retaining an early paint finish) that has fortunately escaped the indignity of being skinned and repolished; it retains the aura of great age. Any subsequent alterations to such a piece are instantly exposed.

Figure 82.
ARMCHAIR.
Oak with cane back panel, old brown over yellow grained paint finish, 1685–1730.
A cheaper version of the expensive caned chairs in walnut or beech that were highly fashionable. Only the back of this piece is caned and the mesh is more widely spaced than on fine examples of this period; the seat (which is quite likely to have been provided with a cushion anyway) is simply panelled in oak. The overall impression is fairly authentic, the chair having scrolled arms, turned H-form stretchers, and the back panel frame and flat front stretcher carved in the 'broken S-scrolls' of the time, but the carving is unpierced and comparatively crude, with strange wheatsheaf-like crowns in central parts, and the rear legs and stretcher are plain. The rear posts are topped by acorn finials. Originally a single wooden upright bisected the caned panel.

caned chairs but even relatively substantial, 'rustic' versions suffered. Most examples found in private homes today are kept more for their decorative value than for practical use.

OTHER TYPES

In 17th-century England bedchambers in rich houses were treated almost as reception rooms. It was perfectly acceptable to receive visitors while lying in bed, and the bed was normally a grand and imposing affair with much expense lavished on the cloth hangings, the most visible part. The bedstead itself would usually be of the tester type. This had a wooden ceiling, or 'tester', which met the top of the high headboard at the back and was supported by two turned posts at the foot. Less expensive tester bedsteads were used in ordinary middle-class houses but they, and the

Figure 84.
CHAIR.
Oak. 1685–1740.

The back echoes the form of caned chairs but the expense and weakness of caning have been avoided altogether here; the back frame contains a fielded panel and the seat is solid. There is a touch of royalist support in the well-carved crown to the crest rail but the chair is otherwise functional with simple ball-turned posts capped by mushroom finials, and an elementary ring-turned front stretcher. Such a high back imposes a great strain on the joints of a chair.

The feet have been restored.

83

84

Figure 83.
CHAIR.
Oak. North, 1690–1740.

Here the expense of caning or carving to the back has been avoided by the expedience of a series of vertical moulded slats; scrolled carving has been reserved solely for the crest rail. Front legs and stretcher are baluster-turned but the back posts are austerely plain, topped by the simplest of ball finials. The height of the back on this example is exaggerated by the fact that the base has been cut down, losing not only the bottom part of the legs but probably also two further side stretchers.[16]

hangings with which they were adorned, were still regarded as important status symbols.

The half-headed bedstead, with a lower headboard and no tester (**Figure 86**), was also used mainly (though not exclusively) by those a little lower down the social scale, while those still less fortunate would make do with a simple, boarded variety. The poorest members of 17th-century society usually slept either on straw pallets on the floor or on no special bedding at

85

all – in chairs or wherever convenient – a rude situation which continued, in many cases, well into the 19th century.

It should be made clear that, strictly speaking, the word 'bed' may refer either to the whole piece of furniture or only to the bedding (we still speak of 'making the bed'); the wooden frame itself is more specifically called a 'bedstead'. The series of holes pierced along the rails of a bedstead (seen clearly in **Figure 37** and the head and foot rails in **Figure 86**) were tightly strung with a network of rope to support the bedding, which generally took the form of a woven mattress, a stuffed 'bed' and blankets. The bedding would often be piled quite high and the head of the bed well provided with bolsters and pillows, as it was the custom at this time to sleep almost sitting up. This is one reason why the lower section of early headboards is rarely decorated; it was very seldom seen.

Figure 85.
FORM.
Oak. 1630–80.
Although most 17th-century joined forms are essentially elongated versions of contemporary joined stools (cf. Figure 70), with the legs splayed in the same manner, the seat of a form often has a much greater overhang at each end, as in this example. It is also common for forms to have only three stretchers in an H-form, an arrangement which is very rarely found in stools.

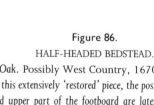

Figure 86.
HALF-HEADED BEDSTEAD.
Oak. Possibly West Country, 1670–1720.
In this extensively 'restored' piece, the posts, side rails and upper part of the footboard are later additions. Only the headboard (excluding the posts) and the bottom rail of the footboard seem to be original. Nevertheless, ignoring the upper part of the footboard and, of course, the modern castors, this piece gives a fair impression of how such a bedstead looked. In its original condition, it probably had no footboard at all above the bottom rail and the footposts would have been much shorter. 17th-century half-headed bedsteads that have not been tampered with are now quite rare.

86

4 EIGHTEENTH CENTURY

ALTHOUGH BRITAIN SPENT MOST OF THE 18TH CENTURY IN A STATE OF WAR with one foreign nation or another, it was a period of relative peace within the borders of England itself and the economy had settled somewhat after the deep disruptions of the previous century. England's exports were increasing rapidly and by the middle of the century this nation rivalled France (with more than three times the English population) as the greatest commercial power. This national prosperity, however, did little to alleviate the conditions of the poorer classes. The enclosure and consequent privatisation of what had previously been regarded as common land was being finalised during the 18th century. The smallholders, whose dependence on common land was essential, and the large number of squatters were reduced to paupers, adding still further to the vast population of rural poor.

Nevertheless, it is evident that the living standards of many people in the lower classes were slowly improving. In richer parts of the country the often ephemeral cottages of earlier times were being gradually replaced by more permanent and weatherproof structures in brick with tiled roofs. The interiors, too, were more refined, with stone, brick or timber floors rather than beaten earth, and plastered walls and ceilings. As glass became ever cheaper, the windows were made larger and more were made to open, often as side-hung casements. Increasingly, almost identical cottages were being built in small groups and repetitive rows, a tendency which reflected the growing concentration of workforces into settlements.

Certainly, the memoirs of James Spershott (1710–89), a joiner living in Chichester, Sussex, paint a fairly pleasant picture of the time. Unlike the proverbial rose-tinted memories of many older men reviewing their youth, Spershott's observations of the past were objective and he was enthusiastic about the way many things had improved during his lifetime. In particular, he extols the improvements in housing, street maintenance and transportation. By the end of his life the frequency of drunkenness had abated, cruel blood-sports were in a decline and religious denominations were more tolerant of each other.

As a joiner – and this is of special relevance here – Spershott obviously had a professional interest in furniture and he gives a detailed and informed account of the furniture most common in his boyhood (i.e. the early 18th century):

I observ'd in those days that the household furniture of the wooden sort was, with old housekeepers, almost all of English oak, viz. long tables, round and triangular ditto, chest of drawers, side cupboards with large doors at bottom and on the top short pillars with a kind of 'Piazer' and small doors within, much carved [press cupboards]. Arm chairs with wood bottoms and backs, joint stools, clothes chest, bedsteads with 4 posts[,] fram'd heads and testers, all of which were much carved with flowers, scrolls, images, &c. Likewise the wainscoting was all of English oak fram'd with a flat moulding, the panels all cleft from the tree.

But with younger people it was now in fashion to have deal dressers with shelves over for pewter, &c. Their tables and chests of drawers of Norway oak called wainscot. With the higher sort, walnuttree veneering was most in vogue and esteem'd for its beauty above anything else. Mahogany was not yet come to be in use. The best chairs were turn'd ash, dyed, or stuffed, with Turkey or other rich covers.

But the cabinet-makers' walnuttree chairs with French [cabriole] legs began now to be made. Bedsteads of beech as English oak began to be scarce and dear, no feet posts, but raised head-board and raised tester hung up to the ceiling, and abundance of lacing on the furniture [hangings and covers].

Spinning of household linen was in use in most families; also making their own bread, and likewise their own household physic. No tea, but much industry and good cheer.[1]

It will be seen that Spershott contrasts the furniture of the older generation (carved English oak) with that of the young (imported oak and other timbers). Carved oak was certainly old-fashioned in the south-east of England by this time but in regions further removed from influential London it was to remain in vogue for some decades.

Interpretations of Classical Greek and Roman architecture, which found perhaps their first mature applications in England with Inigo Jones in the early 17th century, were to dominate the treatment of English buildings in the 18th century. Architectural style had always exerted a powerful influence in the design and decoration of English furniture as well; Gothic tracery motifs frequently decorated chests and aumbries before the mid-16th century and the common application of Classical elements to furniture produced after 1550 resulted in such pieces as tables and chairs being treated like minor Roman temples, their legs turned as columns and their rails embellished as friezes. In the 18th century, it was case furniture which was naturally considered most suitable for architectural treatment and it was mainly to pieces of this genre that the style was applied with academic accuracy; hence the style of the most revered architect of the age, that of the 16th century Italian, Andrea Palladio, came to dominate not only the early Georgian house but also a great deal of the furniture within it. The architectural Classicism of Palladio continued to influence the design of everyday furniture long after his popularity had passed its zenith. Late into the 18th century, corner cupboards, dressers, clothes presses and chests of drawers were commonly presented as miniature Classical buildings complete with quarter-columns, dentilated cornices and, occasionally, a triangular or swan-neck pediment.

Yet the Classical influence was mainly cosmetic and superficial. The most radical inspiration that was to revolutionise fundamental European furniture design during the late 17th and early 18th centuries was not architectural and came not from ancient Greece or Rome or even from

87

Figure 87.
WINDSOR ARMCHAIR.
Ash with elm seat, traces of old paint finish. Thames Valley, 1720–60.
This comb-back armchair, formerly in the collection of Fred Skull of High Wycombe, Buckinghamshire, is one of the earliest known examples of the Windsor type. The pierced crown motif in the crest rail and the 'barley-twist' decoration of the central back members and stretchers are obviously derived from fashionable joined chairs of the second half of the 17th century. However, the latest features (by which any furniture must be dated) appear to be the curved arm supports and the simply turned legs; these suggest that the chair is unlikely to have been made before 1720. Both crown motifs and 'barley-twist' decoration remained popular in more rural areas well into the first few decades of the 18th century. Note the broad saddle-shaped seat. The feet are missing. (cf. Edward T. Joy, The Country Life Book of Chairs, Plate 55.)

Figure 88.

WILLIAM HOGARTH (1697–1764).

The Distressed Poet. Oil, circa 1736.

The painting, intended as a satire on an impecunious poet, depicts a garret in what was probably meant to be a house in London. The poet, seated on the end of a makeshift bed under the eaves, is writing on a rude, square-legged table, possibly of pine. The bookshelf above his head is of ageless simplicity. His wife, sitting on one of two rush-seated ladderback chairs with cabriole front legs and prominent finials to the rear posts, stares at the bill presented by a milkmaid. The hanging food cupboard is of boarded construction and each end is pierced in a pattern similar to that on the door of the cupboard in Figure 129.

By the mid-18th century, it was common to have a lath-and-plaster ceiling under the joists, as here.

88

Europe. Like the most highly prized and imitated ceramics of the period, that influence came from China (and, to a lesser extent, Japan). The chair splat, the cabriole leg, the 'Marlborough' leg and the bracket foot, all basic elements of 18th-century English furniture design, were all of Oriental derivation. Even the flush appearance and the very lightness and simplicity of form so characteristic of 18th-century furniture were to some extent of Chinese inspiration. European admiration for and imitation of Oriental lacquer surface treatments have been known for a long time but only comparatively recently, with the help of more precise dating of Chinese furniture types, is it beginning to be widely realised that Far Eastern influence on European furniture went far deeper than mere applied decoration and was far more fundamental than the superficial chinoiserie of designers such as Chippendale.

Objects from the Far East had been much admired in 16th-century Europe but with the founding of the English East India Company in 1600, the Dutch East India Company in 1602 and the development of Eastern trade in general, Oriental fashion became more widely disseminated and more popularly desirable. Naturally, imported furniture was very expensive and the Europeans who could afford it preferred finely lacquered pieces, which were more exotic and impressive than simpler ones in bare wood. It was the lacquer, not the furniture it was on, that was really prized. Most Chinese furniture forms were considered unsuitable for the European market anyway and the West sent out patterns of their own furniture for the Oriental makers to copy and lacquer. Nevertheless, it was largely the need for furniture with flush surfaces, similar to those of imported Oriental cabinets, on which lacquer, or alternative Euopean treatments such as marquetry, could be suitably displayed, that was to lead to the immensely increased popularity of flush cabinetwork for European furniture from the mid-17th century onwards. In this way, at least indirectly, the Far East played a major part in changing the emphasis of European construction methods and contributing to the supremacy of cabinetmaking. In addition, some basic Chinese design elements (such as splats, feet and legs), not necessarily on actual imported furniture but in depictions of it on ceramic ware, lacquer screens and other items,[2] made a strong impression and modified versions of these elements were being incorporated into some European furniture by the late 17th century. The sophistication of Oriental brass hardware such as handles, hinges and key escutcheons was also greatly admired. It was from this time that the English started to employ brass hardware on any scale for their own furniture, basing the designs (e.g. drop handles and bail handles, with backplates) directly on Chinese prototypes.

Spershott's reference to 'French legs' as a term for 'cabriole' is common at the period and reflects the fact that to a large extent Oriental design elements often reached England only indirectly, via the influence of Continental furniture fashion, and that their ultimate derivation may not always have been recognised even by contemporaries. It is perhaps this old blurring of the Oriental style's true origin that has resulted in our virtual ignorance of the full extent of its impact for over two centuries and a rediscovery that is only comparatively recent. Nevertheless, it is surprising that the full importance of Far Eastern influence on English furniture of the late 17th and early 18th centuries has been largely unrecognised for so long; the style was tremendously comprehensive, encompassing everything from clothes fashions to ceramics and metalware.[3]

The grander ornamental expressions of fashions such as Baroque or Rococo (itself based on Chinese decoration – echoed particularly in its frequent asymmetry) had comparatively little effect on vernacular furniture but by the 1760s a new wave of the Classical style, now called 'Neoclassical', began to exert a widespread influence on furniture design and started to replace the Oriental style which had reigned almost supreme for so long. One of the greatest and most significant novelties of this re-interpretation of the Classical heritage lay in basing furniture design partly on the evidence of ancient furnishings themselves rather than merely adapting architectural features. This new Classicism had received some of its stimulation from the exciting beginnings of systematic archaeology, particularly in the excavation of Roman sites such as Herculaneum and Pompeii at that time, and was epitomised in England by the designs of men like Robert Adam and George Hepplewhite. Essentially, the Neoclassical diverged from the Oriental in its accentuation of height and rectilinear form as opposed to the earlier style's relative squatness and curvilinear fluidity, the substitution of tapering square- and round-section legs for cabriole and 'Marlborough', flush straight or splayed feet tied by shaped aprons for bracket types and the common use of inlaid Classical motifs rather than integral carving in deep relief. The trend also extended to brassware, where stamped backplates, typically of oval or rectangular outline, replaced earlier kinds. Naturally, the Oriental style was not ousted overnight, particularly with regard to vernacular furniture where tradition and natural conservatism played a strong part in retaining archaic fashion. Some elementary tenets of Chinese influence had become so deeply implanted in English furniture design by the mid-18th century that in one form or another they have persisted to the present day.

STORAGE

On the simplest joined furniture of any period, the panel edges are roughly chamfered on the inside in order to fit into the grooves of the stiles, muntins and rails holding them in place, and the front surfaces of the panels

89

Figure 89.
CHEST.

Oak. Probably South-East, 1630–1720.
This chest is entirely undecorated except for central groove and channel mouldings on the front stiles, muntins and rails. It is representative of a very large number of plain joined chests produced over a long period; even simpler versions were still being made until at least the mid-18th century – although many of them received carved ornament in Victorian times (or more recently in an effort to enhance their value). In this example the lower portions of the stiles are missing and tiny early 19th-century bun feet have been substituted. The leaf-shaped brass key escutcheon is old and possibly original.

are flush. Early decorated panels were occasionally neatly chamfered on the *outside*, leaving the carved, central portion of the panel raised, or fielded. Around 1660 the idea of reversing a panel to show the chamfers on the outside was revived for its decorative effect (reflecting contemporary architectural fashion). One normally finds fielded panels and flush panels on the same piece of furniture – finer fielded ones on the front for show and simpler flush ones on the sides and back – as on the chests shown in **Figures 91 and 93**. From the last quarter of the 17th century onwards, fielded panels were occasionally enhanced by a plain, rounded arch (e.g. **Figures 114 and 132**) which after 1700 frequently assumed more elaborate outlines (e.g. **Figures 130, 134 and 135**).

Chests with one or more drawers fitted in the lower part had been made as early as the 16th century and this useful arrangement became increasingly popular in Stuart and Georgian times (**Figure 44 and Figures 93– 95**). More recently the type has come to be known as a 'mule' chest, since it can be thought of as a cross between a simple chest and a chest of drawers.

Figure 89a.
(Detail of Figure 89.)
The unpolished rear surfaces of centuries-old furniture can look startlingly fresh, although the oak has in fact darkened considerably over the years. Note the side-batten nailed under the lid overlap; ideally this should be closer to the chest end to keep the lid firmly in place but it is nevertheless perfectly genuine. To the far left can be seen one of the pair of original iron staple hinges (similar to two linked cotter-pins – one through the top rail of the rear, the other through the lid) undisturbed and still performing their function.

89a

90

Figure 90.
CHEST.
Oak. 1680–1723.
The applied mouldings in a geometric formation framing the panels on the front of this panel-lidded chest, together with the small rectangular mouldings applied to the stiles, suggest a date in the second half of the 17th century. The inscription '17 TB 23' may have been added long after the chest was made. However, this type of decoration actually continued in exactly the form seen on this piece into the first few decades of the 18th century; the inscribed date is therefore quite possibly contemporary with the chest's manufacture.

The term is not contemporary but does no harm as it is not misleading – as long as one does not regard such pieces literally as a short-lived link between two kinds of furniture. The evolution of furniture did not proceed in as orderly a fashion as some earlier writers would have us believe. Plain chests, chests with drawers and chests of drawers all existed at the same time; one type did not automatically or immediately supplant the other.

In 17th- and 18th-century England, linen, blankets and clothing often constituted the more important elements of a newly married couple's possessions and the chest in which to store them assumed an almost symbolic role. The chest and its contents frequently formed part of a prospective bride's dowry and this custom has become especially associated with the kind of chest having one or more drawers – this variety often being dubbed a 'dower chest' to distinguish it from contemporary

91

Figure 91.
CHEST.
Oak. Lake District, dated 1718.
The carved top rail, with the inscription 'IR 1718', comes above three fielded panels which are framed by applied mouldings on only three sides, leaving the bevelled bottom edge free to act as a dust splay. The front stiles and bottom rail are decoratively moulded. Unusually, this chest was never provided with a normal lock, although there are signs that a padlock was fitted at one time. The lid is modern.

Figure 92.
CHEST.
Elm. 1680–1720.
This boarded chest originally had applied mouldings forming two large rectangles on the front to give the impression of panelling. The band of decoration along the top is a rather flat rendition of the deeply-carved gadrooning popular on much earlier furniture.

Figure 93.
CHEST WITH DRAWERS.
Oak. North, dated 1713.
The three fielded panels on the front of this lavishly decorated chest are carved in relief on a plain ground with flowering plants flanked by birds. The central panel bears the initials 'FN' and the others feature the date. The two double-fronted drawers edged by mitred mouldings (some missing on the right hand drawer) are survivals of a 17th-century fashion (cf. Figures 57 and 69). All framing members are enlivened by bands of chequered parquetry — a constantly recurring mode of decoration in the north of England. The handles are replacements.

92

drawerless versions. In fact, any type of chest – with or without drawers – may equally have fulfilled the role of keeping a dowry; in the absence of historical information (perhaps in the form of an inscription) relating to a specific example of whatever variety, it is now impossible even to guess whether a particular chest was ever actually used for the purpose.

94

Boarded chests of this general form continued to be
made into the 19th century. This example is fitted
with a drawer which is simply held in place by the
runners; there is no rail beneath it. The edges of the
front of the chest are notched while those of the lid,
with side-battens, are heavily moulded. Otherwise,
the sole decoration is the large date '1766' delineated
in iron studs below the key escutcheon of the chest
lock.

94a

Figure 94a.
(Detail of Figure 94.)
*Side view of the drawer front, which is rabbeted instead
of dovetailed; note the two large hand-made nails.
Such crude drawer construction is common on
vernacular furniture of all periods.*

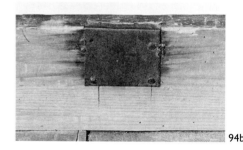

94b

Figure 94b.
(Detail of Figure 94.)
*The steel drawer lock is affixed by hand-made nails,
not screws. Note the staining of the surrounding wood
caused by rust.*

Drawers are basically boxes. Those belonging to boarded and inferior
joined furniture are generally of simple nailed construction; the sophistication of dovetailed drawer fronts was reserved mainly for the better types of
joined and cabinetmade furniture. Up to the early 18th century, the
dovetails were comparatively large and crude, often nailed for extra
strength. After that time, very generally speaking, they became progressively smaller, finer and more closely spaced until, on the finest furniture
of the 19th century, they could be almost paper-thin.

The first chest of drawers illustrated in this chapter (**Figure 96**) retains an
early method of drawer suspension which had become old-fashioned on
finer furniture by this time. The drawers have large, horizontal channels cut
along each side into which fit strips of wood (or runners) nailed on the
inside of the carcase. (The side of one drawer is shown in **Figure 13b, left**). By
1680 the modern method of fitting base runners had begun to supersede
side runners on more expensive furniture and eventually became the norm.
According to whether it runs laterally or longitudinally, the direction of the
grain in drawer bases can occasionally serve as a rough guide to dating fine
furniture. This method cannot, however, be used dogmatically in dating
even expensive pieces and is certainly of little use for dating humbler kinds
of vernacular furniture. It should, however, be noted that it was not until
the 1770s that drawer bases were sometimes divided into two panels with a
central bearer running from front to back. A refinement to drawers which
was introduced on better furniture shortly after 1790 was the fitting of
quarter-round beading to the inside of drawers, between the sides and
base. This practice became almost standard, even on common pine pieces,
by the end of the 19th century.

Figure 95.
CHEST WITH DRAWERS.
Oak with mahogany crossbanding. Lancashire/ Cheshire, 1770–1800.
Intended to double as a low dresser, this good-quality chest, with plain quarter-columns and ogee bracket feet, appears at first glance to have nine drawers; in fact, the upper three are false and the hinged top lifts up to reveal a storage compartment. All the drawer fronts are crossbanded and fitted with handles and keyhole inserts but only the bottom six drawers are real. The clue is the keyhole in the centre of the top rail just below the lid. This trompe l'œil furniture type is fairly common in the north-west of England. (See also Figure 345.)

95

The treatment of drawer fronts and the carcase members framing them, which changed over time, can provide some indication of the earliest possible date for a specific article of furniture. When drawer fronts were commonly attached by through dovetails during the 17th century, there was obviously a strong case for mouldings applied around the perimeter to hide the unsightly joints. By the late 17th century, when lapped dovetails were in more general use, the drawer front could be left flush and attention was concentrated on mouldings applied to the framing members of the carcase, these being usually convex – a single half-round – after about 1680 (e.g. **Figures 96 and 99, left**) or, alternatively, double half-round from the late

Figure 96.
CHEST OF DRAWERS.
Oak. South-East, 1700–30.
From an old house in Farnham, Surrey, and possibly made locally, this joined chest has flush drawer fronts framed by half-round mouldings on the carcase. As with most oak case furniture, the secondary wood (for the back, base and drawer backs and bases) is pine. The original feet (replaced here by modern bun feet) were formed by downward continuations of the corner stiles in the same way as contemporary chests. The brassware is also modern but, judging by residual marks, probably resembles the original. The escutcheon on the top drawer front is a dummy; there is no lock.
Like the gateleg table in Figure 65, this chest of drawers incorporates re-used timber. The inside edges of the corner stiles (the part now inside the carcase and out of sight) are channel-moulded and obviously once formed part of an earlier piece of furniture.

96

98

97

Figure 97.
CHEST OF DRAWERS.
Oak. 1760–1810.
This small chest doubles as a dressing table and is fitted with a brushing slide, a wooden board which pulls out from under the top and forms a useful surface on which clothes can be brushed, for example. A section of the top is hinged and lifts up to reveal a mirror.

Figure 98.
CHEST OF DRAWERS.
Oak. 1750–1800.
This example forms a complete contrast to the chest in Figure 96. The construction is flush rather than panelled; the carcase front is plain and the drawer fronts have an ovolo lip moulding projecting around their edges which hides the gap between drawer and carcase.

In the late 17th century fashionable chests of drawers would often have a pair of half-width (short) drawers at the top and three full-width (long) drawers below them gradually increasing in size, with the largest drawer at the bottom. In the 18th century this arrangement of drawers became almost standard and can be seen on the oak chest here. By the time this chest was made, the dovetails of the drawers had become finer and more numerous on pieces of this quality upwards. The handles are modern.

1690s onwards (e.g. **Figures 99, right, and 101**). In the early 18th century a conscious effort was made to disguise the gap between the drawer and the carcase; this was achieved around 1710 by the use of a small ovolo lip moulding which, projecting around the outside of each drawer front, hid the gap effectively (e.g. **Figures 98 and 103**), the carcase itself being left flat-faced. Lip mouldings have continued to be used on much vernacular furniture up to the present day. Their worst weakness, however, is their tendency to break off if the drawer is slammed in too hard. It was possibly an attempt to overcome that deficiency which resulted in an alternative, known as cock beading, being devised. A cock bead is a thin strip of wood inset all around the outside of a drawer with its edge perpendicular to and standing slightly proud of the drawer's front surface. Unlike a lip moulding, it does not overlap the carcase (e.g. **Figures 107 and 112**). Cock beading had appeared by 1725[4] and gradually superseded lip moulding on better furniture. On lesser pieces, the time and expense involved in making cock beading were frequently avoided by merely simulating it with incised lines. At the same time, a form of ovolo lip moulding existed in which the edges were flush with the drawer sides rather than projecting beyond them, thus solving the problem of breakage.

When veneered furniture came into vogue during the second half of the 17th century, it became the usual practice to frame the main veneered surface of flush areas such as drawer fronts, table tops and doors with a border of veneer set with its grain diagonally or at right angles to the central part. This 'crossbanding', so-named to distinguish it from straight

99

Figure 99.

TWO CHESTS OF DRAWERS.

Oak. Both East Anglia, 1715–50.

Both these chests originally had linen presses mounted above them in the same way as the next piece and the scars are clearly visible on their tops. They also have the same arrangement of two drawers flanked by deep ones in the upper part – an East Anglian feature. The chest on the right displays double half-round mouldings between the drawers while the other retains the slightly earlier single style, although both chests are roughly contemporary. All the brassware has been replaced.

banding, which was cut *along* the grain, also came to be applied to common oak furniture which was otherwise unveneered. The complex herringbone form of crossbanding (with two parallel bands of opposed diagonal grain) seen on the oak chest in **Figure 101**, was popular on walnut furniture during the period 1690 to 1730 (and even up to 1760 in the provinces) although its use on oak is unusual. Crossbanding on oak furniture was normally restricted to the simple cross-grained variety. As a means of decoration on areas such as drawer fronts, table tops and fielded panels crossbanding continued into the 19th century, particularly in the north of England, where a version inset from the edge (**Figure 103**), more in the nature of inlay, also occurs.[5]

Deriving from Chinese prototypes, bracket feet were introduced in the late 17th century and became almost standard on 18th-century case furniture until Neoclassical foot styles ousted them from really fashionable use in the final decades. On dovetailed furniture bracket feet formed separate appendages glued to the bottom boards; their application to joined furniture was effected by simply affixing them to downward continuations of the corner stiles. The ease with which they could be applied seems to have proved irresistible to many Georgians, who saw in them a rapid method of bringing earlier, and to them merely old-fashioned, items of furniture up to date; it is, then, important to distinguish between bracket feet as later additions and those which are original to a piece. On more ambitious articles, bracket feet were sometimes shaped in a double-curved, or 'ogee', form (e.g. **Figures 95, 104 and 117**) – again a close reflection of Oriental prototypes.

100

101

Figure 100 (left).
CHEST OF DRAWERS WITH LINEN PRESS.
Oak, elm and fruitwood. East Anglia, 1740–90.
These large presses, here typically mounted on a chest of drawers, were used to store blankets, bed linen and table cloths while keeping them neatly pressed at the same time. The word 'press' here, of course, has a totally different meaning from that of 'clothes press', in which it is simply a synonym for cupboard. On this joined piece from Carrow Abbey, Norwich, the two small central drawers have deeply moulded fronts and there is a decorative ogee-arched moulding applied beneath the front edge of the top. The main drawers are lip moulded.

Figure 101 (above).
CHEST ON FRAME.
Oak with crossbanding. Probably Midlands, 1710–40.
A type of joined chest of drawers supported by a framed understructure (here with H-form stretchers and baluster turnings) which had long gone out of fashion in London by this time, this piece retains the outmoded double half-round style of mouldings between the herringbone-crossbanded drawer fronts. The thin, overhanging top is also crossbanded and the shaped apron is centred by a starburst inlay. The brass knobs are later.

Figure 102 (left).
BOX.
Oak. Probably Dorset, dated 1753.
The archaic carving on the front of this box includes the initials 'LM' and 'RE'. The box was later in the possession of the 19th-century poet William Barnes and his label, 'WRITINGS', is preserved on one end. Note the staple hinges. The hasp is missing.

102

Figure 103 (right).

CHEST ON STAND.

Oak with fruitwood crossbanding. North, 1735–70.
Both the unconventional style of crossbanding inset
from the edges of the drawers and the bands of
chequered parquetry on the top drawer of the base
section reflect this piece's geographical origin. The
cabriole legs end in trifid feet.

The brass hardware with pierced backplates is original
and is of a style much used in the second quarter of the
18th century although, in common with shaped,
unpierced examples (the so-called 'willow pattern'),
similar types were still being shown in brassfounders'
catalogues much later.

103

104

Figure 104 (above).

CHEST ON CHEST.

Oak. 1760–1800.

The reeded canted corners of the upper section have the
effect of lightening the appearance of what is otherwise
a rather overwhelmingly large piece of furniture.
There is blind fretwork above the three small top
drawers and this specimen on ogee bracket feet has the
added refinement of a brushing slide in the top of the
base section.

Simple brass bail handles of the pattern seen here,
popularly called 'swan-neck' from the S-curve at each
end, became fashionable during the second quarter of
the 18th century. Normally used in conjunction with
brass keyhole inserts, as in this case, they eventually
superseded both the solid and pierced backplate types
with matching key escutcheons over the next few
decades.

Unlike an ordinary chest, access to a chest of drawers did not depend on a hinged lid, and there was therefore no reason to limit its height. The idea of raising a chest of drawers by placing it on a separate stand was popular from the 1680s and was possibly inspired by the even earlier fashion of placing imported Oriental cabinets on stands. Sometimes the stand would incorporate one or more drawers matching those of the chest above it and eventually this practice became standard. At first the legs were turned and tied by stretchers but, in the 18th century, cabriole legs were substituted to give the whole piece a more fashionable Chinese flavour (Figure 103).

It was only a matter of time (by about 1710, in fact) before the idea of increasing the storage capacity of a chest of drawers simply by standing one chest on top of another had evolved. The combination was, naturally enough, called a chest on chest (Figure 104). In anticipation of the occasional necessity of having to move such an enormous piece of furniture, the upper chest was seldom permanently fixed but merely held

Figure 105.
BUREAU.
Oak. London, 1700–30.

Like the Coxed and Woster bureau shown in Figure 2, this simple oak bureau has the very rare distinction of bearing the original trade label of its maker. In this case, the maker is John Gatehouse of '"The Golden Ball" by the Ditch-side, near Holborn Bridge, London', a cabinetmaker recorded in a document of 1695 and known to have made fine furniture for the upper end of the social scale[7]. It is yet another example of so-called 'country' furniture which was actually made by an important London cabinetmaker as part of his range of more moderately priced goods. The bevel-edged drawer fronts are divided by half-round mouldings which continue onto the top of the desk section and a further moulding is applied along the bottom of the fall to serve as a paper- or book-rest. The interior, with a well, is fitted with a series of drawers and pigeon-holes. The brassware and bracket feet are later.

105

Figure 106.
DESK.
Oak. 1700–30.

The two small drawers either side of the top of this desk with half-round mouldings act as lopers to support the fall. Very similar desks, with two pedestals of drawers flanking a cupboard-backed recess to accommodate the user's knees but with a flat top instead of a purpose-built desk section, were probably intended to double as a dressing table. The door panels of the cupboard backing the recess on this piece are only roughly chamfered to field them. The brassware is later, the keyhole inserts anachronistic and the modern feet clumsy replacements of original bracket or bun types.

106

Figure 107.
BUREAU BOOKCASE.
Oak. 1740–65.

Similar to the early piece in Figure 109 but here the well has been replaced by a drawer, there is no horizontal moulding round the carcase and the drawers are cockbeaded. There is an unusual vertical moulding at the rear of the bureau sides. The cupboard doors, again with candle slides beneath them, have pegged mortise-and-tenon joints and contain fielded panels with elaborated arches.

The original 'willow pattern' brassware is of a type introduced in the first half of the 18th century but, as with the pierced variety (Figure 103), identical designs still appeared in brassfounders' catalogues of the 1780s.

107

in place by an applied moulding round three sides of the top of the lower chest.

Both chests on stands and chests on chests are now known as 'tallboys'. The term was certainly in use by the second half of the 18th century (when it was mentioned in the *Dublin Mercury* of 1769[6]) and it was probably used to describe any high chest of drawers, whether on a stand or on another chest. In Gillow's cost books of 1784 'tallboy' refers to what is simply a tall chest of two short and five long drawers.

Desks have been made as portable slope-lidded boxes up to the present day but during the second half of the 17th century it was becoming quite common to attach them permanently to stands. Eventually the flap was hinged at the bottom instead of the top in many examples. When open, the flap was supported by lopers, two extractable lengths of wood, and thus formed a writing surface. The flap became known as a 'fall'. Better-quality desks of this type, often with a leather or baize covering set into the writing surface, were called 'bureaux' by polite society, although the term 'desk'

108

Figure 108.
BUREAU.
Oak with mahogany crossbanding. Lancashire/ Cheshire, 1775–1810.

Reeded quarter-columns are a constantly recurring feature of furniture from the North of England; the rectangular plinths are fronted here by bands of parquetry. The fall has the common characteristic on unveneered bureaux of end cleats, mitred at the top, and both the fall and the drawer fronts are crossbanded in mahogany. The space between the lopers, usually occupied by a well on early pieces, is filled by two drawers.

109

Figure 109.
BUREAU BOOKCASE.
Oak. 1710–35.

A grand (and expensive) piece of furniture; the early practice of using applied mouldings round the carcase to separate visually the chest of drawers and the desk section is retained on this example. The theme of double half-round mouldings seen between the drawers of the base is repeated in miniature on the interior divisions of the upper section. The small central cupboard behind the well in the desk is flanked by half-columns and near them are two small shelves which pull out under the pair of cupboard doors to the bookcase. These slides were intended to support candlesticks which helped to shed light on the writing surface. On finer bureau bookcases the panels of the cupboard doors were often mirrors which reflected the candlelight still further.

The original brassware is of an early type with engraved backplate and centrally moulded bail.

has continued to be used in the provinces and, particularly, North America. 'Bureau' comes from the French word for desk which, in turn, came from an earlier word referring to a baize covering.

By the end of the 17th century it became usual to substitute a chest of drawers for the stand and this developed into the typical 18th-century English bureau (**Figure 105**). Like most early bureaux (up to about 1740 or so in the South-East), this example has a storage compartment, or 'well', in the space between the lopers which is reached via a sliding panel in the floor of the desk section. The interior of the desk is fitted with a series of small concave-fronted drawers below a row of arched open compartments popularly known as pigeon-holes. Often (as here) the arches over the open compartments are the fronts of tiny drawers. Inside many bureaux is a small central cupboard which is generally flanked by two applied pillars and normally each pillar is the front of yet another tall drawer. The variety of unexpected or 'secret' compartments within their inner recesses makes bureaux one of the most fascinating types of furniture. Sometimes there is a hidden drawer behind the more obvious one in front. Occasionally the lopers are hollow and are really unsuspected drawers.

Extra storage space was sometimes provided by the addition of a structure on the level top surface of the desk section. Most frequently this took the form of a cupboard filled mainly with shelves and sometimes a series of small drawers, pigeon-holes or a combination of both, echoing their counterparts inside the desk, and effectively forming an enclosed bookcase (**Figures 107 and 109**). Occasionally the interior is fitted out entirely with drawers, pigeon-holes and, perhaps, a miniature internal cupboard without any shelves at all. Then the validity of the usual term 'bookcase' must be questioned; 'cabinet' may be more appropriate.

110

Figure 110.

LOW DRESSER.

Pine, originally stained brown. West Sussex,
1700–30.

*An early example of an English formal dresser in pine.
Until recently, its significance unrecognised, this piece
was in a dirty, dilapidated condition and served as a
shop counter in the village store at Westhampnett,
near Chichester, Sussex. It possibly had a set of shelves
mounted above it at one time and, as such, may well
represent a local survival of Spershott's contemporary
reference to 'deal dressers with shelves over for pewter,
&c.'.*

*Three drawers, dovetailed and double-fronted by half-
round mouldings, are separated by a bold horizontal
moulding from a central fixed panel flanked by two
cupboard doors in the base. All front panels are fielded.
There are signs that the stump feet had brackets affixed
at some time, though these may not have been
original. It is interesting to note that 18th-century
dressers with enclosed bases were by no means
exclusively confined to the North, as has sometimes
been thought. All the brassware is modern.*

The concept of a formal dresser, mentioned in Chapter 3 (**Figures 55–58**),
remained fashionable for the dining rooms of large houses in some parts of
England, notably in the North and the West Midlands, throughout the 18th
century (although it was in many cases eventually supplanted by the finer
sideboard of 'Adam' type which had become fashionable in London during
the third quarter). In these homes the formal dresser and the kitchen dresser
were usually still quite distinct from each other; while the former, an
elegant piece of furniture, took pride of place in a main reception room, the
latter remained a basic kitchen piece. However, the concept of the formal
dresser had also been adopted lower down the social scale early in the 18th
century; its use spread to much humbler dwellings, where it tended to
merge with its kitchen counterpart, especially in those homes where
parlour and kitchen formed a single room.

It is evident that both the formal and the combined formal/kitchen
types of dresser were regarded as ideal successors to the old press cupboard
and inherited at least some of the latter's prestige in the ordinary house. In
order to retain, and indeed increase, the display capacity provided by the
superseded press cupboard, it became common in many regions to mount
shelves above the dresser, converting it into a 'high dresser'. This
arrangement was perhaps partly inspired by the purely functional versions
in kitchens and sculleries, although now the shelves were used as a vehicle
for display rather than merely as storage space. The provision of a shelved
superstructure was by no means universal, however, and 'low dresser'

91

types (e.g. **Figures 112 and 117**) continued in some regions well into the 1800s.

Both the physical form of the dresser and the status that it was accorded varied enormously from one region of England to another. In the South-East, the concept of a dresser as a display piece was adopted in the homes of less well-off yet fashion-conscious people at an early stage but appears to have been generally regarded as unworthy of serious attention by their social superiors in the 18th century. This attitude is perhaps reflected in Spershott's specific use of the word 'deal' as a description (see page 76 and the dresser, probably from this region, shown in **Figure 110**), although better woods are occasionally found. By mid-century, the formal dresser in the South-East seems to have been mainly restricted to the lower classes, where it merged with the workaday variety. In the West Country, too, the dresser was apparently not considered to be of great importance in the 18th century and few early specimens survive. Likewise, in East Anglia, the dresser does not appear to have achieved real prestige at this time; extant examples tend to be fairly plain pieces of low dresser form.

Figure 111.
LOW DRESSER.
Elm and oak.
North-West/West Midlands, 1730–90.
This piece's line of descent from the type of earlier dresser shown in Figure 55 is obvious; the shaped apron and turned front legs are rough parallels, but here the turning is more restrained, heavy mouldings and panelled ends have been replaced by flush surfaces, the drawers are lip moulded and the rear legs are chamfered. The present set of brassware is a later replacement; the original handles and key escutcheons appear to have been of the 'willow pattern' variety.

Figure 112.
LOW DRESSER.
Oak. North-West/West Midlands,
1760–1820.
Both front and rear legs are shaped, here in a round-section straight form tapering to a pad foot. The end panels are recessed and the three cock-beaded drawers are fitted with simple keyhole inserts to complement swan-neck handles. Apron fretting is kept to a minimum.

113

Figure 113.

LOW DRESSER.

Oak with mahogany crossbanding. North-West/
West Midlands, 1740–80.

The exceptional quality of this dresser is reflected in the
relief-carved edging to the frets between the small
drawers in the apron and the use of four cabriole legs
across the front. The rear legs are chamfered on the
inside edge – in keeping with the 'Marlborough' style
popular at this period. End panels, in this case lip
moulded to match the drawers, applied over the
framing are common on dressers from this region.

The picture is entirely different in the North and the West Midlands, where the formal dresser was embraced wholeheartedly and where its prestige survived intact into the 19th century. While cheaper timbers, such as pine, were naturally used for purely utilitarian or inferior pieces (the possible superstructure in **Figure 194**), the better dressers of these regions were frequently of oak, well made and sometimes lavishly decorated. Those from the West Midlands tended to retain the old open-based low dresser form of their fine 17th-century predecessors (**Figures 111–116**). Their appearance was eventually updated by the substitution, in turn, of cabriole and square legs for the outmoded turned types, and often by the addition of a shelved superstructure on top. Open-based dressers continued northwards into South Lancashire, but the general preference in many parts of the North was for bases enclosed by drawers and cupboards (**Figures 117 and 118 and 121–123**). Unlike in the South-East, where the dresser simply supplanted the press cupboard, some dressers of the North-West appear to have evolved almost directly from the press cupboard itself and retained much of the latter's pre-eminence in ordinary homes.

To some extent, the superior quality of 18th-century dressers (and many other contemporary pieces of vernacular furniture) from the North and the Midlands reflected the increased prosperity that industrialisation brought to these areas. It was, perhaps equally, also a manifestation of the

114

Figure 114.
HIGH DRESSER.
Oak. North-West/West Midlands,
1750–1810.

A high dresser with a base similar to the previous pieces, here with flush ends, three cock-beaded drawers and front and rear cabriole legs ending in a squared foot. The shelves of the superstructure are flanked by cupboards with arch-top fielded panels to their doors and upper arched alcoves. The plain frieze echoes the lack of a shaped apron to the base. The back boards of the superstructure are a modern addition.

Figure 115.
HIGH DRESSER.
Oak with mahogany crossbanding. Probably West Midlands, 1780–1820.

The continued use of cabriole legs on this dresser type has frequently led to the attribution of a much earlier date than is indicated by a closer examination of other features; any artefact must always be dated from its latest original component. In fact, the cabriole leg enjoyed longer popularity on vernacular furniture than is commonly supposed — particularly in its debased form on turned chairs (e.g. Figures 292 and 300) although occasionally on regional joined furniture as well, as here. Though old-fashioned at the time, the cabriole leg appears to have been regarded by many ordinary people as superior to the simple, square type even at this late period. Its survival is paralleled by the retention of archaic bracket feet, of both plain and ogee form, for other furniture from this area.

The shaped frieze of the superstructure matches the apron on the base. The pair of cupboards, their doors inlaid with a shell motif, surmount small drawers. The swan-neck handles on the base drawers are original.

115

116

Figure 116.
HIGH DRESSER.
Oak with mahogany crossbanding. Probably
West Midlands, 1790–1820.
On this example the apron is treated in a different
manner from the fretted frieze and the central
pendants are reminiscent of central bracket feet. The
arrangement of shelves flanked by cupboards is almost
standard, as is a horizontal back board for only the
lowest open cavity, leaving the remainder unbacked
(except for thin horizontal rails on this piece). The
cupboard doors have a crude diamond inlay and the
frieze is parquetry-banded below a mahogany veneer.
A late date is suggested by the simple flat edges of the
top surface of the base and by the quadruple reeding to
the small shelves above the cupboards. The feet are
damaged and the brassware has been replaced.

innate concern for sturdy craftsmanship and love of ornamentation shown by the inhabitants of those areas, traits which had often been revealed in the previous century. A great many low dressers, both the open-based and enclosed types, from these regions have survived and, while a large proportion of them are obviously complete as intended, it is likely that many apparent 'low dressers' (from here and elsewhere) made from at least as early as the mid-18th century onwards were originally provided with a shelved superstructure. Since this was probably fixed to the wall in most cases and merely rested on the lower section, there was no need to attach it permanently to the top of the 'low dresser'. Thus a large number of these superstructures were subsequently separated and, partly because of their unwieldy size and relatively simple, flimsy nature, have been lost.

After the late 18th century, even dressers from the north of England became fairly utilitarian whereas in Wales the demotion was much slower. There, dressers retained their prestigious status well into the 19th century. The large quantity of high-quality examples from that country has

117

Figure 117.
LOW DRESSER.
Oak with mahogany crossbanding. North-West/ West Yorkshire, 1760–1830.
Here a central flush door has been crossbanded down its centre to resemble the usual configuration of double doors seen on the dressers in Figures 118 and 121. The pleasantly long, low proportion has been preserved and this piece stands on ogee bracket feet — particularly common in this region (cf. Figures 95, 121 and 134) as are the crossbanded spandrels, here restricted to the top half of the cupboard door.

118

Figure 118.
LOW DRESSER.
Oak with burr elm and pear crossbanding. North-West/West Yorkshire, 1750–1800.
The top drawers at each end have been crossbanded down their centres to convey the impression of two small drawers and harmonise with those above the central cupboard doors. The fielded panels of the doors are arched whereas those on the ends are simple rectangles. The relationship of both this and the previous piece with the high dresser shown in Figure 121 is obvious. It is certainly possible that these first two low dressers originally had similar superstructures which have since been lost. Nevertheless, low dressers of this kind also appear to have been an established form in this region and it is equally possible that these examples never had shelves[8]. The handles have been replaced.

119

Figure 119.
LOW DRESSER.
Walnut. West Somerset, 1760–1800.
A distinctive regional type; the slab ends, often concave-shaped as in this piece, are common to dressers from around the Quantock/Sedgemoor area of Somerset and can also be seen on those in Figures 120, 124 and 125. Here the slab ends are used for a low dresser form, with an ovolo-moulded top, three lip-moulded drawers and the unusual feature of a potboard, perhaps for storing water crocks and the large cooking pots and saucepans used on open fires. Note the central foot. The swan-neck handles are replacements, but similar to the originals.

120

119a

Figure 120.
LOW DRESSER.
Elm. West Somerset, 1760–1800.
Joined construction at its crudest: careful pegged mortise-and-tenon joints for the front combined with rough through-tenons for the ends – while the two drawers, not provided with locks, are merely nailed together. The top has an ovolo edge moulding and the drawer fronts are lip-moulded. It is quite possible that there were separate shelved superstructures, simple and open-backed, above this and the previous piece originally. The sledge feet have been replaced.

Figure 119a.
(Detail of Figure 119.)
The use of slab ends on dressers from this region apparently has a long history; examples dating from the early 18th century have been noted.

121

subsequently resulted in 'Welsh dresser' being erroneously used as a popular label for all dressers, regardless of their true national origin.[9]

Cupboards made to fit into the corner of a room, making the most of otherwise unused space (particularly important in small houses), became very popular during the 18th century. We are not concerned here with the grander architectural corner cupboards, frequently with concave barrel-backs and intended to complement the panelling of a richly appointed room, which are outside the scope of this book, but with humbler varieties such as those in **Figures 4, 126 and 127**. These were normally sited in one of the main downstairs rooms of the house and probably often served the same purpose as the old press cupboard – primarily the storage of dining articles – although they no doubt had many uses. Loudon, writing in 1833, advocated their use as an accessory to a dresser, for keeping 'cups and saucers, glasses, the tea-caddy, liquors in daily use, &c.'. They were often built in and many therefore had no backs. (A large number of those seen today have had backs added later. Even cupboards originally made with backs have sometimes had replacements because backs were frequently made of softwood or elm, which are very susceptible to woodworm and rot caused by close proximity to what were often damp walls.)

Figure 121.
HIGH DRESSER.
Oak with mahogany crossbanding. West Yorkshire, 1770–1800.

All the best examples of formal dressers must have come from fairly prosperous homes. This impressive showpiece apparently stood all its life in a stately upstairs hallway in the manorial setting of Field House, near Sowerby Bridge, West Yorkshire, until the disposal of the house contents in 1985. It was used to display fine china and was obviously held in high esteem. Certainly, such articles were a far cry from the utilitarian dresser in the kitchen.

The pair of cupboard doors in the base have inlaid paterae and flush panels edged by raised ogee-arched borders echoing the arches of the alcoves above the cupboard doors, with spandrel inlays, in the upper section. At Field House, the base cupboard held more china and the drawers stored bed linen – appropriate for its upstairs location[10].

Figure 122.
HIGH DRESSER.
Oak base with later stained pine (?) superstructure.
Base: North, 1760–1800.
The usual arrangement of drawers around a central cupboard but here in a breakfront form and without any crossbanding; the central recess is flanked by fluted canted corners and the outer corners of the base are simply bead-moulded. The single door panel has shaped spandrels – an ancestral form of the crossbanded varieties seen on other pieces (see Figure 117). The superstructure, with dentil cornice, is probably a 19th-century replacement.

122

Figure 123.
HIGH DRESSER.
Oak with fruitwood quarter-columns and mahogany crossbanding. Yorkshire, 1750–90.
Another breakfront dresser; the central portions of both base and superstructure are recessed and all corners are ornamented with plain fruitwood quarter-columns. The shaping of the brackets under the cornice is echoed in the bracket feet and the top of the cupboard door, which overlaps the carcase in the same manner as the trunk door on a longcase clock. Here, there is no upper row of three drawers to the base; instead, the central door spans the full height, a common arrangement in Yorkshire, where this example was found. As usual with high dressers, the top shelf is extra-deep to allow for the display of large dishes. Since large dishes were used less often than normal dinner plates, it was not as important to store them within easy reach.

123

Figure 124.
HIGH DRESSER.
Elm. West Somerset, 1780–1820.
Although from the same county as the next piece, the three drawers and the dramatic profiles of frieze, apron and superstructure ends reflect a higher quality and give this dresser greater visual appeal. It does, however, share the method of using a single board of timber from cornice to foot for each slab end (although cut through at one time for removal on this example) and the normal extra-deep space above the top shelf. Here, the base fronts of the the slab ends are not shaped and there is a single horizontal back board to the lowest shelf cavity. The drawers, with cock beading simulated by incised lines round the fronts, are merely nailed together and only the centre one has a lock.

The double doors frequently fitted to these cupboards took up little space when fully opened and allowed the contents of the cupboard to be displayed; old pictures occasionally show the doors of corner cupboards left open to reveal a treasured dinner service neatly arranged on the shelves. In more expensive cupboards the doors of the upper section were sometimes glazed. Many humbler versions have had their panels replaced by glass in more recent times to enhance their desirability. Even more deplorable is the modern practice of removing the doors entirely and discarding them.[11] Smaller corner cupboards intended to hang on a wall (Figures 128, 130 and 131) had the advantage of leaving floor space free.

Figure 125.
HIGH DRESSER.
Elm. West Somerset, 1780–1810.
Until the 1950s there were large estates of late 18th-century terraced houses in Bridgwater, Somerset, and this type of dresser (the 'Bridgwater dresser') was a standard fitting in the back room of each of them. For economy, simple boards were merely nailed together and there are no drawers. This example has modern feet and the pine cornice is also possibly later.

Figure 126.
CORNER CUPBOARD.
Oak with mahogany crossbanding. North-West,
1790–1830.
The horizontal dado moulding of the following piece is
repeated here but there is no moulded frame and the
cupboard stands on bracket feet. A mahogany-
veneered frieze is substituted for a dentil moulding and
it comes below a mean cornice – suggesting a late date.
The flush door panels are crossbanded with a quadrant
in each corner – a Classical feature particularly
common at this period (cf. Figures 131, 238 and
240 et al.). The top panels boast oval inlays depicting
vases of flowers.

127   126

Figure 127.
CORNER CUPBOARD.
Ash with cherry crossbanding. Cheshire/North-
East Wales, 1770–1820.
Upper and lower sections are separated by a strong
horizontal moulding which was intended to correspond
with the dado rail in a room and both parts are set
within a moulded frame. All door panels are fielded
and the top panels are half-arched – forming a
complete arch together. The cornice is decorated with
an applied dentil moulding.

In the 18th century clothes presses usually had drawers fitted in the base, the main upper part being left as a large, empty space with hooks or pegs around the top for hanging clothes, as had been the custom in the 17th century. By 1750, the alternative fashion of fitting the main part with sliding trays on which to lay folded clothes had also become common. Furniture with either method of clothes storage was known by the same name, 'clothes press', 'press' simply being an old term for 'cupboard', in this context having nothing to do with its other meaning, that of exerting pressure. On finer furniture, both methods of storing clothes were often combined in a single, large clothes press with one part for hanging and another fitted with trays.

Towards the end of the 18th century, the term 'clothes press' was being dropped from usage in polite society and the new term 'wardrobe' substituted. It is clear that for most people at that time (and for some time

128

Figure 128.

HANGING CORNER CUPBOARD.

Pine, yellow ground painted with a grey vase of red and blue flowers, green foliage and supplementary floral designs, all within brown striped borders.

Probably South, 1720–60.

Bow-fronted corner cupboards, usually of oak, lacquered with chinoiserie motifs and embellished with finely pierced brass butterfly hinges in imitation of Oriental work, were at the height of fashion during the early to mid-18th century. Occasionally there was a demand for a more European character and a range of cupboards decorated with historical scenes or, as here, floral themes was produced, although the Chinese-style hinges were retained. The European patterns were often of a slightly inferior quality and normally on pine, although it would be wrong to regard such cupboards as having been aimed at anything less than a middle-class market. This example, with typical half-round moulding on the door, preserves its shelved superstructure and original brassware.

129

Figure 129.

HANGING FOOD CUPBOARD.

Elm with pine door, traces of original red-brown paint finish. 1710–1820.

A rare survival of the very simplest boarded construction – possibly home-made – from an early date. The door, enclosing a single shelf, is crudely pierced for ventilation and the H hinges are original. Such furniture must have been made over a very long period; it represents a basic version of the boarded cupboards in Figures 28–30 and 62, and should be compared with a faintly similar cupboard in the painting by Hogarth shown in Figure 88.

130

131

Figure 130.
HANGING CORNER CUPBOARD.
Oak. North-West, 1760–90.
*An attractive cupboard; the front is stepped forward
and flanked by fluted quarter-columns. There is a bold
cornice with dentil ornament and the fielded door panel
is ornately arched. The marks of the original H hinges
are still quite visible.*

Figure 131.
HANGING CORNER CUPBOARD.
Oak with mahogany crossbanding. North,
1780–1810.
*A bow-fronted cupboard echoing the simple top and
base mouldings of earlier versions. The double doors,
crossbanded and veneered with quadrants to the base
and double-concaves to the top, come between fluted
pilasters and can be left open to reveal china displayed
on three shaped shelves within. Also inside are three
small drawers. The H hinges and urn-topped key
escutcheons are over-polished but may be original.*

after) the two names were synonymous – both describing either the kind of
furniture with hanging space, the type with sliding trays or a piece
combining both. However, although both Hepplewhite and Loudon
depicted what they named a 'wardrobe' completely fitted with trays or
shelves above one or two drawers and with no hanging space, Sheraton and
some of his contemporaries chose to call this type of furniture only by its
old name, 'clothes press', and restrict the newer term 'wardrobe' purely to
pieces in which the clothes could be hung. Sheraton's arbitrary usage is the
one generally followed in England today; thus the strange situation has
arisen where pieces of either kind which were made before the late 18th
century are called 'clothes presses', while for those of a later date a
distinction is made.[12]

By the present century the practice of hanging larger items of clothing
was much preferred to that of keeping them folded on shelves and many of
the early clothes presses with shelves have subsequently had their shelves

132

Figure 132.
CLOTHES PRESS.
Oak with fruitwood crossbanding. North Midlands,
1725–60.
An early example on stump feet. The simply arched
fielded panels of the doors are crossbanded and include
a starburst inlay, which is quite common on furniture
from this area (though used elsewhere). The two base
drawers come below rectangular fielded panels and the
lozenge bands of parquetry behind their handles are
also in keeping with a northern origin. The piece is
restored.

Figure 133.
CLOTHES PRESS.
Oak. North, 1750–1800.
Stopped fluting appears to have been the forte of this
piece's maker; not only does it appear on the quarter-
columns to the top section and on the canted corners of
the base but it has been given full and spectacular rein
on the wide upright between the fielded panel doors.
The press stands on ogee bracket feet.

133

Figure 134 (right).
CLOTHES PRESS.
Oak. North-West, 1760–1810.
*A series of fluted pilasters runs along the top section of
this press which includes two doors with double fielded
panels flanking a similarly panelled fixed portion. All
the end panels are also fielded. To complement such a
grandiose design, the pilasters are topped by a
mahogany-veneered frieze and a dentilated cornice.
The base section, with central cupboard, is somewhat
similar to that of the dresser in Figure 122. The whole
stands on ogee bracket feet.*

134

135

Figure 135 (above).
CLOTHES PRESS.
*Oak with mahogany crossbanding. North,
1750–90.
More akin to the modern idea of a wardrobe; the
enclosed space dominates this press and the two
drawers are relegated to a small separate stand below.
The arched tops of the fielded and crossbanded door
panels have an Oriental flavour but the fluted quarter-
columns on the corners are decidedly Classical. The
sides of both sections are flush. The stand has an
attractively fretted apron and rests on four short
cabriole legs; the right-hand cabriole on the front has
lost one of its 'shoulder pieces', the projections either
side at the top which were made separately from the
main member. All the hardware is modern.*

removed in order to conform to modern taste.

As with many other types of vernacular furniture (e.g. dressers), the largest proportion of oak clothes presses to have survived appears to be from those parts of the North and the Midlands benefiting from the relative prosperity of industrial progress. Naturally, these extant presses must, for the most part, represent the better grades. It would seem that the lowest classes of the population even in industrial areas and, in particular, those living in poorer regions with agriculturally based economies, such as the far North, the South, the West Country and East Anglia, not only had less varieties of furniture on average per household but also that such pieces which they did own were likely to be of a quality so inferior in most cases as to render long-term survival improbable. In those houses which were provided with neither clothes presses nor built-in closets, clothing was stored in chests, in chests of drawers or merely hung on pegs wherever convenient.

136

Figure 136.
LONG TABLE.
Oak. 1760–1810.
A purposeful table on square-section legs tied by H-form stretchers. The legs are chamfered on three edges and the outer edge is finished with a bead moulding. The top is formed from three planks united by end cleats. No drawer.

Figure 137.
GATELEG TABLE.
Oak. 1710–40.
A late example with ogee-arched ends (no drawer) and rule joints between the top and the leaves. The column legs have a small baluster base and there are large turned feet below stretcher level. The oak is a soft honey colour.

137

Figure 138.
DROP-LEAF TABLE.
Oak. 1750–1800.

A rectangular-topped table on straight legs; as usual, one leg each side swings out to support the leaves. Similar to the cabriole leg in the round turned section and the pad foot, these straight legs were likewise of Oriental inspiration but far easier to make, less wasteful of timber and, of course, cheaper. Very often (though not on this example) the square-section top portion is bead-moulded in the same manner as contemporary 'Marlborough' legs, thus confirming a late date range. The feet are re-tipped.

139

138

Figure 139.
DROP LEAF TABLE.
Oak. 1730–70.

A confident version of its finer cousins in mahogany and aimed at only a slightly lower income bracket, this table with well-proportioned cabriole legs was undoubtedly the product of an experienced cabinet-maker who probably also used fine timbers for his upmarket range. The fretted ogee-arched ends are particularly lively and the edges of the oval top are gently bevelled. A rule joint between top and leaves has now become a standard feature of tables with folding leaves. The secondary timber is pine. (The raised rectangular decoration to each foot recurs frequently on Irish furniture and Irish origin is certainly possible here, although oak is unusual for that country.)

TABLES

The humbler kinds of large dining tables surviving from the 18th and 19th centuries (**Figure 136**) have been dubbed 'farmhouse tables' because of their frequent association with that type of dwelling. They were commonly equipped with either the older four-stretcher (or box-stretcher) arrangement or a distribution of three stretchers in an H-form. In the latter case, the single lengthwise stretcher allowed greater footroom and made it easier for stools, forms and chairs to be pushed in when not in use. In some regions, the tops of these utilitarian tables were often deliberately not fixed; being reversible, the top could be scrubbed on one side for food preparation and polished on the other for dining.[13] Alternatively, in many areas the fixed top would be kept polished for dining and a separate flat cover, or 'table board', placed on the table to protect it when used for ordinary kitchen work. Occasionally, these tables had one or two drawers and those intended purely for the preparation of food sometimes have such a deep frieze under the top that it would be impossible to sit at them comfortably for dining.

The gateleg table continued in use for more elegant dining in the first part of the 18th century. By 1720, the top was not always fixed by pegs from above; instead, it was increasingly common for the top to be secured

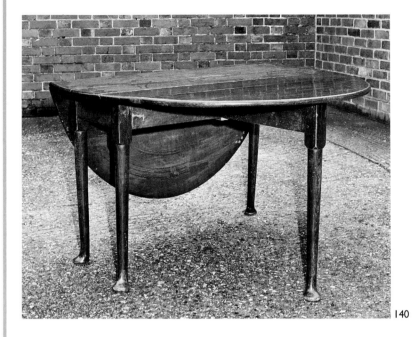

140

Figure 140.
DROP-LEAF TABLE.
Oak. 1750–1800.
An oval-topped example; all mortise-and-tenon joints are pegged. As usual, the edges of the top are simply flush, the secondary timber (for the side rails) is pine and the leaf hinges are wrought iron, secured by screws.

Figure 141.
DROP-LEAF TABLE.
Oak. 1760–1820.
This larger-than-usual drop-leaf table on square-section 'Marlborough' legs has all four corner legs (chamfered inside with a bead moulding on the outer edge) hinged in order to support the extra-heavy leaves. To retain stability there are two more, central, legs fixed to the underframe. This example also has the refinement of ogee-arched ends.
This basic table type, normally with the standard four legs, was still being made in the mid-19th century, although by then the legs were usually not chamfered and were often tapered. Frequently, such pieces formed the central part, with a D-shaped table added to each extended leaf, of a much larger dining table.

by large screws from below, by means of gouges on the inside of the rails (see **Figure 5a**), obviating the presence of unsightly marks on the top surface.

With the increasing European adoption of Oriental style in the early 18th century, traditional forms of furniture had to be modified in order to

141

Figure 142.
TRIANGULAR GATELEG TABLE.
Oak. Probably South, 1690–1750.

An unusual type of table on a triangular frame; the single leaf, butt-jointed to the top, can be supported on the gate to form a square surface when required. This example appears to have been heavily 'restored' at some time and the ovolo-moulded top raised on timber inserted above the frame. The straight-grained oak, particularly visible on the leaf, is likely to be 'wainscot' imported from the Continent.

While both this and the following table were essentially multi-purpose, it is likely that they were intended primarily as tea or card tables. The type is ancestral to the table in Figure 254.

142

141a

Figure 141a.
(Detail of Figure 141.)
The rule joint between the fixed top and the leaf – a working part that is especially vulnerable and commonly repaired. The joint received its name from its resemblance to the hinged joints of folding wooden rulers used by carpenters.

accommodate new elements. In particular, the cabriole leg was uncomfortably allied to a stretcher framework and was certainly unsuitable to the complex gateleg system. A novel form of folding- or drop-leaf table, with swing-legs, was devised to overcome this problem and it gradually ousted the gateleg table from fashionable use. Instead of being provided with special gates, the new type of table had two of its legs (at opposite corners) joined to rails which pivoted on a wooden hinge (or knuckle joint) at the centre of each underframe side so that the legs themselves could be swung out to support the leaves when desired. Not only did this method obviate the need for obtrusive gates but stretchers could also be dispensed with, leaving far more legroom under the top and thus making the table much more convenient for dining.

Although 'cabriole' was not a contemporary term for a curved leg[14], the word is apt since it comes from a French dancing term derived in turn from the Italian word *capriola*, referring to the leap of a goat or horse. The English word 'caper' stems from the same root. A cursory examination of the livelier interpretations of the type shown by the tables in **Figures 139 and 149** readily explains the appropriateness of the name. The manufacture of a good cabriole leg calls for a fair degree of skill and time-consuming labour in shaping it from a solid block of timber. It was therefore natural that an alternative design should also be popular; this took the form of a round-

Figure 143 (above).
TRIANGULAR FOLDING-TOP TABLE.
Yew. 1760–1820.
On this example, with round turned legs and pad feet,
the side-hinged leaf folds over on top. The left-hand leg
is split longitudinally; while the front part is fixed, the
rear half is joined to a rail which pivots on a knuckle
joint in the centre of the rear frieze and can be swung
out to support the leaf when unfolded, thus providing
an hexagonal surface. The flat edge of the top suggests
a late date. The yew employed for this table is a plain
variety lacking the normal figuring. Tables similar to
this type, with the leaf either hanging or folding on top
as here, are now popularly known as 'handkerchief'
tables in North America.

Figure 143a (left).
The table in Figure 143 shown in the open position.
The survival of the thin split leg over two centuries is a
143a *testament to the toughness of yew.*

section straight leg with a pad foot (Figures 138, 143 and 151), which was easier to make and slightly less wasteful of material.[15]

By the 1750s an alternative Oriental design, the so-called 'Marlborough' leg, was in fashion and gradually overtook the cabriole in popularity. This leg was straight and of square section, normally chamfered inside and generally provided with a bead moulding down the outside edge (Figure 141) – although this latter embellishment was frequently omitted on later vernacular versions (Figures 147 and 153).[16] In some instances, this leg had a pronounced convex 'knee' just below the junction with the underframe and the leg ran straight down from this curved projection, standing proud of the rails above it – in the same manner as some round-section straight legs had done. This kneed leg form was not a provincial transition from cabriole to square-section straight legs (as has sometimes been asserted) but was, in fact, a fairly accurate rendition of another Oriental prototype.

Figure 144.
SIDE TABLE.
Oak. 1735–60.
A stocky little side table on well-formed cabriole legs, this example is furnished with one long and two short drawers which are framed within double beaded mouldings applied to the carcase. The top also has a bead moulding around the upper edge and apron decoration is restricted to a small shaped pendant.

145

144

Figure 145.
SIDE TABLE.
Oak and walnut. Probably South, 1720–60.
Although incorporating walnut (a timber also used for 'fine' furniture), this is very much a simple table with functional end cleats to the top. The flush, lip-moulded drawer front and the proportions of the plain column-turned legs, tied by H-form stretchers, confirm an 18th-century date of manufacture. There is no lock nor upper rail to the drawer.

Figure 146.
SIDE TABLE.
Oak. 1700–50.
The preoccupation with fine furniture made in fashionable styles for wealthy clients has led to the popular conclusion that design changes were consistently universal. Thus simple joined furniture, such as this table, has too often been assigned an earlier date than is shown by a study of styles at vernacular level. The general appearance of this table and the ovolo edge moulding to the top look back to the 17th century, but the flush drawer front, the type of stretcher moulding and the style of leg turning suggest the date range given. As with the side table shown in Figure 69, there is no drawer lock (the key escutcheon is a dummy) and therefore no need for a rail above the drawer.

146

III

147

147a

Figure 147.
SIDE TABLE.
Pine, original finish removed. 1770–1820.
A fairly basic side table; although the mortise-and-
tenon joints are stoutly pegged, the drawer is merely
rabbeted and nailed together. The four legs are
pleasantly chamfered on the inside but there is no bead
moulding on the outer edge. This table was probably
stained originally. The base was later painted but the
top appears to have escaped; the table was possibly
demoted to kitchen use at this time as the mellow,
patinated pine grain is deeply ridged — often the result
of scrubbing. There is no lock nor upper rail to the
drawer. The cock beading and handle are modern.

Figure 147a.
(Detail of Figure 147.)
The top, with a generous overhang, is secured by four
large hand-forged nails driven through it into the tops
of the legs, a common means of fixing on vernacular
furniture.

Figure 148.
SIDE TABLE.
Oak with mahogany crossbanding. Probably Mid-
lands/East Anglia, 1740–85.
An archetypal 'lowboy' form, with one shallow and
two deep drawers arranged around a central arch. The
cabriole leg has been presented here in a square-section
form which is very close to Oriental prototypes — an
influence perhaps also reflected in the curved shaping of
the end bottoms, a gentle ogee arch which was by no
means restricted solely to Gothic design but recurred
frequently on early Chinese furniture as well. In fact,
although it is an essentially European furniture type,
this provincial side table conveys the impression of Far
Eastern style far more successfully than many finely
veneered examples. The top has a pleasant ogee edge-
moulding and both the top and the drawer fronts are
crossbanded; yet this is poorly executed, without
neatly mitred corners — a common failure on some
regional forms of crossbanding. The engraved brass
handles are probably replacements.

148

Figure 149 (right).
SIDE TABLE.
Oak. 1725–50.

Perched almost like a spider on its four pronounced cabriole legs with pointed feet, this table is a vigorous interpretation of the 'lowboy' form, but what appears to be the standard arrangement of three drawers, here framed by applied mouldings in an earlier fashion, is in fact just a single drawer. The simple but boldly arcaded aprons, also reminiscent of older styles, add to the dramatic impact. There is no lock nor upper rail to the drawer. The brass pendant handles appear to be original.

Figure 150 (below).
SIDE TABLE.
Oak. 1735–70.

Although this is a fairly standard piece, on pad feet, the round tapered legs are a little unusual in having raised tongues, or lappets, carved on the top portion before the member continues upwards to form part of the frame. The drawers are cock-beaded and the top, with rounded front corners, is trimmed with a bead moulding.

149

151

A specific type of side table with more than one drawer has become known as a 'lowboy' (**Figures 148–151 and 153**), although the term appears to date no further back than the late 19th century. This kind of table was obviously designed for sitting at, with the drawers arranged around a central arch to accommodate the sitter's knees, and they were probably intended as dressing or writing tables, or both.

The tripod table, in which the top (usually circular but sometimes square, rectangular or octagonal) is supported by a single pillar with a pedestal[17] having three legs, had become popular by the end of the 17th century.[18] Small versions served as occasional tables or as candlestands, and larger ones also for the new-fashioned, genteel custom of serving hot drinks, such as tea, coffee and chocolate. (Bearing witness to its increasing popularity, the annual import of tea alone had risen to over 100,000 lbs by 1700.[19]) On all these tables, the three legs are dovetailed into the pedestal and often a metal plate with three arms (a spider) is nailed or screwed underneath to strengthen the joints. Frequently, as on the example in **Figure 154**, the top is made to pivot on the block surmounting the pillar, allowing it to tilt to a vertical position; the table thus takes up less room when not in use or can even double as a firescreen.

Figure 151.
SIDE TABLE.
Oak. 1750–1800.
A late example on tapering round-section legs ending in pad feet. The frame ends are inset in the same manner as the drop-leaf tables on similar legs seen previously (Figures 138 and 140). The top edge is simply rounded and the apron shaping perfunctory. The drawers have only a very rough lip-moulding.

152

Figure 152.
TRIPOD PEDESTAL TABLE.
Oak with elm top. 1730–60.
A small version ideal for supporting a candlestick (hence the generic term 'candlestand'); similar pieces were also used to support a tea kettle. This example has a tapering, ring-turned column and the concave caps, or lappets, at the tops of the cabriole legs tend to be an early feature. The small top is in proportion to the base on a stand of this size but the use of elm may indicate that it is a replacement for an oak original.

Figure 153.
SIDE TABLE.
Pine, original red-brown stain imitating mahogany.
1770–1820.

With a dramatic mosque-like profile to the central arch, this humble pine table stands on square-section legs which are only slightly chamfered on the inside and without a moulding down the outer edge. Cock-beading is merely simulated on the drawer fronts by incised lines top and bottom, and there are no locks; nevertheless, the drawers are properly dovetailed and they retain the original brass swan-neck handles.

153

154

Figure 154.
TRIPOD PEDESTAL TABLE.
Oak. 1785–1820.

Tilt-top. A full-size table with scrolls under the cabriole legs where they join the pedestal on this example. The Neoclassical urn shape of the pillar was a motif beloved of this era, occurring on everything from sword pommels to candlesticks.

SEATING

The joined chairs most common in many parts of England during the early 18th century were high-backed types with turned posts, legs and stretchers, examples of which are shown in Chapter 3 (**Figures 80, 81, 83 and 84**), with Oriental design elements exerting an occasional influence (**Figure 12, right**). As a purer Oriental form was adopted by the richer classes during the first decades of the period, a joined chair with solid splat and cabriole legs became the ideal model;[20] early examples generally retained the high back of their late 17th-century turned-leg predecessors and substituted an H-form stretcher arrangement for the 'box' stretcher system usual on genuine Chinese prototypes. In accordance with the European preference for matching the design of seat to table furniture, stretchers were eventually relinquished altogether on finer chairs, a development occasionally extended to humbler types as well (**Figures 163 and 165, left**). Stretchers were, however, retained on most vernacular chairs in consideration of the likely necessity for greater strength than their statelier counterparts.

By the 1730s, chair backs had been reduced in height and it was becoming common to pierce the splats. Within two decades this trend had evolved into the so-called 'Chippendale' style, particularly characterised by a splat pierced in a variety of Classical, Chinese or Gothic designs and a crest rail flourishing into outward projections or 'ears' – in common with some

155

156

Figure 155 (left).
WINGED ARMCHAIR.
Oak. Pennines, dated 1707.
The panelled wings above the horizontally scrolled arms of this chair not only lent a sense of grandeur but also afforded some protection against cold draughts in a region subject to severe winters. The wings are trimmed with applied split turnings and their panels are carved on the outside. The decorated crest rail overlaps the uprights and is finished with pierced earpieces; the upper panel of the back itself is carved with the initials 'MC' within applied geometric mouldings. A central ball-turned strut comes between similarly turned front legs. (cf. Victor Chinnery, Oak Furniture. The British Tradition figures 4:54 and 4:55, which share some characteristics.)

Figure 156 (above).
WINGED ARMCHAIR.
Oak. North-West, 1750–90.
A humble vernacular version of the fine upholstered wing armchairs renowned as 'Queen Anne'. Instead of being upholstered all over, only the seat has rope webbing to support a loose cushion. The panelled back, slab arms, ogee-arched aprons and turned front legs all hark back to earlier times but there is an indisputable hint of the 18th century in the pointed nipples to the crest rail — vestigial reminders of scrolled cresting (cf. Figures 159 right, 162 and 163). Apart from the rope webbing to the seat, this armchair echoes contemporary settle types in the panelled back, the slab arms, the turned legs and the round-arched tops of the rear posts. The feet are missing.

Oriental prototypes[21] and to some extent a reflection of contemporary Rococo taste. It was at this time (the 1750s) that the 'Marlborough', or straight square-section, leg was being used as an alternative to the cabriole type and later gradually came to supersede it. Although most of his designs were essentially conventional rather than innovative, Thomas Chippendale's *The Gentleman and Cabinet-maker's Director* of 1754 (republished several times), along with other pattern books by contemporaries such as Robert Manwaring or the partnership of Ince and Mayhew, must have had tremendous influence in promulgating the fashions of the day; even makers who had never seen a pattern book themselves copied furniture made by someone who had. It is the enormous number of everyday chairs, conforming only roughly to the most basic features – pierced splat and projecting crest rail – of the style and generally made long after its heyday, which have come to be popularly named 'country Chippendale' (**Figures 164 and 165**).

A kind of vernacular chair with a humped crest rail which came into fashion in the last quarter of the 18th century (represented here by **Figures 168–170**) is commonly known as the 'camelback' type, from its distinctive

Figure 157.
ARMCHAIR.
Oak. Lake District, dated 1742.
In spite of the panelled back and archaic carving, a mid-18th century date for this piece should not really come as a surprise in view of the plain, square legs and high stretchers of the base. The crest rail bears the letters 'RSR' separated by oak leaves while a panel at the base of the back and the front seat rail are decorated with foliage. The slab arms owe more to the 17th century than to later times. The finials have been replaced[22].

157

Figure 158.
CHAIR.
Oak. Probably North/Wales, 1720–50.
The mature vasiform splat and square-section back members contradict the early date suggested by the turning and construction of the base. The maker has incorporated a fashionable back but was apparently loath to abandon a base form inspired by cane-seated chairs — one which had probably become a well-established convention in his region (cf. Figure 12, right).

CENTRE TABLE.
Oak. 1740–1820.
Furniture of this simplicity is almost impossible to date with any precision on style alone. The central stretcher of the H-form is simply lap-dovetailed to those at the ends, all mortise-and-tenon joints are pegged and the top is provided with end cleats (resulting in a large degree of splitting in the top boards).

158

159

Figure 159.

Left:
CHAIR.
Oak. 1760–1800.
This chair retains the solid splat, high back and rounded crest rail of the earlier style shown in Figure 162 but here the uprights and crest rail are square-sectioned, there is no curve to the back and the base adopts the 'Marlborough' front legs, bead-moulded on their outer edges, common from the mid-18th century onwards. It is far more utilitarian in concept and the legs are amply tied by stretchers for strength[23].

Right:
CHAIR.
Elm with oak seat. 1770–1820.
A much less substantial chair which demonstrates the vernacular persistence of the solid vasiform splat into the 19th century. Splat-shaping is minimal, the legs are not bead-moulded and the thin seat is simply nailed onto the frame, overlapping it. The lower back reflects a later fashion and, while the two nipples on the crest rail are vestigial remnants of early scrolled cresting, the ends flourish into 'Chippendale' 'ears'[24].

shape, or as 'country Hepplewhite' since it is loosely similar to finer chairs, in which the humped crest rail forms the top of a shield outline, illustrated in George Hepplewhite's *Cabinet Maker and Upholsterer's Guide* of 1788. The basic styles shown by Hepplewhite were in production before the posthumous publication of his pattern book and reflected the Neoclassicism promoted so enthusiastically by Robert Adam from the 1760s onwards. On common 'camelback' chairs, Neoclassical principles were usually strongly diluted; typically, the splat assumes a 'balloon' outline with a narrow waist and the front legs are occasionally tapered on their two inner faces.

The armchair shown in **Figure 171** is a late survival of an ornately turned chair tradition going back to the Middle Ages; the constructional type is more commonly represented in the 18th century by simpler turned chairs, typically with rush seats, which had been made at least since the 16th century and which were affordable by nearly all classes. These simpler chairs are characterised by four continuous posts, two of them extending well above the seat and tied by horizontal members to form a back. The majority of turned chairs of the 18th and 19th centuries may be broadly classified into two types, based on the formation of their backs: the spindleback, in which the back consists of various arrangements of turned spindles, and the ladderback, which has a series of horizontal, flattened slats, usually bowed for comfort. Seventeenth and early 18th-century

160

Figure 160.
CHILD'S HIGH CHAIR.
Ash and elm. Probably North, 1740–90.
This high-chair version of a common chair type retains several early features: rear legs with an octagonal mid-section, semi-slab arms with turned supports, and turned stretchers. At first glance, it looks almost transitional – between cane-panelled chairs and the splat-back with cabriole legs – and therefore early 18th-century. However, a comparison with other vernacular furniture types (settles and turned chairs) suggests that it is more likely to be merely archaic.

Figure 161.
'CORNER' CHAIR.
Elm. 1770–1810.
The popular term 'corner chair' as a description of this type is probably something of a misnomer as it is unlikely that such chairs were designed specifically to stand in a corner. A contemporary term was 'smoking chair' and, to some extent, this joined type may be regarded as related to the Windsor 'smoker's bow', fulfilling much the same function – i.e. frequently as an office or tavern chair. The three-piece arm bow is combined with two solid splats.

161

162

Figure 162.
CHAIR.
Oak. North, 1735–70.

The quality of this chair suggests that it was more likely to have been one of the more down-market products of a good cabinetmaker or chairmaker than the ordinary output of an inferior craftsman — and therefore probably closer to the period when its style was highly fashionable. The S-curve of the back and the round-section uprights are direct copies of Chinese prototypes and are generally an early sign — as are the shaped C-scrolls on the upper insides of the cabriole front legs, vestiges of an even earlier 'broken cabriole' type. However, the relative crudity of the square-section rear legs and other features indicate a later date and it is certainly likely that oak chairs of this style were still being made at least into the 1760s. Note the single turned stretcher between the rear legs. The shoulder pieces to the cabriole legs are missing.

163

Figure 163.
ARMCHAIR.
Elm. 1740–70.

Of exceptional quality for furniture made from elm, this armchair has an S-curved back and well-shaped arms, and the cabriole front legs and round-section rear legs are unencumbered by stretchers — in common with 'fine' chairs of this period. The chair has a drop-in upholstered seat held by rebates on the seat rails. Pierced splats of this type came into vogue during the 1730s; here it is combined with a scrolled crest rail.

examples of both types tended to have pronounced and fairly elaborate finials to the rear posts, but this feature was generally abandoned later.

In most cases, turned chairs continued traditional styles over a very long period and they are notoriously difficult to date with any real accuracy. For at least the first half of the 18th century it was still quite common to inscribe a date upon vernacular furniture having some special significance, but this practice was seldom extended to turned chairs. Two rare and historically valuable exceptions are the similar armchairs of ladderback type shown in **Figure 174**, which are both clearly incised with a date on the top slat. It would be dangerous to jump to the conclusion that inscribed dates on furniture, even if original to the piece, are necessarily indicative of its date of manufacture. Dates were frequently added to items in order to commemorate some event, either past or present, which could be totally

Figure 164.
CHAIR.
Elm. 1770–1820.

Again with square-section 'Marlborough' legs, in this case chamfered inside but without a bead moulding, tied by stretchers, this chair displays 'Gothic' splat piercing of a more competent variety than that of the right-hand chair in Figure 165. The crest rail is fully integrated with both the splat and the curved uprights. The applied convex moulding around the seat was possibly intended to help keep a cushion in place, although it also gives a more finished look to the chair (cf. Figures 159 left and 162).

Figure 165.
Left:
ARMCHAIR.
Elm. 1770–1820.

An archetypal 'Chippendale'-style armchair, with elaborated crest rail and a splat pierced in a 'Gothic' design at variance with the Oriental 'Marlborough' legs. Like the piece in Figure 163, this chair displays several signs of good craftsmanship: part of the intertwining splat pattern is raised, the arms terminate in carved scrolls and the legs, again without stretchers, are embellished with spandrels formed from the seat rails. It is provided with a drop-in seat which, in common with most Georgian armchairs, is generously proportioned. It almost seems a pity that the maker did not take the trouble to add a bead moulding to the front legs.

Right:
CHAIR.
Oak with fruitwood splat. 1770–1840.

In a different class altogether, this humble chair pays only vague homage to the illustrious styles which inspired it. The 'eared' crest rail sits starkly atop the splat and uprights rather than being integrated with them, the proportions have become mean, even for a single chair, and the square-section legs are united by functional box stretchers[25].

165

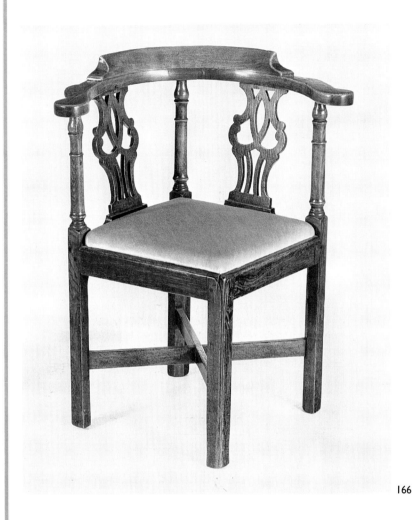

166

167

Figure 166.
'CORNER' CHAIR.
Oak and elm. 1770–1820.
Similar to the 'corner' chair in Figure 161, but having pierced splats and stretchers arranged in an X-form, all legs being chamfered inside to accommodate them. The front leg is bead-moulded. In this instance, the arm sections are centrally united by a lapped joint and the scrolled top section is simply mounted over them.

Figure 167.
COMMODE CHAIR.
Elm. Probably East Anglia, 1780–1830.
The exceptionally wide seat rails conceal a chamber pot which is mounted beneath the removable rush-woven seat. This type was described as a bedside chair by Loudon in 1833. It was not intended primarily for invalids but for general use at a time when inside toilets were extremely rare.

Figure 168.
PAIR OF CHAIRS.
Elm. 1790–1830.
Apparently chairmakers saw nothing wrong with combining 'Gothic' splat piercing with an essentially Neoclassical style, and this design is a common one. The front legs of these chairs are of straight square section; tapering them involved an extra cost. Pegging is confined to the mortise-and-tenon joints of the side seat rails. The curved uprights and humped crest rail hint at the 'shield back' design source.

168

Figure 169.

ARMCHAIR.

Elm. 1790–1830.

This armchair with drop-in seat owes much to 'Hepplewhite' designs. On this vernacular version, a balloon-shaped splat and humped crest rail are typically combined with square-section front legs tapered on their two inner faces — a Neoclassical influence, although on finer chairs the legs were often of round section instead. Stretchers have been retained although in an H form here. The horizontally scrolled arms are particularly out of keeping with this chair's patrician ancestry.

The Prince of Wales Feathers design in the pierced splat was a common stock motif of the period (much beloved by Hepplewhite) and is unlikely to have any specific commemorative significance.

170   169

Figure 170.

CHAIR.

Elm with fruitwood seat. 1790–1840.

Relying for its appeal on its very rusticity, this chair repeats the square-section front legs of the chair in Figure 168 but the pierced design and profile of the splat are more naïve and the uprights are merely splayed rather than curved. The side and rear stretchers are slightly inset and the seat overlaps the frame instead of being flush and neatly trimmed with a bead moulding. One of a set of six.

unconnected with the item itself. Nevertheless, the calligraphic style of the dates incised on these two chairs is particularly consistent with the second quarter of the 18th century and we may assume that, in this instance, they are likely to indicate the age of the actual chairs, giving the year in which each was made. The top slats of both chairs are also incised with stars and that of the chair on the left bears two prominent crescent moons, talismanic symbols of Islamic derivation which were a popular motif on sword blades of the period, though their significance here is not known.

Makers of turned chairs did not always adhere to spindleback and ladderback types but sometimes created back styles echoing those on fine, joined chairs – solid splats with shaped crest rail (**Figure 178**), pierced splats of 'Chippendale' style with eared crest rail, 'camelbacks', and so on – while

171

Figure 171.
ARMCHAIR.

Cherry. Probably Devon/Somerset, dated 1718.

An 18th-century specimen of a venerable and elaborately turned chair type which was waning in popularity by this time. This piece has a trapezoidal seat and, unusually, a slat is inscribed with initials 'GM' and a date. Rather than having continuous uprights, the rear legs and back posts both tenon into a horizontal rail above seat level. This method allows a pronounced rake to the back and a little more comfort for the occupant. As usual on chairs of this ornate type, the seat is wooden.

retaining a somewhat incongruous traditional turned construction for the base. Like the vernacular joined chairs discussed previously, these chairs are usually much later than the style of their backs would seem to indicate.

Three chairs of turned construction with rush seats illustrated here (Figure 179), although quite likely to be of 19th century manufacture themselves, are included in this chapter as they are descended from much older styles and representative of basic types that must have been common in the second half of the 18th century.

Wedged construction (see page 22) must have been one of the earliest techniques employed to make rudimentary furniture and its use has continued through the ages, although normally restricted to utilitarian pieces of the 'primitive' category. Around 1700 professional turners used

173

Figure 172.

ARMCHAIR.

Ash with rush seat. 1660–1710.

An early English example of a simpler turned chair with rush seat; the type must have been common enough in the late 17th century and probably long before, though far more examples appear to have survived in New England (where vernacular furniture has been more highly regarded for a longer period and, hence, is more likely to be preserved). Although it is basically a spindleback chair, the flat horizontal members of the back are broader than those of later versions from the North-West (see Figure 179, left) and are closer to the slats of ladderbacks. The left arm-support finial is damaged.

Figure 173 (opposite).

ARMCHAIR.

Ash with rush seat. 1680–1740.

Another alliance of spindles and slats; the spindles here echo the profile of the flanking uprights and the style is highly reminiscent of American 'banister-back' chairs where the spindles are generally of flat section rather than round. The slats reflect the back members of caned chairs. The 'sausage' turning of the rails below the arms is repeated on the two front stretchers, connected by a series of short spindles. A delicate chair which was probably well-regarded when new and it possibly represents the species referred to by Spershott as 'turn'd ash, dyed, or stuffed, with Turkey or other rich covers'. Although there is evidence that turned chairs with rush seats existed in England at a much earlier date[27], the concept appears to have received a fresh stimulus from Holland in the 17th century; both this and the chair in Figure 172 are very similar to contemporary chairs from that country and the adjective 'Dutch' recurs constantly in early inventories as a generic description of chairs with rush seats.

172

this form of construction, refining it to produce a sophisticated type of chair, often painted green and perhaps intended primarily for outdoor use – although it was widely used in both domestic and public indoor locations as well. These chairs were, and still are, called 'Windsor' chairs. Today, 'Windsor' is a generic term for any chair which has both the legs and the uprights wedged into holes bored in a slab seat. Whereas in most other chairs the back legs and back uprights are of one piece, in a Windsor chair they are separate. The old belief that the chairs were named after George III having had copies made from an example he saw at a Windsor cottage can be dismissed. John Brown, a chairmaker (or possibly just a retailer) of London, was advertising 'all sorts of Windsor Garden chairs of all sizes painted green or in the wood' as long ago as 1727[26] – eleven years before

125

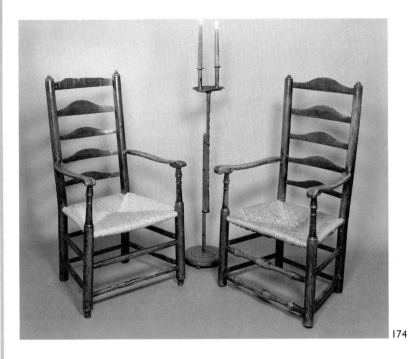

174

If the inscribed dates on the top slats of these two chairs are accepted as contemporary with their manufacture (see pages 120–123), they represent early survivals of an austere, plain type with turned decoration restricted to the column arm supports and front stretchers, and with rear post finials reduced to vestigial domes. The unusual use of yew for the right-hand chair supports the likelihood that these pieces were both regarded as important when new, their plainness perhaps being a fashionable virtue rather than a failing. The top slat of the left-hand chair is damaged and its front stetchers may be replacements[28].

Centre:
CANDLESTAND.
Oak with iron fitting. 1750–1820.
The concentrically ring-turned base on ball feet has an almost ageless simplicity but the iron candleholders with ejector slots indicate the date range given. The height is adjusted by a rachet mechanism. Along with rushlight holders, such simple lighting devices continued to be made later than is generally recognised[29].

George III was born. The probable explanation for the term is that the chairs may have first appeared for sale in the market town of Windsor, Berkshire, an ideal distribution centre for the Thames Valley area where the earliest ones appear to have been produced. Windsor was situated on the Thames, a convenient location at a time when the easiest transportation of goods to London was by river. Buyers (trade or private) from London and elsewhere would then naturally refer to the type as 'chairs from Windsor' or 'Windsor chairs'. The two earliest known Windsor chairs still bearing the original maker's label beneath the seat were both made in Slough, Buckingham-

175

Figure 175.
Left:
ARMCHAIR.
Ash with rush seat. 1760–1820.
A basic ladderback form echoing the two previous chairs. Here the arms are gently dished and end in scrolled handrests while the arm supports are baluster turned. Domed finials. The two front stretchers may be replacements and the feet have been re-tipped.

Right:
ARMCHAIR.
Ash with rush seat. Probably Lincolnshire, 1790–1850.
A low, squat style that is probably 19th-century. The horizontally scrolled arms thicken above the baluster-turned suppports and the two front legs, joined by a single turned stretcher, terminate in turned feet.

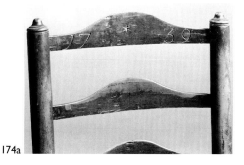

Figure 174a.
(Detail of Figure 174, right.)
Incised dates can occasionally be authenticated by subtle variations in the shape of numerals at different periods. The style certainly suggests contemporaneity in this case.

176

Figure 176.
'CORNER' CHAIR WITH HEADREST.
Ash with rush seat. Lincolnshire, 1770–1820. A turned version of the joined 'corner' types seen previously, this chair has a single 'ladder' slat, with ogee-arched shaping to the underside, curved between the outer posts and rebated into the back one. The posts and stretchers are turned in a regional style, here with ball feet. Unusually, there is a 'comb' headrest mounted above the three-piece arm bow and this design of chair has been associated with barbers' shops — in the days when patrons were normally shaved. There is possibly some truth in that connection.

shire, (a mere two miles from Windsor) around the middle of the 18th century.[30]

The first Windsor chairs appear to have been the comb-back type, in which the spindles of the back are topped by a horizontal crest rail (**Figures 87, 181–183 and 185**). By mid-century, the bow-back type had been developed, in which the crest rail was replaced by a bent hoop, the ends terminating in either the arm bow or the seat (**Figure 184**). Cabriole legs, as an alternative to turned front legs, and bowed front stretchers (a curved stretcher linking the two front legs and connected to those at the back by short, straight stretchers) had also appeared by that time.

These bowed front stretchers have been referred to in the past as

177

Figure 177 (left).
CHAIR.
Ash with rush seat. Lancashire/Cheshire, 1780–1840.

A triple-row spindleback chair with back uprights flattened and curved to meet an 'eared' crest rail with vestigial cresting – an attempt to emulate the 'Chippendale' style. Surprisingly, the hybrid works very well, resulting in an appealing chair. Particular care has been taken to make the 'ear' scrolls stand proud of the surface. The upper spindles are splayed and the top blocks of the front legs have been carved in imitation of earlier lappets. The lower side stretchers are joined by a central one.

178

Figure 178.
CHAIR.
Elm with rush seat. Probably Lincolnshire, 1785–1820.

Apart from straight turned front legs with pad feet a conservative influence is apparent in the imitation of a back type (solid shaped splat complete with 'shoe' at seat level) found on older joined chairs. The splat has been inverted. The correct way up, it has the profile of an urn – confirmation of the date range given (cf. F. Gordon Roe, English Cottage Furniture, fig. 12). Ash is the usual timber for the frame of turned rush seat chairs but the wood here appears to be elm.

'crinoline' stretchers, presumably because they were thought to have been made to accommodate that women's fashion. In fact, these chairs were intended for either sex and the bowed front stretcher has nothing to do with dress. The H-form stretchers are equally commodious for the clothes of the sitter and, at any rate, crinolines did not arrive until the 1830s (first as material, later as petticoats) – roughly a hundred years after bowed front stretchers had been introduced. The only concessions that the design of Windsor chairs made to the bulkier clothes of an earlier period are the frequently bowed arm supports (seen in **Figures 87, 181 and 184**) and normally wide seats, common to all types of 18th-century chairs.

In Saxon times, settles took the form of fixed benches ranged along the walls around the central hearth. After chimneys became popular at the end

Plate I.
CHEST.
Oak, with stained details. Dorset/Devon/
Somerset, 1650–70.

*A geometric pattern, including stylised tulips on the
panels, has been incised on the front of this joined chest
and parts of it have been stained in red, black and
white. This distinctive decorative style is particularly
associated with Dorset, but variations of it are also
found in neighbouring Devon and Somerset, and as far
away as the Hertfordshire/Essex border. The lock and
hasp are later.*

Plate II.
STOOL.
Oak, old dark over pale brown scumble finish.
1630–80.

*A joined stool with fluted decoration on the seat rails.
While obviously of considerable age, the paint finish is
unlikely to be contemporary to the date of manufacture of the stool and was probably added during the
18th century. The graining has mostly worn away to
reveal the pale ground.*

Plate III.
CHEST.
Oak. West Country, 1630–80.
A chest of traditional boarded construction. Chests of this type are normally smaller than those that are joined. This example exhibits the West Country characteristic of continued saw-cuts on the ends (see Figure 40). The front board is carved with a series of stylised leaves within an ornate arcade. The hasp is missing.

Plate IV.
DESK.
Pine, old brown over yellow grained paint finish imitating oak. 1790–1830.
In the 18th and 19th centuries, pine was widely used for functional furniture such as this clerk's desk, the interior of which is fitted with pigeon-holes. Pine was a considerably cheaper timber than oak, but was held in lower esteem. The simulation of an oak finish on a pine carcase, seen here, was a device commonly used throughout the 19th century. The handles are modern.

Plate V (right).
CHEST OF DRAWERS.
Oak, black over brown paint finish on drawer front mouldings imitating tortoiseshell. 1670–1720.
Real tortoiseshell (actually made from turtles) was a highly fashionable veneer on furniture of the late 17th and early 18th centuries; it was also very expensive and the crude painted blotches on the drawer fronts of this chest represent a passable substitute.

Plate VI (above).
WINDSOR ARMCHAIR.
Ash with elm seat. Thames Valley, 1750–80.
An exceptionally fine example. Windsors of this quality were intended mainly for wealthier customers, often for use as library chairs, and were beyond the means of most people. The pierced splat and crest rail reflect the 'Chippendale' style and the flat arm supports tend to be an early sign. The broad and deeply shaped seat is supported by cabriole legs which end in pointed feet.

Plate VII (right).
CHEST OF DRAWERS.
Oak, later blue-green paint overall with front portions patterned in red over yellow and end panels chequered.
1680–1720.
A remarkable use of paint to enliven an otherwise conventional chest. The paint scheme, although similar in some respects to that on several American pieces of this period, does not appear to be contemporaneous in this English instance and was probably added long after the chest was made. The uppermost pair of drawers are double-fronted while the three matching long drawers below bear a rounded moulding in the centre of each 'panel'. Original bun feet.

Plate VIII.
CHEST ON STAND.
Elm with walnut crossbanding. North, 1740–90.
The striking grain of elm wood is clearly seen on this
attractively small piece (just under 5 feet tall). The
cock-beaded drawers are crossbanded in figured
walnut, enhancing the overall effect. The base conceals
a 'secret' drawer and stands on cabriole legs ending in
'trifid' feet. The acanthus carving on the knees may be
modern.

Plate IX.
WINDSOR SETTEE.
Elm with beech legs. West Country, 1800–35.
(See Figure 309)

Plate X (right).
CHEST OF DRAWERS.
*Pine, brown over yellow grained paint finish imitating
oak. 1865–1900.*
(See Figure 211)

Plate XI (above).
CHAIR.
Elm. 1770–1820.
*A humble elm chair, with rush-woven seat, which is
decidedly vernacular, yet whose back design successfully manages to express a great deal of the elegance of
far more expensive pieces. The crest rail is competently
integrated with the splat and part of the scroll pattern
is raised.*

Plate XII (right).
*The open hall of Bayleaf, a medieval yeoman's house
originally at Chiddingstone, Kent.*
*The house has been re-erected at the Weald and
Downland Open Air Museum, Singleton, West
Sussex, and furnished as it may have appeared in about
1540, using modern reconstructions. A food cupboard, a chest and a stool, all of boarded construction,
stand near the large window to the left. A long dining
table on a pair of trestles takes pride of place at the
'high' end of the hall behind the central hearth.
Turned stools of the type seen in the foreground,
although shown in contemporary illustrations, do not
appear to have survived.*

Plate XV.
HIGH DRESSER.
Oak. Probably Lake District, 1750–90.
This magnificent dresser came from a house in the Lake District and the configuration of the base – a pair of full-height cupboard doors flanking a bank of drawers – appears to be fairly typical of dressers from the North-West. Here the base is of breakfront form and the corners are embellished with fluted quarter-columns, while the fielded door panels are ornately arched. The fluted pilasters of the superstructure, although popularly associated with Yorkshire, were a common feature on high dressers throughout the North of England. The row of small drawers along the base of the superstructure provided useful storage space for smaller items such as herbs and spices.

Plate XVIII.

MARY ELLEN BEST (1809–91).

A Cottage Interior, York. *Watercolour, 1836. The dual functions of kitchen and parlour are comfortably juxtaposed in this interior; curiously, the gilt-framed portrait (possibly a 'cast-off' from a grand house) does not seem too incongruous hanging above a pine kitchen table with three drawers on which food has been prepared. The simple stool under the table has the seat pierced for a hand-hold; the stool on which the girl is sitting appears to be a 'primitive' cricket. Further seating is provided by a solid-seated chair and the sleeping dog has sensibly chosen an armchair with a cushion. A large chest of drawers with a shaped apron, dating from a slightly earlier period and now missing some of its bail handles, stands beneath a wall clock. China is displayed in a glazed corner cupboard, in front of which a tripod table has been placed with its top raised in the vertical position.*

Plate XIX (opposite).
CHEST WITH DRAWERS.
Pine, black over brown scumble finish imitating rosewood, brown over yellow scumble 'panels' imitating curly maple, and black striping imitating ebony stringing. Probably North Midlands, 1830–60.

Pine furniture with this high quality of paint finish was much used to furnish the inferior rooms of large houses. This dovetailed chest with two drawers came from a town house in Blythe Bridge, near Stoke-on-Trent, Staffordshire.

TESTER BEDSTEAD.
Oak, original polychrome (red, blue, green, yellow, brown, white and black) paint finish. Kirkbride area, Cumberland, dated 1724.

Paint finishes on English furniture are seldom as spectacular as that on this bedstead; the decoration includes birds, flowers, a serpent and simulated curtains and valances. A hinged panel in the headboard originally gave access to a wall niche behind the bedstead and bears what may have been intended as a representation of the Tree of Life. Above that are the date and the initials F^{H}A for Francis and Anne Hall, who were married in 1713 and owned the house in Kirkbride, Cumberland, where the bedstead was found.

Plate XX (above right).
SIDE TABLE.
Oak, dark over pale brown paint finish imitating walnut. 1690–1720.

The single drawer, its front visually divided by paint into two 'panels', comes between an ovolo-moulded top and an applied moulding. The ball-turned legs are tied between the base balusters and the bun feet by the flattened X-form stretcher arrangement that was fashionable at this period.

Plate XXI (right).
CHAIR.
Oak. North, 1690–1740.
(See Figure 84)
TRIPOD PEDESTAL TABLE.
Fruitwood. 1815–50.
(See Figure 261)
DESK.
Oak. Dated 1600.
(See Figure 27)
SIDE TABLE.
Pine, original finish removed. 1770–1820.
(See Figure 147)

Plate XXII.

LOW DRESSER.

Oak with mahogany crossbanding. South Lancashire, 1760–1800.

Although open-based low dressers were fairly widely distributed, the imitation quoins decorating the corners of this example are a particularly recurrent feature on the bases of longcase clocks made in the Liverpool area and strongly suggest a South Lancashire origin for this dresser. The inner border of stringing to the crossbanding on the drawer fronts hints at a Neoclassical influence.

Plate XXIII.

CLOTHES PRESS.

Pine, original blue paint finish. Probably North-West/Wales, 1770–1820.

A joined example with panelled ends and fielded panels on the doors. The careful removal of later paint has revealed the original finish. The cornice and waist moulding are restored.

Plate XXIV (right).
WASHSTAND.
Pine, greyish blue-green paint overall with striping in blue, white and black; paint finish on top surface imitating marble. 1800–25.
(See Figure 325)

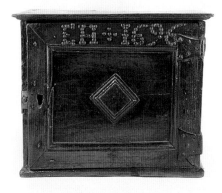

Plate XXV (above).
SPICE CUPBOARD.
Oak. Dated 1696.
A mitred frame has been nailed to the front surface of the door, giving the impression of superior joined construction.

Plate XXVa (below).
(Interior of the cupboard in Plate XXV)
Despite the appearance of its outer side, the door is actually boarded. The lock is missing.

Plate XXVI.

SPOON RACK.

Pine, dark over pale brown scumble finish.
1790–1840.

A humble household object that has been enhanced by
a fretted frieze and sides and by an imaginative paint
finish. The unusual effect of the latter was probably
achieved by the application of a vinegar- and sugar-
based glaze over an oil- or milk-based ground.

Plate XXVII.

WINGED ARMCHAIR.

Pine, elm and sycamore, dark red paint. Lancashire /
Yorkshire Dales, 1800–60.

A distinctive form of armchair which is specifically
regional (cf. Figures 275, 276 and 344). This
example retains much of the red paint which
originally disguised the diversity of timbers used in its
construction.

Plate XXVIII.

CHEST.

Oak. 1590–1680.

A late example of the use of 'clamped-front'
construction, this chest has a band of Classical fluting
across the front board. The vertical bands of concentric
circles decorating the stiles were possibly intended to
represent a guilloche pattern. (Lid repaired; hasp
missing.)

179

Figure 179 (above).
THREE TURNED CHAIRS.
Left:
Ash with rush seat. Lancashire/Cheshire, 1780–1850.
A standard double-row spindleback.
Centre:
Ash with rush seat. Lancashire/Cheshire, 1780–1840.
A 'wavy line' ladderback.
Right:
Ash with rush seat. South Lancashire (Billinge/ Pemberton/Wigan area), 1780–1870.
A 'bar top' ladderback.
All three chairs have straight turned front legs ending in pad feet, while the rear legs are either turned or chamfered, neither type being exclusively confined to any one chair style. These examples retain the wooden strips around the edges of the seats, which are so often missing.

Figure 180 (right).
ARMCHAIR AND TWO SINGLE CHAIRS.
Ash with rush seats. Lancashire/Cheshire, 1780–1840.
One of the most attractive styles of turned chairs, this 'wavy line' ladderback pattern has for long been associated with Yorkshire, although evidence suggests the North-West as a more likely origin.

of the 16th century, a settle or two was frequently integrated in the structure of the large fireplace, or 'inglenook'. These seats, flanking the warmest and busiest part of the house, must have been of prime importance in the past, and are still almost irresistibly inviting when they are found in an old house or inn today. Their snug position next to a crackling fire on a cold winter's day is magnetic and it is small wonder that in days gone by they were often also used as beds at night.

Settles were, of course, by no means exclusively confined to the fireside; both fixed and free-standing types were situated in any convenient location. The earliest surviving examples of movable domestic settles

180

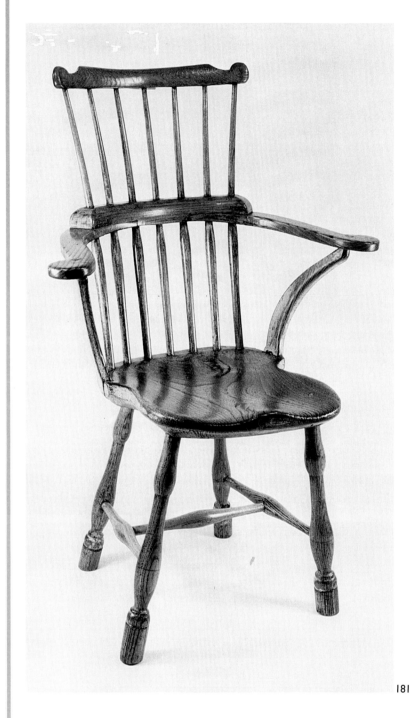

181

182

Figure 181.
WINDSOR ARMCHAIR.
Ash with elm seat. Probably West Country,
1760–90.
Similar to a comb-back chair bequeathed by Oliver
Goldsmith in 1774[32], this example lacks the bracing
spindles and 'bobtail' of the Goldsmith chair. It has a
specific type of three-part arm bow construction which
is a West Country feature: both the thin horizontally
scrolled arms are lap-jointed to, but separated by, a
thick central section. The curved arm supports join the
waisted, saddle-shaped seat near the back, making
ample allowance for the occupant's clothing. The four
baluster-turned legs are linked by H-form stretchers.

Figure 182.
WINDSOR CHAIR.
Ash with elm seat. Thames Valley, 1740–90.
A single chair of the comb-back type[31]. Two
rectangular-section uprights and a shaped crest rail
frame a series of spindles, a feature contemporaneous
with the central-splat-and-flanking-spindles style.
On this example, the back is supported by two bracing
spindles running between the crest rail and a 'bobtail'
– a rear extension of the seat. The saddle-shaped seat
stands on four turned legs, the front ones with a short
baluster turning near the base, tied by H-form
stretchers.

appear to be mostly of panelled construction and date from around 1500. Many have box-like bases with lidded compartments and look a little like contemporary panelled chests with back and arms added. There is, however, no reason to subscribe to the old theory that settles actually evolved from chests. It is far more probable that both forms of furniture developed independently. Fixed settles are ancient and the advent of lighter joined construction simply made the production of domestic free-standing settles an attractive alternative.

The settles illustrated in this chapter (**Figures 186–189**) are of an essentially settee form, in that they are to some extent elongated versions of

Figure 183 (right).
WINDSOR ARMCHAIR.
Elm. West Country, 1790–1820.
'Primitive' construction by no means invariably indicates an early date; frequently the reverse is true, crudely made furniture often being a later downmarket copy of finer originals. In fact, this chair is more competently made than might initially appear and was certainly the product of a professional craftsman. It has the same regional form of three-part arm bow construction as the chair in Figure 181, with a central thick section stepped between the arms, and curved arm supports, although here they join the seat towards the front. The thick seat is shaped and stands on four octagonal legs.

184

183

Figure 184 (above).
WINDSOR ARMCHAIR.
Yew with elm seat. Thames Valley, 1780–1810. An attractive bow-back armchair which, in yew and having cabriole front legs linked by a bowed front stretcher, would have been quite expensive when new. A similar type has spindles instead of a central fretted splat. Short baluster turning as in the chair in Figure 182 has here been relegated to the rear legs. (cf. Bernard D. Cotton, The English Regional Chair, Figure TV18, which bears the trade card of 'W. Webb. Newington, Surrey'.) One arm has been replaced.

a single armchair. While occasionally adopting more fashionable styles for legs, stretchers and decorative details, they also display a particularly long-lived retention of some characteristics of 17th-century joined armchairs in their backs and (apart from **Figure 187**) their arms.

Figure 185.

WINDSOR ARMCHAIR.

Elm with oak seat. Probably West Country, 1760–90.

As with the piece in Figure 181, this chair is also similar in general form to a provenanced and datable example – a low comb-back Windsor acquired by the Bodleian Library, Oxford, in 1766[34]. Again, however, the chair shown here was probably made further away from London than the documented example and possibly, though not necessarily, somewhat later. The use of elm for every part but the seat is a reversal of the norm and the unusual oak seat is flat rather than shaped. The scrolled arms are simply butt-jointed to the rear section and their front supports are thickened at the base. The rear legs are square-sectioned, those at the front being shaped in a rudimentary cabriole form with hoof-like feet – one of the earliest cabriole foot types on joined furniture. The 'primitive' stretcherless construction of this chair harks back to the probable ancestors of the Windsor type, although by the date span given it represents merely a less sophisticated version.

Figure 186.

SETTLE.

Oak. South-West Yorkshire, 1680–1720.

Fully-panelled joined settles were made from the 15th to the 19th centuries. Typically, as on this example, the seat is composed of lids giving access to storage in the box base. All the main panels of this settle are fielded, those of the back being carved with diamonds which are elaborated by a regionally specific form of pennant-like ornamentation. The thick slab arms are supported by squat turnings.

Figure 187.
SETTLE.
Oak. North-West, 1740–1800.
Both the shoulders of the cabriole legs and the arched tops of the fielded panels on this settle are shaped in a manner typical of (though not exclusive to) the Cheshire area (cf. the panels of the clothes press in Figure 134). The ends of the crest rail are similarly shaped. Another regional trait is the conservative tendency to retain earlier stylistic forms, seen here in the five cabriole legs tied by turned stretchers and the 'shepherd's crook' arms.

187

Figure 188 (right).
SETTLE.
Oak. Lancashire/Cheshire, 1705–30.
A late date is suggested by the shell carving on the crest rail and front stretchers – a Baroque motif which was particularly popular during the early 18th century. Very similar to a pair of settles in Trinity College, Oxford, one of which is dated 1715 (see John C. Rogers, English Furniture, Figure 26).

189

188

Figure 189 (above).
SETTLE.
Oak. Cheshire/South Lancashire, 1770–1820.
A robust settle type still frequently found in old inns. In this example, with arch-top fielded panels to the back, all the mortise-and-tenon joints are pegged in the usual way for strength, a necessity also reflected in the archaic slab arms and sturdy legs. The cabriole front legs are tied by turned stretchers to those at the back. Often, settles of this type are embellished with inlaid designs typical of the Neoclassical period.

OTHER TYPES

While the bedstead continued to hold a rank of some importance in the middle-class home, both its stocky proportions and exuberant decoration were pared down in common with other furniture during the 18th century. Spershott noted that the popular type of this class in his area was a half-tester form 'of beech as English oak began to be scarce and dear'. The tester bedstead from Kirkbride, Cumberland, (Plate XIX) is of oak and is remarkable for its unusual decorative paint finish. This piece stood in the principal bedchamber of a yeoman's house and opposite it, built in over the staircase, was a box bed – probably intended for some of the chilren.[33] The humblest bedsteads were naturally of boarded or the very simplest of joined construction – unenclosed except perhaps by curtains suspended from the ceiling (the garret bed in Hogarth's painting – Figure 88).

One of the most popular forms of cradle throughout the ages has been the basketwork bassinet which stood upon the floor. Wooden cradles appear to have been invariably provided with some means of allowing them to be rocked and thus pacifying the occasionally exasperating occupant. Two primary methods of permitting such a rocking motion were

190

Figure 190 (left).
CRADLE ON ROCKERS.
Oak. 1690–1740.
Joined cradles of this basic panelled form, with a canted hood, were made over a long period; the complete absence of decoration on this example suggests an 18th-century date. The generous depth of most early cradles was necessary to accommodate the large amount of bedding used for babies in those days, often incorporating a deep underlay of loose rushes or rush matting which could be changed daily as it became damp. Draughts were believed to be a major cause of infant mortality; the baby was therefore well covered by blankets and a coverlet, and the hood at the head of the cradle provided extra protection. The head finials have been restored and modern castors have been added to the base.

used from the Middle Ages onwards: either the cradle itself was fitted with wooden rockers under the base (**Figures 190, 191 and 321**) or it was suspended on a stand (**Figure 323**).

During the 18th century the longcase clock came to fill a place in vernacular homes that was the equivalent in terms of prestige to that of the

Figure 192 (opposite).
LONGCASE CLOCK.
Oak. Chichester, Sussex, 1755–68.
A fairly typical case style from the South-East; clocks of this period from the north of England tend to be more imaginative in their treatment. Columns attached to the hood door, as opposed to being freestanding, and a straight top to the trunk door are indications of southern origin by this time, as are the thinness and consequent lightness of the oak boards. The case would not, of course, have been made by the clockmaker but it is likely to have been a local product. This example has been stained red-brown to resemble mahogany, like so much 18th-century oak furniture. The two features of plainness and sparing use of oak are not confined to clock cases but are characteristic of most southern vernacular furniture. (Thirty-hour 'birdcage' movement made by John Frost (c. 1697– 1768) of St. Pancras, Chichester.)

Figure 191 (below left).
CRADLE ON ROCKERS.
Oak. 1700–60.
A simple form of joined construction in which the width of the rails obviates the need for panels. Although this cradle is somewhat shallower than the previous one, the baby would nevertheless have been heavily covered; overheating or suffocation were probably more frequent causes of cot death than the dreaded draughts. The prominent finials were conve- nient for hand-rocking the cradle.

191

press cupboard or bedstead in previous times. The fact that only two examples (**Figures 192 and 331**) are illustrated in this book is in no way a proportional reflection of their importance. Since longcase clocks have received a great deal of attention elsewhere, most space is devoted here to those items of furniture which have received somewhat less.

Enclosing a clock in a tall wooden case roughly coincided with the adoption of the pendulum and the anchor escapement in the third quarter of the 17th century. Apart from acting as a dust cover, it served two purposes: the weights and, particularly, the long pendulum of the clock were protected from interference by children or pets and the floor-standing case was necessary to support the often heavier weights required to drive clocks which could now be made to run accurately for a longer duration.[35] Such clocks were naturally very expensive at that time and ordinary households, if they could afford a clock at all, owned the so-called 'lantern'

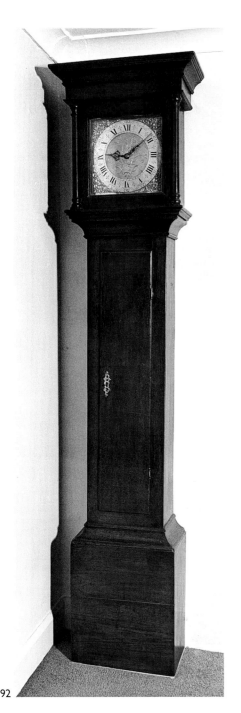

192

192a

Figure 192a.
(Detail of Figure 192.)
The obvious open frame of a 'birdcage' movement is instantly distinguishable from 'plate' types. The movement sits on a horizontal seatboard which in turn rests on the two upright extensions, or 'cheeks', of the case sides. There are no signs of alteration made to fit the movement into the wrong case. This, and other evidence, indicates that the two components are original to each other. The secondary timber (for the seatboard and backboard, etc.) is pine.

193

Figure 193.
HANGING SHELVES.
Oak. North Country, dated 1707.
The pediment is decorated with scrolling tulips, flanking an anthemion-like motif, on a crosshatched ground. The carved initials at the top of the central splat are in the standard triangular marriage format and the letters 'SS' are also stamped further down, below the inverted heart piercing and above the two carved S-scrolls. The absence of backboards was normal at this period.

variety, which hung directly on a wall without a wooden case. In 1700, when the average *per capita* income was around £8 or £9 a year[36] (little of which could be saved for luxuries), a thirty-hour lantern clock would cost about £3 while a good eight-day longcase clock might be about £20 – well beyond the reach of most people. Gradually however, as the 18th century progressed, wages rose a little and cheaper longcase clocks became more widely available, the most expensive ones running for eight days or more and cheaper thirty-hour versions normally being aimed at the less affluent.

Eighteenth-century thirty-hour longcase clocks, particularly those made in the south of England, often retained an old-fashioned 'birdcage' form of movement, a modified version of that used in lantern clocks (**Figure 192a**).

194

Figure 194.
SHELVES.
Pine, old blue-green paint finish. North-West, 1770–1830.
The arrangement of shelves flanked by 'pilasters' of arched niches was a common style for the super-structures of high dressers from the North; it is tempting to dismiss this piece as being such a superstructure that has become separated from its base. Nevertheless, there also exist several examples of identically arranged shelves which, judging by size and proportion, were actually intended as complete entities in their own right. This piece is just as likely to be one of them. The horizontal rails indicate that the plates were meant to be displayed leant forward, collecting less dust on their front surfaces, while the shelf fronts bear scars of the rows of hooks used to display cups and small jugs.
Pine appears to be an unusual timber for 18th-century high dressers from the North, but probably only because it has a low survival rate and not necessarily because it was an uncommon type at the time. If this piece was in fact originally a superstructure, it is quite possible that the base was discarded when it became infested with woodworm or had rotted beyond redemption.

195

Figure 195.
DOUGH BIN.
Elm. 1730–70.

A larger example (over four feet long) possibly made for the kitchen of an important house. The quality of this dough bin is evinced by the fine dovetailed construction of the box and the well-finished base consisting of column-turned legs tied by moulded stretchers. The interior is divided.

Northern longcase clocks, of whatever duration, almost always had a more sophisticated 'plate' movement, wherein the gears (or 'wheels') were mounted between a pair of vertical brass plates. It is a popular myth that longcase clocks with 'birdcage' movements are necessarily older than those with 'plate' movements. Both types were produced contemporaneously; in fact, 'birdcage' clocks were still being manufactured at the beginning of the 19th century in some regions.

Longcase clocks have been of inestimable value to the student of 18th-century vernacular furniture. They possess an almost unique attribute – that of consistently bearing the name of the maker and the town in which he worked – whereby the clock can be dated fairly accurately and set within a specific area. While these details on the dial refer only to the movement rather than the case, which was not made by the clockmaker, it may be assumed that (if the case is undoubtedly original to the movement presently within it) the case was probably a local product and thus provides a definite chronological and regional reference for other furniture types.

Early examples of large wall shelves (**Figure 193**), primarily intended for the storage and display of plates, are known as 'Delft racks' as most better ceramic plates in the average middle-class household at that time were of tin-glazed earthenware, usually decorated in blue, and collectively termed 'Delft', whatever their actual origin, after the town in Holland which was one of the most important producers and exporters. (When used purely as a generic label, 'Delft' later came to be spelt with a small 'd'.) These shelves were sometimes provided with horizontal rails fixed to the front a little way

Figure 196.
Left:
SPICE CUPBOARD.
Oak. 1680–1740.
Of basically boarded construction, this piece has a joined door edged by mitred mouldings. The interior is fitted with an arrangement of six drawers.

Centre:
SMALL CUPBOARD.
Oak. West Country, 1660–1720.
A cupboard of boarded construction fronted by a joined frame, within which is a plank door embellished with carving and affixed by butterfly hinges.

Right:
SMALL BOX.
Oak. Dated 1711.
The moulded edges of the lid, affixed by staple hinges, match those of the base. The front has notched ends overlapping the sides and bears the inscription 'IW 1711' between bands of gouged decoration.

above each shelf as it was a common practice before the modern day to display plates leant forward, preventing dust from collecting on their surfaces. Many early wall shelves of this type must originally have been mounted on the wall above a low dresser while a great deal of the later ones probably once formed the actual superstructure of a high dresser and have since been separated.

Herbs and spices were of great importance in past times, not only for cooking, but also for their (real or supposed) medicinal properties. Before they were commonly kept in separate jars or other containers in domestic environments, they would generally be stored in specialised small cupboards which were fitted inside with an assortment of little drawers (Figure 196, left, and Figure 197, centre). These cupboards were normally kept in a warm location near the fireplace to protect their contents from dampness. In the Lake District and some other areas it was particularly common to build small cupboards for storing such dry goods as spices and salt actually into the chimney.

Figure 197.
Centre:
SPICE CUPBOARD.
Oak. North West/North Wales, 1760–1800.
These small cupboards were intended to be either hung on the wall or stored on a convenient surface. On this example, the base is fretted with ogee arches and the fielded panel of the door has quadrants in the upper corners – a style common over much of the region indicated. Here, the mortise-and-tenon joints of the door frame are not pegged. The hinges are at the side, allowing the entire front to open and reveal two drawers below a shelf inside.

Left and right:
TWO CUTLERY BOXES.
Both oak, the left-hand example with mahogany crossbanding. Both North West/North Wales, 1770–1830.
The pierced extensions for hanging are particularly ornate.
The wide regional attribution of each of these pieces reflects the fact that general, broadly based traditions did not stop at national boundaries. Several other items illustrated in this book, although attributed to English regions in the captions, may equally be of Welsh origin when their stylistic type overlaps shared borders.

5 NINETEENTH CENTURY & LATER

THE RAPIDLY ACCELERATING GROWTH OF INDUSTRY, AIDED BY NEW inventions and mechanical power, during the course of the 18th century was to change the face of England in the 19th. The very word 'industry', which had generally been merely a description of personal character in 1700, had by the 19th century acquired the wider connotation of a whole branch of the national economy. Not that industry in the more modern sense had not existed before 1700; it was then more a matter of large workshops and collective home crafts than of enormous factories with their attendant employees' towns that had arisen by the start of Queen Victoria's reign.

The hub of this phenomenal industrial expansion was centred in the Midlands and North of England, the chief providers of the natural resources (such as iron and coal) required. Many places lying within this area, like Leeds, Bradford, Manchester and Birmingham (all of which had been smaller than towns such as Oxford or Cambridge in the 17th century), grew so rapidly that in the 19th century they were large, bustling cities. Most of the inhabitants of these industrial settlements had deserted their agricultural roots and gone in search of a more secure living; England was increasingly becoming a nation of town-dwellers. Out of a total population of just under 9 million in 1801, over 76 per cent lived in rural areas. By 1901, when the population had shot up to over 30 million, less than a quarter were still dwelling in the countryside.

The quality of new housing provided for the workers in industrial towns was governed not only by the high cost of urban land but also by the rapidly escalating price of building materials after the French wars of 1793–1815. Economics dictated that as many houses as possible were built on one plot and that bricks were saved by constructing party walls. Most workers and their families lived in small 'two-up, two-down' houses in long, narrow terraces. Sometimes, in order to reduce the cost still further, rows of tiny houses would be built back-to-back. These were generally 'one-up, one-down', that is, a single living room on the ground floor with a bedroom above. With these, there was no yard or garden; a small number of privies would be set up nearby for several houses to share. Even this standard of new housing was beyond the means of many people and they were forced to live in older buildings which had been subdivided into cramped tenements; the poorest families often existed in damp, single-room cellars with neither a window nor a fireplace. Naturally, living conditions in these overcrowded homes were frequently squalid. In mid-century, there was usually no running water; what drains and sewers there were would often be open and refuse collection was limited. Diseases like cholera and typhus were rife. Nevertheless, for many people the better examples of urban terraced housing were probably an improvement over the homes in which they might have lived in the countryside. Although 19th-century rural England has been much romanticised, farming was in fact in decline during much of this period, offering only poverty and insecurity to a large number of its dependents.

The massive population boom, referred to above, provided a hungry demand for cheap, mass-produced goods which English industry was not slow to fulfil. It had been discovered that the larger the workshop or factory, the easier and more economical it was to produce large numbers of finished items. By concentrating workers together and organising and co-ordinating their efforts, the output of goods could be multiplied many times. A large factory warranted the high, initial expense of costly but labour-saving machinery to expedite production. Increasingly, goods manufacture became the province of large-scale operations, self-employed craftsmen with small workshops becoming eclipsed by cheaper, quicker competition from large businesses.

Figure 198.

George Hardy (1822–1909). The Sailor's Return.
Oil on panel, dated 1877.

Dedicated to a sentimental theme that was highly popular during the Victorian period, this painting depicts the combined kitchen/living room of an idealised cottage. Judging by the design of the turned ladderback chair, provided with a cushion, below the window and that of the Windsor high chair supporting the little girl, the scene was painted in the Midlands, possibly Lincolnshire. The meal is being served on a simple cricket table, with low stretchers, covered by a table cloth. A joined stool with four tapered legs stands in the foreground. The fireplace contains a cast iron hob grate for burning coal over which is suspended a large cauldron; a cloth screen has been hung between the fireplace and the doorway for privacy and for protection from draughts. Note the bellows hanging to the left of the mantelpiece, the hearth mat on the brick floor and the curtains at the window.

With regard to furniture, mass-produced brass fittings had been available in the 18th century, production being centred in Birmingham during the last part of the century. By 1800, the furniture itself was often made by very large firms, sometimes employing several hundred craftsmen.[1] These businesses would often sub-contract self-employed part-makers, or 'piece-workers', to supply certain components. These smaller workshops might specialise in only one kind of component (such as drawers or legs) or, later in the century, complete items like tables or wardrobes. By 1900, many of the largest furniture businesses were purely retailers, putting their label on stock supplied by other firms.[2]

Transport improved immensely in the 19th century, with all major towns served by good roads, canals or railways. The old provincial insularity was no longer possible. New furniture could be easily transported from its place of manufacture to almost anywhere in the country. Retailers might now purchase their standardised merchandise more cheaply from large suppliers far away; thus the local product was often ousted.

The average *per capita* income was £22 a year in 1800; by 1860 it had doubled.[3] The standard of living for most people was rising and it was becoming easier to buy finer furniture in mahogany made to the latest designs. This fine furniture tended to follow standard, national styles; local furniture in native timber with its regional characteristics was scorned as crude and vulgar by those with pretensions. This attitude was deplored by William Cobbett (1763–1835), when he wrote of a Surrey farm sale which took place in 1825:

> Every thing about this farm-house was formerly the scene of plain manners and plentiful living. Oak clothes-chests, oak bedsteads, oak chests of drawers, and oak tables to eat on, long, strong, and well supplied with joint stools. Some of the things were many hundreds of years old. But all appeared to be in a state of decay and nearly of disuse . . . One end of the front of this once plain and substantial house had been moulded into a 'parlour'; and there was the mahogany table, and the fine chairs, and the fine glass, and all as bare-faced upstart as any stock-jobber in the kingdom can boast of.[4]

The cost of making fine (and vernacular) furniture was moderated to some extent by the introduction of machinery such as mechanical circular- and band-saws and planing and mortising machines, which were all in use by the 1850s. Even patent carving machines were being employed at this time which enabled the operator to produce several identical carvings simultaneously.[5]

Of course, while showy mahogany, walnut or rosewood furniture was the coveted ideal, a large range of cheap imitations of fine furniture was made in pine or beech, stained or painted to resemble the real thing, to cater for a mass market. Even in households which could afford more expensive furnishings for the parlour or other public rooms, cheap painted pine furniture might be used in servants' quarters and secondary bedrooms – and, naturally, the kitchen would be fitted with utilitarian pieces. The gradual abandonment of traditional furniture in native timber for the modern equivalent in pine appears to have irked Cobbett as much as the increasing use of mahogany in farmhouses. In 1822 he advised that 'In household goods the warm, the strong, the durable, ought always to be kept in view. Oak-tables, bedsteads and stools, chairs of oak or of yew-tree, and never a bit of miserable deal board.'[6] Cobbett would perhaps be surprised to find that, 170 years later, the pine furniture he abhorred has in its turn become the subject of nostalgic admiration. Indeed, much of it was better made than he allowed. At its best, painted pine furniture retained a simplicity of line and form and was eminently suitable for its purpose, avoiding the over-elaborate excrescences of some 'fine' furniture of the Victorian age.

Nowadays, a great deal of largely mass-produced Victorian and Edwardian pine furniture has been stripped of its correct finish, polished and is being sold off as 'country furniture'; in fact the majority was urban-made for urban use and has little or no connection with either the countryside or, in many cases, local vernacular traditions. True regional furniture, with traditional characteristics peculiar to the locality in which it was made, was in danger of becoming extinct after 1860. In the event, some traditions did survive, turned and Windsor chairs being obvious examples.[7]

The spectacular extremes of fashions such as 'Chinese' or 'Gothic' (epitomised architecturally in the Brighton Pavilion and the Houses of Parliament respectively) have naturally excited the popular imagination and have occasionally come to dominate our perception of the major influences on 19th-century style. These fashions were, however, mainly superficial conceptually and, in the cases where they were manifested in totality, almost exclusive to those who could afford to indulge in eccentricities. The most profound influence on general design, particularly that of furniture, during the century was a more prosaic offshoot of the Neoclassical style which had dominated taste in the last quarter of the previous one. A growing desire to base furniture designs on actual Classical prototypes (both real and as depicted on murals and vases) with greater historical exactitude coincided with the expansion of archaeological activity beyond Italy and into Greece and Egypt around 1800. It was Greece, with its fashionable connotations of objective philosophy and democracy, that emerged as the supreme influence and triumphantly pervaded English applied arts throughout the 19th century. Its initial stages are normally termed 'Regency' in this country and 'Empire' in France and the United States, where, in its architectural form, it is also known as 'Greek Revival'. However, since the style was by no means restricted to the nine years of the actual Regency (1811–20) and was only vaguely connected with either the French or the British empire, it is perhaps best labelled by the term used extensively by Loudon and his contemporaries and called simply 'Grecian'.

The Grecian style, with its emphasis on horizontal proportions frequently allied to rounded arches and turned feet or plinths, was readily adaptable to the economic needs of vernacular furniture and formed the underlying current of its design until after 1900. Simultaneously, however, 19th-century England was being bombarded with a plethora of often impossibly exotic inspirations from other nations and other periods. Furniture designers and manufacturers turned from one to the other in their search for new ideas. Some of the elements that they incorporated into their own products were occasionally well integrated but were perhaps more often a combination which equalled or even surpassed in its eclecticism anything of the Chinese/Gothic/Classical genre produced in the Chippendale era. When necessarily reduced to the simplicity demanded by economically viable and usually mass-produced vernacular furniture,

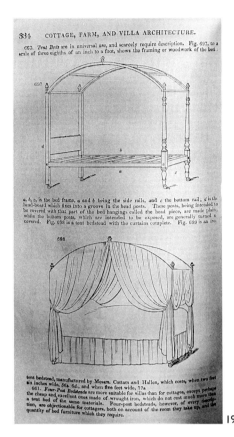

199

Figure 199.
ILLUSTRATIONS OF A 'TENT' BED
From J.C. Loudon's Encyclopaedia of Cottage, Farm and Villa Architecture and Furniture, London (1846 edition).
One of the first works of which an entire section was devoted to furnishings for the lower classes, Loudon's book went through several editions between 1833 and 1867 and was immensely popular on both sides of the Atlantic. An assiduous worker and prolific writer who at one time averaged only three to four hours' sleep a night, Loudon died literally on his feet in 1843.
The italicised letters accompanying the bedstead in Loudon's Figure 697 are explained: ' a, b, c, is the bed frame, a and b being the side rails, and c the bottom rail; d is the head-board which fixes into a groove in the head posts. These posts, being intended to be covered with that part of the bed hangings called the head piece, are made plain; while the bottom posts, which are intended to be exposed, are generally turned or covered.'. Loudon's Figure 698 shows the bedding and curtains in position.

however, such frivolities were pared down to a minimum and seldom showed themselves as more than a cosmetic decoration or finish to an otherwise basic object which, as often as not, essentially held true to the mainstream Grecian style.

It was perhaps inevitable that there should be a reaction to the standard mass-production of every aspect of the applied arts, from architecture to pottery, with the corresponding loss of character and individuality that came with the machine age. By mid-century, the Middle Ages were increasingly being seen by one group of intellectuals as a Utopia to be resurrected. Since the mid-18th century, Gothic design had been appreciated by many but, by the 1850s, it was an idealised vision of medieval life itself that inspired a new kind of enthusiasm. Modern products were perceived as shoddy, fussy and deceptive; those of the Middle Ages as the perfection of craftsmanship, simplicity and honesty.

One of the chief exponents of this movement was William Morris (1834–96). Morris, a socialist, despised mechanised mass-production as debasing mankind and destroying the appreciation of beauty. In 1861 he founded the firm of Morris, Marshall, Faulkner & Co. (Morris & Co. from 1865) and put his principles into practice. Among other things, the firm produced items of furniture which were loosely based on what was felt at the time to be the medieval ideal. Some designs, notably his range of rush-seated chairs, were inspired by more recent 'country' furniture.

Morris's taste was echoed by Charles Lock Eastlake in his influential book *Hints on Household Taste* of 1868. Like Morris, Eastlake advocated well-made furniture with a medieval flavour and was much in favour of 'honest revealed construction'. The movement rapidly became popular among the better-off middle classes and an increasing number of designers catered to their wants. Some makers carried the principle of revealed construction to extremes of self-conscious 'honesty' in the form of large through dovetailing, heavily and ostentatiously pegged joints and elaborate, oversized metal hardware cratered almost out of recognition by the marks of the hammer.

One of the most important branches of the Arts and Crafts Movement, a reformist group inspired by Morris, was the Cotswold School, founded by Ernest Gimson and the brothers Ernest and Sidney Barnsley, in the 1890s. Many of their products were based on vernacular types, beautifully executed and startlingly modern in their simplicity.

Nevertheless, although some Arts and Crafts furniture shared much in common with earlier vernacular furniture (the frequent use of native materials, simplicity, form of construction and so on) and, indeed, was in several cases directly inspired by it, a large amount of Arts and Crafts production was entirely alien to it in certain fundamental respects and cannot really be considered as 'country furniture'. Whereas the bulk of true vernacular furniture was usually the product of a minor (generally anonymous) craftsman catering to a general market in order simply to make a living, Arts and Crafts furniture was normally designed by educated (and sometimes wealthy) middle-class intellectuals for the most part deliberately avoiding mainstream furniture fashion in a conscious effort to create an original work of art. Price was sometimes almost irrelevant and the product could often be afforded only by rich clients. In common with art pottery, Arts and Crafts furniture was frequently intended to be essentially utilitarian, yet its basic sophistication elevated it to the ranks of

200

Figure 200.
LINEN PRESS.
Pine, brown over yellow paint finish imitating curly maple. 1860–1900.
The doors open to reveal a set of sliding trays. This austere piece, with a simple half-round moulding instead of a fully fledged cornice and a plain plinth, relies almost solely on its attractive paint finish for decoration. The white ceramic knobs are original.

'fine' furniture and the often high cost of hand-crafted construction put much of it well beyond the reach of ordinary people.

Some Arts and Crafts furniture, particularly many of the products of Morris & Co., *was* affordable, however, and reached a wide, popular market. Even the expensive pieces had a strong influence on contemporary design and, by the end of the century, were being imitated by mass-producing factories. Ironically, it was the use of machinery which allowed much of this 'vernacular' style to become truly accessible to the general public.

A division of furniture into 'fine' or 'vernacular' merely according to whether it is made of mahogany or of oak is at best a simplistic system. It becomes completely untenable when dealing with the Victorian period. By the mid-19th century, many working people could afford mahogany, at least for the parlour. Oak, on the other hand, had become quite expensive and very fashionable – even for the upper classes. From the mid-century onwards, then, this chapter concentrates mostly on the very cheapest forms of furniture – which, as far as case varieties are concerned, were almost inevitably made of pine and originally stained or painted. From that, of course, one must not presume that pine furniture was invariably cheap; some of the most fashionable pieces were occasionally constructed from that timber (e.g. **Figures 243 and 325**). Nevertheless, ordinary pine furniture, although fulfilling secondary functions in grand houses as well, was the genre most readily available to both the urban and rural lower classes for their homes. In its furnishing role for the staff quarters and kitchens of rich households, it was also that most familiar to servants, a very large proportion of the working population at that period.

Pine furniture made after 1850 is often excluded from studies of vernacular furniture on the grounds that a great deal of it was produced in factories. In fact, three points require consideration:

1 Factory-made does not necessarily imply machine-made. On the contrary, evidence of the use of machinery on a large proportion of Victorian (and later) pine furniture is confined solely to saw marks (mechanical frame and circular) on the timber itself, while the actual manufacture of the piece shows every sign of hand craftsmanship (hand-cut dovetails, scribe lines on joints and so on). Labour was cheap enough in England until well into the present century and the purchase of expensive machinery was not always felt to be warranted.

2 Even in cases where machinery was used to produce factory-made furniture, that machinery was still guided by hand, in essentially the same way as any other tool; machinery is merely a more complex form of tool. If furniture is to be despised solely on the grounds that machinery aided its production, such an attitude must condemn every piece which incorporates turning – from 16th-century 'thrown' chairs and 17th-century gateleg tables to 18th-century Windsors – since a lathe is unquestionably a machine; whether its driving force was human, wind or water mill or steam engine is irrelevant.

3 It is certainly likely that the various skills involved in the production of a factory-made piece – turning for the feet or legs, dovetailing for the drawers, final assembly, and staining or painting – were the contributions of different specialists. But there was nothing entirely new in that; even in the 16th century a single piece of furniture might well represent the combined skills of several craftsmen – the sawyer, the joiner, the turner, the carver and the blacksmith. During the 19th century the main

novelty lay in the sheer scale of output – when many specialised workers might work under one employer and produce hundreds of identical components day after day on an assembly-line basis. Even then, this was only the natural culmination of the system of large workshops, often creating enormous numbers of mass-produced goods, which had existed since at least the 17th century (or, in the case of pottery, since prehistory). It was the scale of mass-production, not mass-production itself, that was a 19th-century phenomenon.

STORAGE

Both plain chests and chests with one or more drawers in the base were still being produced as household furniture well into the 19th century. (An attractive painted pine example can be seen in Plate XIX.) Generally, however, they had long since lost the prestige they had had in the past and the increasing availability of more convenient chests of drawers and wardrobes diminished their popularity.

The one-off chest made by Ernest Barnsley (1863–1926) at the end of the century (**Figure 202**) may be viewed as a consciously archaic revival – produced perhaps more for its aesthetic effect and as a tribute to past craftsmanship than as a strictly utilitarian piece of furniture in its own right. At this early period the aim of the Cotswold School, of which Barnsley was a founder-member, was to make simple domestic furniture, and indeed this

Figure 201.
CHEST.
Elm. 1790–1830.

Of exposed dovetail construction and possibly once painted, this chest stands on a plinth shaped to form integral, rather than applied, simple bracket feet. The lid, attached by strap hinges, has applied edge mouldings which are shaped and mitred to resemble those of the plinth. There is an internal till and the original lock survives behind the inlaid key escutcheon.

202

Figure 202 (left).
CHEST.

Oak inlaid with fruitwood and stained oak. Pinbury, Gloucestershire, circa 1896.

Designed and made by Ernest Barnsley, one of the founders of the Cotswold School, this conspicuously dovetailed chest has corner brackets and three large ornamented hinges of wrought iron – a vague gesture towards medieval types. The charming inlaid decoration includes two hens and twelve dark chicks wandering in every direction among sprays of flowers.

The notch-edged plinths are free-standing.

Figure 203 (below).
CHEST.

Pine, brown over yellow scumble finish imitating oak. 1850–1910.

Little care or expense has been committed to the production of this box – in which the boarded construction does not even have the refinement of rabbeting. Both the iron bands reinforcing the corners and the iron butt hinges of the lid are merely nailed on rather than screwed and the crude brass key escutcheon looks almost like an improvisation. The lid edges are fitted with a half-round moulding which overlaps the carcase when shut. Both this and the box in Figure 204 bear original iron carrying handles at each end.

chest was intended for Barnsley's own household use,[8] but the piece lies far outside the mainstream of vernacular furniture production at that time.

The most common chests, or boxes, of the 19th century are those without feet and often fitted with a carrying handle at each end (**Figures 203 and 204**). These were, of course, primarily intended as travelling chests but, in the home, they naturally fulfilled the same functions of older domestic chests. Many would have served as 'lodging boxes', the chest and its contents constituting the only possessions carried by adolescents leaving home to go into domestic service or take up other work. As such, they may

203

Figure 204.

CHEST.

Pine, original red paint. Probably Oxfordshire,
1810–30.

The lid of this boarded box is fitted with long wrought
iron strap hinges and the lock is affixed by early V-
slotted screws. The interior is equipped with a small
lidded compartment, or till, to one side in the same
manner as the earlier large domestic chests. Victorian
floral wallpaper lines the interior, but where this has
peeled away in places can be seen the remnants of a
previous lining– an Oxford newspaper dated 1810. It
is dangerous, of course, to rely too heavily on evidence
like this for dating – earlier newspapers can be pasted
inside later chests, and vice versa – but in this case
the newspaper does appear to be original and roughly
contemporary with the box's likely period of
manufacture.

204

well have provided the only storage, seat and table in sparsely furnished
staff accommodation.

While oak became progressively more expensive in most areas of
England (particularly in the south), mass-produced furniture made from
pine correspondingly became ever more widely available and filled the
vacuum. The vast numbers of pine chests of drawers surviving from the
19th century testify to their ubiquitous popularity (**Figures 207 and 209–212**).
They were fashionably up to date, usually painted in attractive finishes and
reasonably priced. Loudon, writing in the 1830s, gave the cost of one

Figure 205.

CHEST.

Pine, brown over yellow paint finish imitating oak.
1850–1900.

So many old, originally plain pine chests have
subsequently been painted with bogus nautical themes,
such as compass roses, ships and fictitious captains'
names, and deliberately 'antiqued', over the past two
decades in order to cater to the furnishing decor market
that there is now some danger of rejecting anything
remotely of that genre as inherently spurious. This
chest is in fact entirely genuine; while the exterior
bears an ordinary simulation finish, a nautical scene
has been sensibly located inside, on the underside of the
lid, where it would suffer least from the rigours of
shipboard life[9]. The style and colouring of the amateur
artwork is especially similar to that occurring on other
examples of sailors' craft from the turn of the century
(e.g. ships in bottles) and was probably added to this
utilitarian chest by its owner around that time.
The chest is well-suited to a rough lifestyle: it has long
iron strap hinges, a robust lock and large iron handles
attached to shaped wooden blocks bolted to the ends.
The interior has been lined with later wallpaper but the
lid of the till is just visible on the right.

205

206

Figure 206.
CHEST OF DRAWERS.
Elm. 1800–40.
The narrow reeded moulding around the top and the high, delicate bracket feet help to emphasize the impression of lightness given by this piece. Judging by marks, the present brass knobs on the cock-beaded drawers are probably similar to the originals. As usual, the secondary timber is pine.

207

Figure 207.
CHEST OF DRAWERS.
Pine, dark over pale brown scumble finish imitating mahogany. 1840–1930.
A monochrome photograph does scant justice to the dramatic paint finish on this standard pine chest of drawers with ovolo-moulded top. The knob-fitted drawers are without cock beading or any other form of edge treatment – a legacy of the Grecian trend. The 'turnip' turned feet, based loosely on those depicted on Classical antiquities, are one of the earlier styles but were also still being shown in trade catalogues of the 1930s. This is a piece that is extremely difficult to date with any precision – hence the long date-range given – although the lock details on this specimen suggest a probable 19th rather than 20th-century origin.

Figure 208.
CHEST OF DRAWERS.
Oak. 1800–40.
The drawer fronts are carefully trimmed with cock beading as on the example in Figure 206 but the reeded moulding around top and base is wider and the overall proportions are heavier. The modern brass handles replace wooden knobs; the bracket feet are restored with elm.

TEA CHEST.
Oak, traces of original red finish. 1780–1830.
Roughly made with through dovetails, this piece has later feet and a handle has been added.
This type of tea chest either contains two or three removable boxes, or 'caddies', each holding different kinds of tea, or the chest itself acts as a 'caddy' and is divided into foil-lined compartments.

208

209

Figure 209.
CHEST OF DRAWERS.
Pine, brown over yellow paint finish imitating curly maple. 1850–1900.
As with the piece in Figure 207, chests similar to this one were being advertised in the 1930s; it is the curved-base keyhole inserts which suggest (though do not prove) a 19th-century date here. The more complex turned feet were probably of a standard size made separately by a specialist supplier; they look disproportionately large on this diminutive chest. The white ceramic knobs, original here, became fashionable after 1850.

'painted wainscot colour, with real oak knobs' as 'from £3 to £4' in London – still a large slice of the average annual income at that time but at least within the reach of many.

Drawered case furniture of the early 19th century conformed mainly to the Neoclassical principles which had gained momentum since the 1760s or retained earlier styles. In general, the 'Hepplewhite' influence was expressed in feet (often splayed) which were flush with the carcase and linked by shaped aprons (e.g. the bureau in Figure 216) and the frequent substitution of inlaid key escutcheons for brass inserts (also seen in Figure 216). By the 1830s, the Grecian style was achieving almost total supremacy; both turned knobs and turned feet virtually became standard, although bracket feet remained, and plinths were increasingly adopted, as alternatives, particularly on heavier pieces. Knobs, both brass and wooden, had become a fashionable alternative to handles before 1800 but were at first comparatively small and elegant, not evolving into full-blown bulbous 'mushroom' knobs until around the 1820s. Early knobs were normally fixed either by a screw from inside the drawer front or by means of a small dowel. Knobs with integral, threaded wooden dowels did not become common until later. Loudon, writing in 1833, illustrated a wooden knob incorporating what is probably meant to be a metal screw (which would simply go into the exterior of a drawer front) and extolled the virtues of wooden knobs on chests of drawers:

210

Figure 210.
CHEST OF DRAWERS.
Pine, original finish removed. North, 1850–1900. Found in Yorkshire, this low chest, with rounded corners and heavy moulding to top and base, has mitred mouldings applied to the perimeters of the drawer fronts in a manner strongly reminiscent of much earlier fashions. The squat turned feet are in accord with the proportions of the chest. Pressed glass knobs appeared in a more delicate form earlier in the century; the robust ones seen here (they are original) date from the second half of the century. There are no locks.

Knobs of the same wood as the furniture . . . are now generally substituted, as in most other pieces of furniture, for brass. They harmonise better, and do not tarnish; besides, the fashion is, at present, comparatively new in London, and this confers on them a certain degree of factitious elegance, viz., that of novelty and fashion.

As learning was universally esteemed in the 19th century, more attention was paid to the education (and therefore literacy) of even the working classes. Books were no longer expensive and the introduction of standard penny postage in 1840 encouraged still further the writing of

211

Figure 211.
CHEST OF DRAWERS.
Pine, brown over yellow grained paint finish imitating oak. 1865–1900.
With feet shaped from the solid ends in a manner similar to that on earlier boarded chests (cf. Figure 94), this attractively painted chest has an applied apron shaped in a fashion which was possibly intended loosely to represent the Louis XV style. Both the upper edge of the apron and the complex edge moulding to the top are broadly striped in maroon, while the freehand (not stencilled) patterns on the top and the drawer fronts are in maroon and black accompanied by narrow black striping. The drawers are finely dovetailed with quarter-round beading inside and bear 'early' curved-base keyhole inserts. The added white ceramic knobs conceal paired holes for the original handles.

Figure 212.
CHEST OF DRAWERS.
Pine, brown over yellow grained paint finish imitating oak. 1870–1915.
The top and the drawer fronts are accentuated by black striped borders and floral stencils in black and red to each corner; the chamfered edges of top, corners and plinth are painted red. The chunky design of this chest, with plinth, chamfers and stencil patterns, vaguely suggests an 'Eastlake' influence[10], placing it towards the end of the century. The straight-base keyhole inserts are consistent with such a date. The white ceramic knobs may be replacements.
The drawers are fitted with quarter-round beading inside, between the sides and base – a refinement introduced around 1790 on better furniture.

212

letters. Loudon appears to have felt nothing incongruous in recommending several designs of bookcases for the lower classes. On some that he illustrated, the apparent drawer front was hinged and the interior was fitted as a desk – a secretaire bookcase. Loudon stressed that 'bookcases and escrutoires, secretaries, or bureaus, are extremely useful . . . and, therefore, no cottage parlour ought to be without one'. Virtually the only obvious

Figure 213.
DESK.
Pine with plywood base, original finish removed. 1900–30.
Although desks of this basic boarded form with sloped lid were being made at least as far back as the 16th century, the type has continued to the present day. The use of plywood on this example dates it probably to after 1900. The interior is fitted with pigeon-holes.

213

Figure 214.
BOX WITH DRAWERS.

Pine, black over brown scumble finish imitating rosewood and cream-painted borders imitating maple or boxwood. 1820–45.

This small box would have rested on a table and was probably intended either as a work box or jewellery case. The hinged top reveals a shallow, paper-lined compartment. This bears a conventional lock; the two drawers below, similarly paper-lined, are both secured by one metal rod inserted into a hole running vertically from the top compartment down through the drawer fronts. A remnant of the original turned bone knobs survives in the front of the bottom drawer.

Figure 215.
BOX.

Elm. East Devon, dated 1813.

The notched ends and scratch decoration round the inscription are traditional but unlike most earlier boxes this one has a deep moulding fixed around the lid. The initials 'TP' stand for Thomas Pring of Hemyock, Devon, and his box remained in the family's possession until 1972.

Figure 216.

BUREAU.

Oak with mahogany crossbanding. 1790–1830.
The simple elegance of the 'Hepplewhite' style has been well expressed in this bureau with flush feet linked by shaped aprons and key escutcheons (or, more accurately, kite-shapes) inlaid in bone or ivory. The mahogany crossbanding to the fall has been combined with an inner frame of straight banded oak while the crossbanded drawer fronts come above a bordered inlay band round the base which visually separates the carcase from the apron-tied feet. The fall encloses a mahogany interior of drawers and pigeon-holes surrounding a central cupboard.

216

217

Figure 217.

DESK.

Ash with inlays and mahogany stringing. West Midlands/Wales, 1810–50.
Here the inlaid key escutcheons are shield-shaped and wooden. This desk was probably intended for commercial rather than domestic use and would require a high stool to sit at. Construction is basic, with no dovetails anywhere – even the drawer is merely nailed together – but the inlaid lozenge and mahogany stringing, combined with the heart-pierced brackets, show a concern for decorative effect. The tops of the pigeon-holes inside pull out as little drawers and there is one secret drawer. The modern brass handles on the exterior drawer replace original wooden knobs.

distinctions between his Grecian and 'Gothic' designs lay in the form of the arches – rounded in the Grecian, pointed in the Gothic – and in the sections of the astragals – again rounded in the Grecian, but trefoil in the Gothic. Other differences lay mainly in turned (Grecian) or bracket (Gothic) feet and in ornamental details. It was perhaps ironic that the Oriental bracket foot, which had been one of the most radical breaks from archaic traditions only a hundred or so years before, had now come to represent an even earlier fashion than those which it had replaced. Some of the best 19th-century furniture was based on classic styles with scholastic authenticity, but it was typical of mainstream design to show a complete lack of concern for even a shadow of historical verisimilitude.

Loudon's observations on dressers are particularly illuminating:

Dressers are fixtures essential to every kitchen, but more especially to that of the cottager, to whom they serve both as dressers and sideboards. They are generally made of deal by joiners, and seldom painted, it being the pride of good housewives, in most parts of England, to keep the boards of which they are composed as white as snow, by frequently scouring them with fine white sand. The dishes, plates, &c., which they contain are also kept perfectly clean and free from dust, by being wiped every day, whether used or not. In old farm-houses, the dressers are generally of oak rubbed bright, and the shelves are filled with rows of pewter plates, &c., polished by frequent cleaning, till they shine like silver . . . When there is a pot-board affixed to the dresser, it is usually painted black or chocolate colour; and when the shelves and fronts are painted, it is generally white, or, what is in better taste, the same colour as the walls or doors of the apartment. Gothic dressers would be more appropriate if made of oak, or painted to resemble that wood. The price of a deal dresser, in London, is from £2 to £5.

218

Figure 218.
BOOKCASE.

Pine, original finish removed. 1860–90.

The drawer front of this pine bookcase is moulded in an ogee curve (in this instance, strictly speaking, inverted), a common feature of the Grecian style whose influence is also seen in the round arched tops of the glazing and the applied panels of the lower cupboard doors. The handles on the drawer are modern additions; originally the drawer front was devoid of any form of handle or knob, being provided only with the hidden finger-holds cut into the projecting undersurface. The large expanse of undivided glazing and the absence of a formal cornice suggest a late date.

219

Figure 219.
LOW DRESSER.

Oak. Probably West Midlands/East Wales, 1810–50.

A standard low dresser form but with two smaller drawers flanking a central raised portion – an arrangement slightly reminiscent of contemporary 'fine' sideboards which almost gives this piece the look of a hybrid of two related types of furniture. The contrasting dark cock beading of the drawers adds a note of sophistication and the apron shaping is dramatic, though perhaps a little undecided. The end panels have been merely nailed on over the framing – a common regional feature (cf. Figure 113). The drop handles on the small drawers are certainly anachronistic replacements, and it is possible that all the drawers were originally provided with knobs.

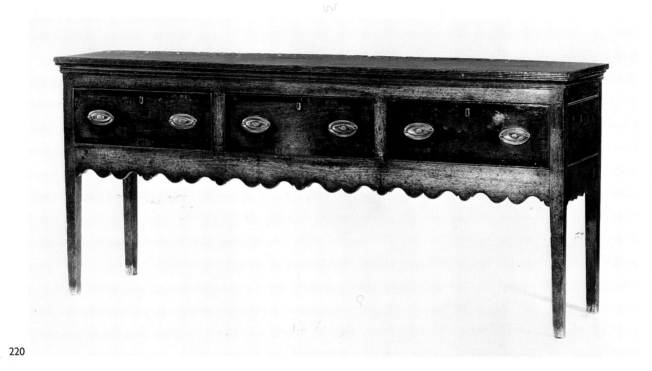

220

Figure 220.
LOW DRESSER.
*Oak with mahogany crossbanding. North-West/
West Midlands, 1790–1830.*

*The earlier dressers from this area (Figures 111–
116) are represented here in an updated form —
mainly achieved by the simple substitution of
Neoclassical square legs tapered on their inner sides for
the turned and cabriole varieties. The reeded moulding
to the top also conforms to early 19th-century
fashion. The standard number of three cock-beaded
drawers comes above a repetitively shaped apron which
is continued on the flush-panelled ends. The slightly
protruding keyhole inserts seen here are an early
pattern that was seldom used after the date range given
for this piece.*

Figure 221.
HIGH DRESSER.
*Oak with mahogany crossbanding. Probably West
Midlands, 1800–40.*

*With an identical superstructure arrangement to that
of the dressers shown in Figures 115 and 116, this
piece has a simply moulded top crossbanded to match
cupboards and drawers, square tapered legs and flush
ends. The exact match of the shaping under the
mahogany-veneered frieze with that of the apron
nicely confirms the originality of superstructure and
base to each other. The handles are modern.*

221

222

By the early 19th century, dressers with enclosed bases were generally superseding the open-based variety in many parts of England. Loudon gave designs for either type, basing his example of a version with three drawers above two cupboards and a central fixed panel on those 'used in the better description of cottage dwellings in Cambridgeshire'. This piece, and two others shown in his book, are fitted with plate rails across the front to allow plates displayed on the shelves to lean forward, thus preventing dust from settling on their front surfaces. The other dressers illustrated have a strip of beading fixed along each shelf so that the plates can safely be leant backwards. The shelves on all his specimen dressers have hooks fixed along the front edges 'on which jugs and any small articles having handles may be hung'.

Figure 222.
HIGH DRESSER.
Oak with mahogany crossbanding. Probably West Midlands/East Wales, 1800–50.
Superficially similar to the previous dresser but here the flanking cupboards have been replaced by a row of small drawers (not exclusively for spices) at the bottom of the superstructure and they are graduated to reflect the unusual wide central and two narrower drawers in the base section. The mahogany cross-banded base drawers are adorned with bands of parquetry – a decorative theme repeated on the small drawers in the superstructure, on the cornice and above the shaped apron. Parquetry banding was a favourite device of later dealers seeking to 'improve' antique furniture – but there is no need to doubt its originality on this dresser. The back boards of the superstructure and all items of brassware are modern.

223

Figure 223.
HIGH DRESSER.
Pine. Devon, 1820–45.
A West Country open-based dresser on turned front legs; this example has three equal drawers although the central drawer is frequently narrower than those flanking it on dressers from this region. The drawers are cock beaded and all mortise-and-tenon joints are pegged. There are no locks.

Figure 224 (right).

HIGH DRESSER.

Elm. East Somerset, 1810–45.

A simple, enclosed-base dresser from a cottage in Wincanton, Somerset. The base ends are formed by slabs rather than panelled, echoing an earlier regional tradition (cf. Figures 119, 120, 124 and 125), and it stands directly on the floor with neither feet nor a plinth. The protruding keyhole inserts are an early type but the fairly large knobs suggest a later date.

225   224

Figure 225 (above).

HIGH DRESSER.

Pine. Penzance, Cornwall, 1810–40.

A superb piece in which the entire superstructure, including the large overhanging cornice, is bow-fronted and embellished with reeded pilasters. The width of the back boards is remarkable. This dresser came from a house in Penzance and a base entirely filled by drawers is typical of the area. Note the narrow central drawer at the top.

It is interesting to note that in a late Victorian mention of dressers it was still being recommended that a potboard should be black:

Of the [kitchen] fixtures, the dresser is the most important. This has, as a rule, besides the racks for plates and dishes, its table-top and three drawers, and cupboards below; but sometimes, instead of these cupboards there is a pot-board, which should be kept brightly black. The ledges should have hooks of different sizes, and different distances apart upon each ledge, for the hanging-up of cups, large and small, and jugs of various sizes.[11]

Convenient and space-saving corner cupboards (**Figures 232–237**) continued in popularity well into the 19th century although, as time wore on, less care was lavished on them and by the end of the century, apart from fine 'reproductions' (or, rather, interpretations) of Georgian styles intended for rich drawing rooms, the true vernacular variety had been almost entirely supplanted by dressers, larders and pantries. Certainly, in their heyday, corner cupboards were well-regarded and proudly displayed. Loudon stated: 'In small rooms these cupboards are very convenient, as they occupy very little space, and, for a moderate sum, supply a handsome article of furniture'. Loudon was much in favour of the pine specimens shown in his book being 'grained to imitate wainscot' (i.e. painted in oak

226

Figure 226.
HIGH DRESSER.
Pine. 1800–50.

Over 7 feet long, this large dresser possibly stood in the kitchen of a grand house. The drawers, doors and fixed side panels are trimmed with mitred, grooved mouldings and the top of the lower section has cleated ends. The backboards are certainly modern and it is probable that the entire superstructure is a later replacement. The multi-knotted timber of the frieze is particularly inconsistent with that used for the base. The plinth is missing.

Figure 227.
SIDEBOARD.
Pine, original finish removed. Probably North Midlands/South Yorkshire, 1830–90.

Though very similar to the piece in Figure 231, having turned feet and the same arrangement of drawers surrounding a recessed cupboard below a shaped arch, this one is probably later and is made entirely in pine. The carcase has rounded outer corners and top and base mouldings identical to those on many contemporary chests of drawers from the North. A low backboard is mounted behind the top surface. The sideboard was found in Lincolnshire. There are no locks.

227

Figure 228 (right).
GLAZED HIGH DRESSER.
Pine, stain and varnish finish. Possibly West Country, 1880–1915.
Kitchen cupboards with completely drawered bases are recorded as far apart as the West Country and Northumberland by the end of the 19th century; this example is virtually just a chest of drawers with a cabinet on top. Its austerity is relieved by the round-arched glazing and the use of large split turnings to decorate both sections. The Gothic brass key escutcheons and the glass knobs are original.

229

228

Figure 229 (above).
GLAZED HIGH DRESSER.
Pine and elm, original finish removed. Probably West Country, 1850–85.
Here, the dresser has developed into the ubiquitous 'kitchen cupboard' – a type which never entirely superseded the old open-shelved version, becoming a standard fixture in many kitchens by the end of the century. This piece (upper and base sections are separate) still has pegged mortise-and-tenon joints but the large glazing areas suggest a date after 1850. Here there are three doors below the three drawers to the base; in many high dressers the central door is replaced by a fixed panel. The brassware is modern.

'scumble') and, apart from one piece with no doors at all, all the illustrated examples have their upper doors glazed. Glass had become cheap in the 19th century, but Loudon noted that, whereas the items shown would cost from £2 to £5, 'the cost will be considerably diminished by having the upper doors in single wooden panels, instead of being glazed'.

One type of furniture which has survived in considerable quantities from the 19th century is a specialised variety of large cupboard, with a combination of drawers and doors enclosing shelves, which was intended for the storage of household linen and other articles and which was likely to have been situated in the servants' quarters or upstairs in a large house. These imposing pieces have come to be termed 'housekeepers' cupboards', although an alternative description – 'housekeeping cupboard' – is perhaps preferable since it is more general and does not imply individual

230

Figure 230.
SIDEBOARD.

Pine, original finish removed. Probably North, 1850–90.

A variety of sideboard with a curvilinear high back, edged in applied, scrolled carvings, which reflects the French Rococo designs shown in contemporary publications such as The Cabinet Makers' Assistant of 1853 and lends presence to a piece of 'status symbol' furniture. The single shelf above two small drawers retains a fraction of the superstructure facilities offered by the high forms of the old 'formal dresser'. In order to restrict the overall size, symmetry has been dispensed with in the base, which is divided into three graduated drawers on one side and a cupboard on the other. The outer corners are rounded and a heavy plain moulding comes above the turned feet. Curiously, the Classical moulding which frames the cupboard door panel is arched at the base; this is apparently intentional and the door does not appear to have been subsequently inverted. The brassware is later.

possession. The bases of two of those illustrated here (**Figures 238 and 239**) are obviously related to the formal dressers of their region (**Figures 117, 118 and 121**) and it is significant that the dresser from Field House (**Figure 121**) fulfilled more of a housekeeping function than that of either a sideboard or a conventional kitchen dresser.

231

Figure 231.
SIDEBOARD.

Oak and sycamore (?), red-brown stain. Probably North Midlands/South Yorkshire, 1810–50.

This piece was found in Derbyshire and was probably intended for use mainly in the parlour rather than the kitchen. Whether it was called a sideboard or a dresser was largely a matter of local custom; in its own region it was probably referred to as a dresser.

Drawers surround a central cupboard which is stepped back below an ogee-arched frieze. A corresponding arch is repeated on the panel of the door itself. Although the drawers are lip-moulded and traditional fielded panels are retained for the carcase ends, the carcase has assumed the rounded corners and base mouldings typical of the 19th century and stands on turned feet. The present brass handles replace original knobs. There are no locks on the drawers.

Figure 232 (right).
CORNER CUPBOARD.

Pine, original finish removed. North, 1790–1835. The deliberate intention of using even an unglazed corner cupboard as a display vehicle is well shown by this example found in Yorkshire. The door panels are neatly fielded internally as well as on the exterior, indicating that the double doors were designed to be left open if desired. The shelves are attractively shaped and there is also an internal shaped arch at the top. Despite the sad loss of its correct finish, the good proportions and the bold dentil moulding below the cornice still give this piece considerable presence.

233

232

Figure 233 (above).
CORNER CUPBOARD.

Pine, traces of original red-brown paint on the exterior, brown inside the doors. 1790–1840.
A rudimentary piece with neither cornice nor plinth, this cupboard retains the double-door arrangement for the upper part seen on the previous example but the base door is single. All doors are affixed by iron butt hinges; that on the upper left is closed by an iron bolt while the others have turn catches. Only the base cupboard was provided with a lock. The lower door panel has been replaced by later boarding.

The cupboard in **Figure 239** displays a particularly fine selection of the intricately detailed inlays which were fashionable during the Neoclassical period. (Further, though less exalted, examples can be seen in **Figures 115, 121, 126, 236 and 240**.) Despite the obviously high standard of craftsmanship involved in making this cupboard, neither the various paterae nor the narrow bands of intricate parquetry are likely to have been the actual work of the cabinetmaker himself. They would have been bought ready-assembled, ready-coloured and paper-backed (or, in the case of the parquetry, sometimes glued parallel in lengths, like sticks of rock candy, which could be sawn off in sections) from a specialist supplier and then merely applied by the cabinetmaker to his own product.[12] Unfortunately, similar inlays were also readily available in late Victorian and Edwardian

234

Figure 234 (left).
HANGING CORNER CUPBOARD.
Ash. Possibly Cheshire/North-East Wales, 1790–1840.
The all-round edge framing and the dentil moulding to the cornice are highly reminiscent of the style of the cupboard in Figure 127, suggesting a similar origin. The impression at least of Welsh influence, if not actual origin, is reinforced by the use of ash and the inlaid wooden key escutcheon in the shape of an elongated heart. While the lower door panels are simply fielded, the roundels of concentric circles on the upper panels closely resemble a similar motif used on the splats of Windsor chairs of the same period or somewhat later. Early blue paint finish to interior. (Blue was often favoured for both the walls and the furniture of kitchens since the colour was widely regarded at the time as an effective fly-deterrent.)

235

Figure 235 (above).
HANGING CORNER CUPBOARD.
Pine, original finish removed from exterior, traces of old green paint inside. 1810–50.
A basic example in which the top is distinguishable from the bottom only by a wider frieze member above the door and a minimal cornice. The single panelled door opens in the conventional direction — i.e. the hinges are on the right; this tradition was observed with amazing conformity through the ages (cf. Figures 3, 28–30, 59, 62, 128, 129 and 130 et al.) and only rarely broken. The original pressed brass key escutcheon is affixed by steel nails. Portions of the moulding are missing from top and base.

times for application to reproduction furniture or to enhance antique pieces. Although they are not normally of such fine quality as genuine Georgian examples, they can sometimes be difficult to distinguish from original embellishments when used on suitable antique items.

Abiding by Sheraton's usage (see page 103), the piece shown in **Figure 242**, with its top section fitted with trays, would be termed a 'clothes press'. As clothes came to be more commonly kept in wardrobes with hanging space or in chests of drawers, this type of furniture was often used only for storing household linen. Thus, by the end of the 19th century, it was more likely to be called a 'linen press'[13] – in effect, a small, specialised version of a housekeeping cupboard (see **Figure 200**).

Loudon states: 'Wardrobes are as essential in a bed-room, as a dresser is in a cottager's kitchen, or a cupboard, or sideboard of some sort, in his parlour'. The deep drawer in the base of one that he illustrates (called by him a 'wardrobe', though without hanging space – so Sheraton would have said 'clothes press') is 'for bonnets, &c. In this drawer are commonly fixed bonnet-holders . . . and against its sides cap pins [hooks]'. Loudon also shows an example of a wardrobe with a central division – hanging space on one side, shelves on the other – which was to become the most common type in the 19th century (**Figures 243 and 244**). He gives the price of painted pine wardrobes as from £3 to £5 in London.

Figure 236 (right).
HANGING CORNER CUPBOARD.
Oak with mahogany veneers and crossbanding.
North, 1790–1830.
A fine example in which the entire front of the carcase is veneered in mahogany, leaving only the canted sides and doors in oak. The frieze is picked out with parquetry banding and lies below a cornice with a narrow carved moulding at the top. The panels of the double doors are centred by superbly detailed shell inlays which are complemented by shell inlay spandrels in the corners of the crossbanding. Each door is provided with a bone inlaid key escutcheon in Neoclassical fashion – one real, the other (on the left) a dummy for symmetry. The interior is fitted with shaped shelves.

236

237

Figure 237 (above).
HANGING CORNER CUPBOARD.
Oak. Probably Midlands, 1800–50.
Mahogany veneer has been restricted here to the frieze and the drawer fronts, where it is edged by boxwood stringing. Again there is an inlaid diamond-shaped key escutcheon, this time in wood, but only a single door. The maker of this cupboard has also avoided the cost of buying ready-made inlays and has instead created simple lozenges of burr walnut with boxwood borders on the door panels. Only the central drawer is real. Corner cupboards frequently have drawers fitted internally.

Most wardrobes at this period were provided only with hooks for hanging clothes; although rails with coat-hangers were sometimes fitted in fine wardrobes in the late 18th century,[14] this refined arrangement was not to become common in lesser pieces until one hundred years later.

By the end of the 19th century, wardrobes were increasingly being retailed as part of a coordinated suite of bedroom furniture, comprising matching dressing table, chest of drawers, washstand and so on. Apart from those conforming to the dominant Grecian trend, these suites were also made in the other derivative fashions of the period – either emulative of foreign styles or retrospective, i.e. a Victorian perception, normally wildly inaccurate, of earlier traditions. It would be wrong, however, to perpetuate an attitude prevalent some years ago and regard the lack of originality in the ornamental details of Victorian furniture as an indication that as far as the evolution of furniture was concerned the period was one of stagnation. In most cases, the ornamentation on Victorian furniture was no more derivative than the Renaissance carving on furniture of the 17th century or the eclectic influences on that of the 18th. The 19th century, for all the superficial clinging to earlier decorative styles, was an era of dynamic change and innovation in basic furniture design, creating not only novel constructional techniques but entirely new types of furniture.

238

Figure 238.
HOUSEKEEPING CUPBOARD.
Oak with mahogany veneers and crossbanding.
North-West, 1780–1835.
A magnificent piece with a breakfront upper section; the mahogany-veneered friezes to both sections are trimmed with narrow bands of intricate parquetry and the crossbanded door panels have mahogany corner inserts or spandrels. The lower section, with crossbanded and cock-beaded drawers surrounding a pair of cupboard doors, is flanked by square reeded columns – a feature particularly associated with the Cheshire area. The whole stands on attractive ogee bracket feet, although those at each front corner are slim to the point of looking precarious. Original green paint inside cupboards.

Housekeeping cupboards from this region and North Wales, in common with dressers from the same areas, occasionally incorporate a clock in the upper section.

Figure 239.
HOUSEKEEPING CUPBOARD.
Oak with mahogany veneers and crossbanding.
North-West, 1790–1835.
The friezes of both sections are veneered in mahogany with parquetry banding and ornamented with a series of finely detailed paterae, the central one on the lower frieze bearing a representation of Britannia and the British lion. The base repeats the configuration of that in Figure 238 with crossbanded and cock-beaded drawers surrounding a pair of cupboard doors, here displaying central urn inlays, and flanked by square reeded columns. The upper doors enclose shaped shelves.

This is a piece of furniture that has suffered badly from Victorian updating; the later bulbous knobs and turned feet are starkly at variance with the cupboard's essential Neoclassical design[15]. The correct feet would have been flush or bracket (possibly ogee as on the previous piece) and traces of the original oval or 'swan-neck' brass handles remain on the drawers. Strictly speaking, of course, bracket feet and 'swan-neck' handles were not Neoclassical either but they were traditional and were felt to be in keeping with that style. The brassware on the upper doors is also later.

239

Figure 240 (right).
CUPBOARD.
Oak with mahogany crossbanding. North-West,
1780–1830.
The vertical rectilinear form of the Neoclassical style is
exemplified in this cupboard, which stands on bracket
feet and has two pairs of doors separated by a bold
horizontal dado moulding. The flat pilasters have
crossbanded borders edged by fine parquetry banding
and embellished with crossbanded quadrant spandrels
in the same manner as the fielded door panels. The
theme of inlaid paterae on the mahogany-veneered
frieze is repeated on the two upper door panels and the
key escutcheons are inlaid diamond shapes. The
interior is fitted as a hanging space.
The overall configuration of this piece is much like that
of the front doors of houses of the same period.

241

240

Figure 241 (above).
HOUSEKEEPING CUPBOARD.
Pine, original finish removed. Probably North,
1830–80.
A slightly eclectic pine example, found in Lincolnshire,
which combines a Grecian rounded arch to the panel of
the single cupboard door in the base with ogee-arched
tops to the flat members applied on the uprights
between the three doors of the upper section. All door
panels are trimmed with applied, mitred mouldings.
The whole rests on a simple plinth and is topped by a
large cornice of a Grecian flat-faced style particularly
popular at this period. The brassware is modern.

242

Figure 242 (left).
CLOTHES PRESS.
Oak. 1785–1830.
A design of restrained elegance; decoration has been confined to the large oval mouldings superimposed on the pair of door panels. These doors enclose the shelves of the upper section, which rests on a base of two short and two long cock-beaded drawers.

Figure 243 (opposite, above left).
WARDROBE.
Pine. 1876–90.
Not made of 'fine' timber but not really vernacular either, this wardrobe bears a label indicating that the design was registered in 1876. It is an expression of the 'Japanese' fashion which swept England during the late 19th century; pine has been used here not as a substitute for expensive timber and disguised by paint, but deliberately for its aesthetic effect and decorated with pseudo-Oriental motifs. It would have been far more expensive than ordinary pine furniture when new.
The interior has the standard arrangement of a hanging space on one side with a pull-out frame fitted with hooks at the top, sliding trays and drawers.

Figure 244 (opposite, above right).
WARDROBE.
Pine, brown over yellow paint finish. 1870–1910.
With heavily moulded cornice and rounded corners, the dark striping and stencilled designs, including a 'key pattern' on the frieze, accentuate the basic Grecian style of this wardrobe, which probably once formed part of a bedroom suite with matching decoration. The finish is possibly intended to represent satinwood. As usual, the wardrobe dismantles easily for removal and the interior is divided into hanging space, sliding trays and drawers.

TABLES

The leg forms found on 19th-century tables are, in general, characterised by a progression from Neoclassical to Grecian to more bulbous, sometimes debased, Grecian types. While the simplest of plain, square-section legs are naturally found on the simplest pieces of functional furniture throughout the ages (e.g. **Figures 32 and 158** and the table in **Figure 88**), and were a form universally relegated to rear legs even on fine pieces, it was an easy matter to confine them to narrow proportions and taper the two inner sides in order to conform at least basically to the current Neoclassical principles of the late 18th and early 19th centuries.

Although the Neoclassical style can be said to have come into vogue around 1760, only later, as with earlier styles, was it applied to vernacular furniture and most instances of tapered square-section legs are indicative of a date after 1780 or, more likely, in the early decades of the 1800s. Again, turned legs were also a Neoclassical element but were even later in their widespread application to vernacular tables, seldom being used before 1800 and thereafter conforming more to Grecian influence. In common with the turned feet on case furniture, turned legs on tables began to broaden into more robust forms shortly before the Victorian era – a style that continued on functional pieces into the present century.

243

244

Figure 245.
SMALL TRESTLE TABLE.
Elm top on pine trestles. 1830–90.
A small version with curved top which would neatly
serve a correspondingly curved settle in a tavern and
tempts conjecture. The roughly boarded frieze provides
a measure of sophistication and the trestle members,
crudely screwed together at their junction, curve
outwards in a simple curule-form highly reminiscent
of the crossed legs on some early 19th-century sofa
tables. The Classical allusion was possibly intentional
and it is interesting to note an academic influence on
even the most utilitarian of furnishing objects.

245

246

Figure 246.
TRESTLE TABLE.
Sycamore top on pine trestles. 1840–1920.
An enormous single plank of sycamore rests on a pair of X-form pine trestles, braced by means of iron rod brackets screwed to the underside of the top and bolted to the centre of each trestle. Strictly speaking, a 'trestle' should be free-standing, but the term has long been extended to include a variety of crude beamed supports for tables. Many examples similar to this and the following piece bear the branded names or initials of the breweries which originally owned them.

Figure 247.
TRESTLE TABLE.
Pine. 1810–1910.
Here the X-form trestles rest on batten feet and the crossed bracing is of timber. The corners of the top are curved and a copper edging strip has been applied all round the perimeter as protection — possibly at the time of manufacture.

In North America the type of table standing on X-form trestles and seen in **Figures 246 and 247** would be called a 'sawbuck' table from its resemblance to the simply-constructed frames used to support timber when sawing. In England it is more likely to be called a 'tavern' table after the place in which it was so often found. Indeed, tables of this kind, cheaply and easily made,

247

Figure 248 (right).
KITCHEN TABLE.
Pine, dark stain finish to base. 1880–1920.
The untreated top is edged by a concave moulding and
the robust legs bear a late form of incised turning. A
victim of heavy use, this table has had strips of wood
applied under the rails at some time to strengthen them
and the drawer has been replaced. Truly utilitarian
furniture can deteriorate very rapidly within a
relatively short space of time, and it is small wonder
that so little has survived from a period prior to the
second half of the 18th century.

248

249

Figure 249 (above).
SMALL DROP-LEAF TABLE.
Oak. 1820–70.
The legs are slightly tapered on their inside faces in late
18th-century style but other evidence proclaims a
much later date for this piece, and the type was
certainly made over a very long period. The brass knob
on the single drawer has replaced a large wooden one.

Figure 250 (right).
SMALL DROP-LEAF TABLE.
Pine, original finish removed. 1860–1910.
In this simple kitchen piece, the leaves are merely butt-
jointed to the top and the single drawer nailed together.
An air of sturdiness suitable to its purpose, however, is
perhaps conveyed by the disproportionately robust
legs. The leaves are supported not by hinged brackets
but by wooden strips which pivot in a gap in the frame
just under the top, swivelling out when required.

250

251

252

Figure 251 (above).
DROP LEAF TABLE.
Chestnut top on oak base. 1830–70.
A drop-leaf table in the 18th-century tradition but now with turned legs. The flat-edged top suggests a relatively early date for the type and the rounded corners of the leaves indicate that this dining table is unlikely ever to have formed the central part of a larger combination (see Figure 141). However, it is, of course, not difficult to round corners off and remove connecting lugs or pins in order to present the central part of a combination as a complete entity.

Figure 252 (left).
SMALL DROP-LEAF TABLE.
Oak with mahogany crossbanding. North, 1820–50.
Of a fairly sophisticated 'Pembroke' style, this oak table stands on slim turned legs. Both the real drawer at one end and the mock face at the other are decorated with mahogany crossbanding inset from the edge in the same manner as the chest on stand in Figure 103, although here the drawer fronts are cock-beaded rather than lip-moulded. The photograph shows the mock drawer; the wooden knobs of the real drawer have been replaced by later brass ones.

Figure 253.
SIDE TABLE.
Pine, brown stain. 1790–1840.
The top of this table can be enlarged when required by means of a short leaf at the back which can be supported on a pair of brackets hinged to the rear underframe. In this utilitarian piece, in which the tapered square-section legs are provided with side stretchers, the joints are pegged and the drawers are merely nailed together. The left-hand swan-neck handle is original.

253

254

Figure 254.
FOLDING-TOP TABLE.
Oak. 1780–1830.
Tables of this kind were popular in the 18th and 19th centuries as 'tea' or card tables, although any occasional use was likely. Those specifically intended only for games sometimes had a baize covering inset into the top[16]. This humble oak example has no baize and could be used for either purpose. The side-hinged leaf, polished on both sides, normally rests on the top but can be unfolded when desired and supported by one of the rear legs, which swings out on a wooden knuckle joint in the same manner as the legs of a large drop-leaf table. It represents a later development of the type of table shown in Figure 142.

would have been employed in almost every conceivable situation where a rough, sturdy table was needed – from inns and taverns to shops and market stalls. They have been made over a very long period; examples are shown in early illustrations and similar items are still produced at the present day.

In the 19th century, the vast majority of the population lived in small houses with no separate dining room. If the house had a front parlour, this would normally be kept as an immaculate showpiece for receiving visitors and seldom used for everyday family living. Family life centred on the kitchen and a standard kitchen table, such as the one shown in **Figure 248**, served every purpose. The tops of these tables were usually left unfinished to allow them to be used for preparing food and the surface would be kept clean by regular scrubbing. The bases, however, were normally stained or painted so that the table presented a reasonable appearance when covered with a tablecloth and used for dining. For the kitchen of a Victorian house large and affluent enough to keep servants, it was recommended that the table

should be sufficiently large, and very firm and substantial. The best kind is one with a deal top, not less than $1\frac{1}{2}$ inch[es] thick, with stained and varnished frame and legs. The deal should be constantly scrubbed and kept white, but there should be a table-cloth provided for covering it when work is over . . .[17]

Apart from these primary intended functions, the average kitchen table has also occasionally served as work bench, school desk, washstand or ironing board and has, at one time or another, been hammered on, carved on, sat on and stood on. Their powers of endurance are truly remarkable.

Small drop-leaf tables with two short leaves and usually a drawer at one end had been found useful since the mid-18th century. Each leaf is supported when open by two small brackets which swing out from the frame sides on wooden 'knuckle joint' hinges and, unlike the majority of the earlier gateleg tables, the drawer on these tables rests on side runners fixed on either side of the frame. Finer examples of the type, which often have a mock drawer front at the opposite end for the sake of symmetry,

255

256

Figure 255 (left).
SIDE TABLE.
Chestnut top on elm and pine base, brown over yellow scumble finish. 1820–50.
Good proportions achieve elegance in a table which lacks any form of decoration other than its attractive paint finish. The top has been merely nailed on in the same way as that in Figure 147 but here the nails are finer and the scars in the top have been carefully filled and disguised. The drawer simply fits in a rectangular hole cut out of the centre of the frieze, automatically providing upper and lower rails. There is no lock.

Figure 256 (above).
SIDE TABLE.
Oak. 1780–1830.
This dressing table/desk, with a concave moulding to the top edges, retains the three-drawered 'lowboy' form of much earlier pieces but stands on square-section legs tapered on their inner faces. The dovetailed drawers with cock-beaded fronts come above a gently undulating apron. The brassware is later.

Figure 257 (left).
SIDE TABLE.
Pine, traces of old blue-green paint finish. 1790–1835.
A well-constructed table, in which the top is secured by screws inserted through gouges in the rails underneath and in which the drawer is dovetailed, but retaining old-fashioned pegged mortise-and-tenon joints on the frame for strength. The edges of the top are neatly moulded and there is a narrow applied moulding round three sides of the frieze above the square tapered legs. The drawer, with its front edges incised to simulate cock beading, bears a lock and there is an upper rail above it. The present handles replace original swan-neck versions.

257

Figure 258.
SIDE TABLE.

Pine, dark over pale brown paint finish imitating curly maple. 1860–1920.

A delicate piece intended as a dressing table for bedroom use on which a separate swing mirror would have been placed. Tables identical to this one are extremely common and were undoubtedly mass-produced in factories; an illustration of a very similar table appeared in the store catalogue of George Maddox, a London retailer, in 1882. The construction is economical: the top is merely nailed on, there is no lock to the drawer and the rear legs are unturned. Nevertheless, apart from marks left by a mechanical frame saw on the timber itself, the table shows every sign of have been made entirely by hand, including the dovetailed drawer.

The original wooden knobs of this table have a threaded hole in the shank which receives a domed, threaded wooden screw from inside the drawer front – a common means of fixing knobs after mid-century. Knobs were seldom made by the furniture maker but, like earlier brass hardware, were bought wholesale from specialist suppliers.

258

were being called 'Pembroke' tables (sometimes spelt with a small 'p' at first) by the 1770s and Sheraton asserted that they were named after 'the lady who first gave orders for one of them' – possibly a countess of Pembroke. They were intended for lesser meals and were frequently also termed 'breakfast tables'. Their general usefulness was soon recognised and it was not long before humbler versions were being made for vernacular use, their small size rendering them ideal for cottages (**Figures 249, 250 and 252**).

Loudon was enthusiastic that tables in kitchens should, if possible, be 'contrived to fold up, or otherwise go into little space, when not in immediate use, in order to afford more room for carrying on the business of the kitchen', and went on to illustrate a variety of ingenious designs. Although a table of 'Pembroke' type is not shown in his book, it was to become common in kitchens during the 19th century (**Figure 250**).

Any table having three feet may be called a 'tripod table', but the kind without a single pillar (**Figures 6 right, 267, 268 and 270**) has acquired the popular name of 'cricket table'. Much picturesque speculation has arisen as to the etymology of this term. Perhaps because so many of these utilitarian tables have been used outside inns near village greens, some people have concluded that this type of table was named after the sport so often played there, a few even going so far as to suggest a connection between the three legs of the table and the three stumps of the game. In fact, the probable real origin of the term is quite simple, although its use may be comparatively modern. As mentioned in Chapter 3 (page 66), the word 'cricket' was in

259

259a

260

Figure 259 (left).
TRIPOD PEDESTAL TABLE.
Oak. 1810–35.

Tilt-top. *A deliberately low-angled view showing the fine baluster-turned pillar and the well-finished shaped bearers under the top. This table could be 18th-century in almost every detail but one. The spur on the knees of the legs is a feature typical of the first half of the 19th century. Note the correct proportion of top to base on a full-size tripod table.*

Figure 259a (above).
CAST BRASS CATCH.
(Detail of Figure 259.)

The superbly-made and decorative brass catch which secures the top when horizontal is identical to those illustrated in brassfounders' trade catalogues of the late 18th and early 19th centuries; it was an expensive piece of hardware.

The scars on the underside of the top exactly match details of the block — a welcome sign of originality. Note how even the outer edges of the bearers are bead-moulded on this good-quality table.

Figure 260 (left).
TRIPOD PEDESTAL TABLE.
Oak. 1800–40.

A small fixed-top example in which the pillar includes the urn shape seen on earlier pieces but here heavily supplemented by multiple ring-turnings indicative of the 19th century. The flat edge of the top also tends to be a late feature.

Figure 261 (right).
TRIPOD PEDESTAL TABLE.
Fruitwood. 1815–50.
Tilt-top. *A humbler fruitwood example which in terms of quality provides a strong contrast with the table in Figure 259. The pillar has assumed the heavy turning typical of the 19th century while the cabriole legs retain a traditional form. Since fruitwood is difficult to acquire in wide widths, the top has been made from several planks; here it is finished with a simple flat edge.*

261

261a

Figure 261a (above).
WROUGHT IRON CATCH.
(Detail of Figure 261.)
This crude catch was undoubtedly much cheaper than that in Figure 259a. But it may still have been the product of a large specialist supplier and, contrary to popular belief, not necessarily made by a local blacksmith — any more than were the screws used to affix it.[18]

Figure 262 (right).
TRIPOD PEDESTAL TABLE.
Oak. 1810–60.
The top of this small, simple table is fixed to a plain column decorated only with a single ring-turning near the top and at the base. The legs of the earliest tripod tables were flat-sided before rounded legs became standard; the flat-sided cabriole legs of this table, however, are an entirely 19th-century type, a provincial concession to Neoclassical influence, and are also easier to make.[19]

262

263

264

common use in earlier days to describe a small stool. Since the archetypal stool had a circular top and three legs, a table of essentially the same form as a 'cricket', only larger, has been dubbed, naturally enough, a 'cricket table'. Loudon (1833) depicted a stool of joined construction with three legs tied by stretchers, basically similar to the table in **Figure 270** but without the shelf.

The possible functions of such a sturdy, convenient table are almost infinite and their distribution, from cottages and farmhouses to inns and taverns, must have been extensive. Examples, conforming to the prevalent style of their period, have survived from the 17th century (**Figure 68**) and the type, occasionally fitted with a drawer or a cupboard, has remained popular up to the present day. Although the name 'cricket table' is normally reserved for tables with three legs, there is no reason not to extend the convenient generic term to tables of the same stool-like character which are provided with four (**Figure 269**), as they are identical in every other respect.[20]

Small tables with one or more drawers, designed specifically as 'work tables' and convenient for women doing sewing or other needlework, had come into popular fashion during the late 18th century. Storage was important for the paraphernalia connected with these activities, of course, and during the 19th century this function occasionally obliterated that of the table to the extent that, in some instances, a work 'table' was little more than a box on a stand. At a vernacular level, work tables and boxes often

Figure 263 (left).
TRIPOD PEDESTAL TABLE.
Fruitwood top and column, mahogany legs.
1820–45.
Tilt-top. The crossbanded top of this elegant table is decorated with a central inlay of rosewood and curly maple. Arched legs of this form, with a downward turn, are of Neoclassical inspiration and had been introduced by the 1780s.

Figure 264 (right).
DUMB WAITER.
Elm. 1790–1840.
Essentially a tripod table form but with intermediate tiers, which would be placed conveniently near a dining table for extra courses, plates, cutlery and so on. This example has only two tiers, dished to provide a rim in the normal manner but, unusually, the largest is at the top. The double ring-turning to the pillar just above its junction with the cabriole legs suggests a 19th-century date.
It may be thought that the term 'dumb waiter' is modern; in fact it was used in the first half of the 18th century, though possibly for another type of furniture.

265

Figure 265.
TRIPOD PEDESTAL TABLE.
Pine, original finish removed. 1830–80.
Tilt-top. The rectangular top with double-ogee sides and the kneed cabriole legs of this small stand echo earlier types but the column turning and pendant at the base make a Victorian date more likely. The original wrought iron catch is similar to that in Figure 261a.

Figure 266.
STAND.
Pine and chestnut, later black over old brown paint finish. 1840–90.
The use of greenery in interior decoration became extremely popular during the Victorian period and this tall stand was probably intended to support a potted plant rather than a lighting appliance. The base retains an early leg form while the turning of the pillar is decidedly Grecian.

266

appear to have been home-made. In these cases, they were either made by the user or may sometimes have been a personal gift from husband to wife, in much the same way as other love-tokens. The home-made article in **Figure 274** certainly stands out as an exception in a period during which furniture was increasingly being produced on an assembly-line basis and losing its individuality.

Tables intended to contain needlework and its accessories took various forms and Loudon included several designs in the 'Parlour tables' section of his book. One that he illustrates is similar in concept to that shown here in **Figure 273** and Loudon suggests that it 'may be made by any joiner, out of

267

268

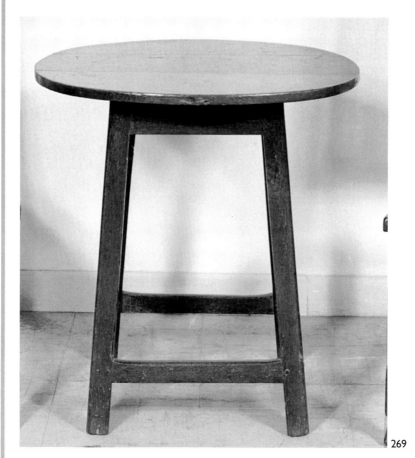

269

Figure 267 (above left).
CRICKET TABLE.
Elm. 1790–1840.

A humble table type of wide-ranging domestic and public use; the old ogee-arched shaping of the friezes on this example is allied to tapering legs of Neoclassical inspiration. The top, made from a single plank of elm, has inevitably warped and cracked.

Figure 268 (above right).
CRICKET TABLE.
Pine, original finish removed. 1860–1910.

The legs of this example are turned as on much earlier cricket tables (cf. Figure 68) but the turning here, with multiple rings to the upper portion, is distinctly 19th-century and there are no stretchers. The mortise-and-tenon joints of the legs on this piece are still pegged for extra strength even at this late date.

Figure 269 (left).
CRICKET TABLE.
Oak. 1780–1840.

A four-legged variety of essentially the same typological group as the foregoing tables. A three-plank top with flat edges rests on square-section legs which are chamfered on their inside edges and tied by stretchers. The joints are pegged.

Figure 270.
CRICKET TABLE.
Pine, dark brown stain. 1810–70.
An extremely common form of cricket table, found on both sides of the Atlantic, in which the stretchers support a convenient shelf and the legs taper below them.[21] Often the joints are pegged for extra strength, as here, and it is perhaps this archaic factor which has led to this variety being popularly (and erroneously) attributed to the 18th century. A closer appraisal reveals a much later date.

270

271

Figure 271.
PEDESTAL TABLE.
Elm and ash, old red-brown paint finish. Probably Cornwall, 1800–50.
This low table, found in Cornwall, has a 'primitive' stool-like base, and the type is believed to have been intended as a lampstand for Cornish lacemakers. The legs of the base are of roughly square section with chamfered edges, the platform is deeply bevelled and the pillar is simply turned in a manner similar to that of regional Windsor chairs. The single bearer is secured under the top by large, hand-forged nails. The pillar has been crudely repaired.

the common woods of the country, at a very trifling expense'. Another example, described by Loudon as a 'plain parlour work-table', is a stocky version of a two-leaved 'Pembroke' form with two drawers, one above the other.

A further type of work table advocated by Loudon is one of those ingenious and space-saving combinations of which he was so fond. In addition to a rising leaf and a sliding bag frame mounted underneath, the table is provided with a writing slope inside the drawer. Loudon was characteristically optimistic: 'we trust that the time will soon come, when not only every cottager's wife will be able to write as well as read, but will have leisure to do so'. His suggestion that the table may be made cheaper by constructing it 'of common deal' and by not turning the legs is significant. Square-section legs, plain or tapered, were often regarded merely as a cheap alternative to turning throughout the 19th century and are not in themselves necessarily an indication that the piece on which they occur is of the Neoclassical period (e.g. **Figure 249**).

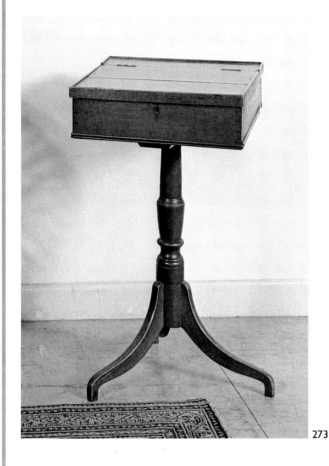

273

274

272

Figure 272 (left).
WORK TABLE.
Oak, top surface veneered on pine. 1830–60.
An unusually sophisticated form for oak at this period but still a workaday piece and not in the fine '19th-Century Oak Revival' class; the construction details of this table are somewhat crude and suggest that it may have been a one-off piece. The style is unashamedly Grecian but the small scrolled feet to the platform are rudimentary shadows of their designer-made counterparts. One end of the box-top is equipped with a finger-hold on the bottom edge and pulls out as a drawer. The oak veneer to the top surface is set within a mitred border but the pieces are ill-fitting and it would seem that the craftsman was unfamiliar with the technique.

SEATING

The publication of Thomas Sheraton's *The Cabinet-makers' and Upholsterers'* *Drawing Book* in three parts from 1791 to 1794 and his *Cabinet Dictionary* in 1803 had an impact on furniture design similar to that which the works of Chippendale and Hepplewhite had produced earlier. Other designers, such as Thomas Hope and particularly George Smith, also had great influence in their day but it is Sheraton who has achieved the greatest fame. Almost any early 19th-century vernacular chair of generally squarish shape and with a straight crest rail has come to be popularly labelled 'country Sheraton', regardless of its real derivation. In fact, many of the chair designs in Sheraton's *Drawing Book* reflected the same Neoclassical fashions shown by Hepplewhite only shortly before and included 'shield back' types as well as the square-backs for which he is better known. Conversely, Hepplewhite's editions also contained square-back designs.

·The essentially Neoclassical, vertical accentuation of the single chairs shown in **Figures 277, 278 and 280** rapidly gave way to a progressive tendency for squatter, more horizontally accentuated, chairs with slats and broad crest rails which stressed a Grecian inspiration. This is particularly strongly expressed in the wide, overlapping crest rails of some varieties (**Figure 281**),

276

Figure 276.
WINGED ARMCHAIR.
Pine, light stain. Lancashire/Yorkshire Dales, 1820–80.

A specifically regional form of vernacular winged armchair which is related to that in Figure 156 and possibly also to the early winged armchair in Figure 155. Frequently this type has a drawer under the seat, at the side or in front (as here), and normally a panelled back. While styles are diverse, this and the preceding example appear to be typical of many pine versions at this period in that the wing boards and side boards under the arms continue down to enclose the space under the seat in place of alternative panelling. On this piece the rear panel is framed by mitred mouldings, the crest rail and frieze are shaped in opposite ogee arches and the drawer is dovetailed. The arms are horizontally scrolled.

Armchairs of this type were apparently intended only as comfortable fireside seats. The popular generic term 'lambing chair' seems to have no relevance other than that, since the Dales were a sheep-farming region, many of them would have belonged to shepherds.

a direct reference to the Ancient Greek *klismos*. The splayed 'sabre' front legs of finer Grecian-style chairs seldom reached a vernacular level and the alternative turned front legs were generally late in their arrival (**Figures 282 and 283**). Curved arms with vertically scrolled handrests were also a common expression of the prevailing fashion on armchairs (**Figure 281, left**) and were sometimes effected in a highly pronounced form (**Figure 282**). The virtual demise of the joined solid-seat chair over most of the country in the latter part of the 19th century is perhaps explained by the ever more accessible upholstered mahogany pieces for parlour use, caned chairs for bedrooms and the eventual supremacy throughout England of turned and Windsor types for the kitchen.

Following Classical precedent, it became fashionable in the late 18th and early 19th centuries to apply painted decoration to furniture. Chairs treated in this way were known as 'fancy' chairs; expensive joined examples were intended for wealthier homes and medium-priced versions with rush seats (**Figures 285, 289 and 290**) were also aimed at the popular market. Being a fashionable rather than conservative furniture type, their

Figure 277.
CHAIR.
Cherry with elm seat. East Anglia, 1800–30.
Chairs having a concave, or 'hollow', wooden seat
appear to have been peculiar to East Anglia (cf.
Figures 278 (left) and 279). This example, in
desirable cherry, represents the upper range of chairs in
its class. The concave seat and tapered front legs were
more expensive than flat and straight versions and the
H-form stretchers are a more sophisticated arrangement than the box stretchers seen in Figures 278 and
279. The rear uprights are stepped above seat level
and, most significantly, the back is carved: the narrow
splats broaden at the top as in the chair in Figure 280
but here the surface is carved in a manner closely based
on the design source. The crest rail and lower rail are
groove-moulded; the uprights are carved with inset
reeding and topped by pyramidal finials.

277

Figure 278.
Left:
CHAIR.
Elm. East Anglia, 1790–1830.
*Another version of the 'Sheraton' Neoclassical style;
the crest rail curves downwards at the corners and this
chair has a box-stretcher base. The original concave
wooden seat survives under later upholstery.*

Right:
CHAIR.
Elm. 1790–1840.
This simple chair with straight crest rail is roughly
similar in general appearance to an example with a
curved crest rail illustrated by Loudon in 1833 and
described by him as 'the commom kitchen chair about
London. It is generally made of deal, but sometimes of
birch or beech, and is usually painted'. In fact, very
few English chairs made from pine survive from before
1900. The chair shown here is of stained elm and
probably of more rural origin.

278

279

280

Figure 279 (left).
CHAIR.
Elm. East Anglia, 1800–40.
This chair repeats the Neoclassical tapered front legs and the regional concave seat of the example in Figure 277 but the stretchers are of box form and the back shows a decided progression away from the earlier Neoclassical and towards its later development into the Grecian style. The broad crest rail, here flush with the uprights, complements the horizontal accentuation of the pair of central rails joined by three turned balls.[23] *Later triangular blocks have been added at the junction between seat rails and uprights for strength.*

Figure 280 (above).
CHAIR.
Fruitwood. 1790–1830.
A vernacular chair which conforms to the fashionable square-back style promoted by Sheraton. Tapered square-section front legs support a drop-in upholstered seat.

The dimensions of hand-made chairs always differ slightly, even in chairs forming part of a set. Matching Roman numerals were often inscribed by the maker on both the inside of the seat rail of a chair and on the drop-in seat frame made for it, so that seats would not be accidentally interchanged. Forcing the wrong seat frame into another chair from a set could easily weaken or even split the joints.

style features generally followed the latest trends of the day instead of preserving archaic traditions. Rush-seated fancy chairs attained widespread popularity, particularly in North America, and were employed in both parlours and bedrooms.[22] It is regrettable that their painted decoration, an essential part of the design, has all too often been removed or overpainted.

The turned chair-making tradition of the West Midlands produced one of the very few makers of vernacular furniture who achieved a fair degree of fame – Philip Clissett (1817–1913) of Bosbury, Herefordshire. In common with other makers of wood-seated chairs in the region, Clissett often stamped his initials into the tops of the back uprights of his products (**Figures 294 and 294a**) and he is known to have made both spindleback and ladderback varieties with rush seats as well. Clissett was not an innovator but, with the exception of special commissions, appears to have produced only chairs which were of established and conventional design for his area. He is likely to have remained in relative obscurity had it not been for his

281

Figure 281.
ARMCHAIR AND SINGLE CHAIR.
Elm. 1810–45.

Wide, overlapping crest rails of this klismos form had appeared by 1800; on these chairs they are set on back uprights which are scrolled and round-fronted above seat level and combined with boldly carved slats. The bases have tapered front legs tied by stretchers, here of H form. The arms of the armchair rest on urn-shaped continuations of the front legs.

These chairs are from a set of six. It is likely that the single chair originally had a drop-in seat matching that of the armchair, although the present upholstery of the latter has been stuffed a little too high.

Figure 282.
ARMCHAIR.
Mahogany. Possibly North-West, 1810–80.

Despite the use of mahogany, the turned front legs and the lack of stretchers, this armchair retains a charmingly rustic character that is partly achieved by its somewhat awkward proportions. The squat turnings below the boldly scrolled arms are similar to those on some turned chairs from the North-West and suggest a possible regional affinity, given that this chair recently came up for sale in Cheshire.

282

283

Figure 283.
CHAIR.
Beech and birch with alder seat, dark brown stain.
1850–90.

The final development of the joined solid-seat chair. The rear uprights are scrolled and round-fronted as on the chairs in Figure 281 but the overlapping crest rail has broadened into the deep, heavy shape characteristic of the mid-19th century onwards. The front legs are turned in the fashion of the same period. Stretchers have been dispensed with.

STOOL.
Elm seat, ash legs and stretchers, old black paint.
North, 1870–1920.

A turned stool of Windsor form; a type commonly used at the turn of the century in factories and commercial premises as well as recreational and domestic locations. On this example, one thin stretcher is mortised through the central swelling of the other.

Figure 284.
ARMCHAIR.
Fruitwood. 1820–70.

A turned chair in the Grecian style; the seat was originally rushed. While retaining the traditional round stretchers for the base, the rear uprights are of square section and the back and the scrolled arms reflect the contemporary fashion for joined chairs.

284

Figure 285.
ARMCHAIR.

Beech with rush seat, natural ground painted with foliage in dark and light green, flowers in rose/plum and striping in dark green and black. 1790–1820. A sophisticated type of turned chair with rush seat (obscured by a loose cushion in the photograph) which was known at the time as a 'fancy chair'. The style was highly fashionable rather than traditional; this example displays typical late Neoclassical features — 'Sheraton' back form, tapered arm supports, bowed front seat rail and flat sections to the spindles and front stretcher — and is almost identical to many contemporary American specimens. Unusually, the freehand decoration here appears to have been painted directly on to the bare wood rather than applied over a base coat[24].

285

286

Figure 286.
CHAIR.

Fruitwood (?). 1810–50.

This chair, on a box-stretcher base with tapered front legs, has reeded uprights stepped above seat level and rising above the crest rail. The front of the crest rail is embellished with a gouged rectangle bordered by beading. The similarly treated rectangular panel in the central slat is intentionally reminiscent of the winged tablets appearing on Classical monuments. Later upholstery conceals the original flat wooden seat.

association with the Cotswold School of the Arts and Crafts Movement in the final decades of his long life. Because of the fame brought by that connection, his role as a simple country craftsman was to serve as an idealised model for later times.

In the 1880s Philip Clissett's work was seen by a young architect, James MacLaren, who made a few alterations to his traditional designs and commissioned him to produce the chairs for the meeting hall of the Art Workers' Guild in London. Ernest Gimson (1864–1919) saw these chairs while still an architectural student and, in 1890, spent a few weeks in Herefordshire with Clissett learning the techniques of chairmaking. In 1902 Gimson and Ernest Barnsley established workshops for the production of furniture of vernacular inspiration at Daneway House near the village of Sapperton, Gloucestershire. The armchair seen in **Figure 299**

288

289

290

287

Figure 287 (left).

CHAIR.

Ash with birch crest rail and rush seat. Lancashire/
Cheshire, 1790–1840.

A distinctive variety of spindleback chair with a shell
motif in the centre of the crest rail. The type has long
been known as a 'Liverpool' chair and was so described
in Gillow's cost book of 1801 – where, incidentally,
it was intended to be stained red (a mahogany colour)
and costed at 4/11d. (just under 25p). Of course,
these chairs were not produced purely in Liverpool
although they may have originated there (the firm of
Gillow's was based in Lancaster). They were in fact
made over quite a wide area, occasionally with local
variations (cf. Bernard D. Cotton, The English
Regional Chair, Figure NW138, which is stamped
'C. LEICESTER' of Macclesfield, Cheshire).

Figure 288 (opposite, above left).
CHAIR.
Ash with rush seat. North-West, 1810–50.
An eclectic combination of 'Sheraton' crest rail, regional turnings and 'bamboo' front legs, this chair is one of a set of six. The multiple ball turning seen in the central rails of the back was a popular feature of chairs from this area (cf. Bernard D. Cotton, The English Regional Chair, e.g. Figures NW50 and NW56).

Figure 289 (opposite, centre).
CHAIR.
Beech with rush seat, original finish removed. 1790–1835.
Another fancy chair, unfortunately lacking its paint, which repeats the simple ring-turned front legs of the piece in Figure 285, but here the flat section of the front stretcher is thicker and circular. A further flat section adorns the central spindle while those flanking it are turned with multiple rings. The seat probably had edge strips originally.

Figure 290 (opposite, right).
CHAIR.
Beech with rush seat, grey paint overall with crest rail pattern in white and in dark and light green, and striping in dark green. 1810–25.
The Oriental style, a revival of interest in which occurred in the early 19th century, often assumed a more delicate interpretation than that of previous times and was characterised by the frequent imitation of bamboo — typified by the turnings on this fancy chair.

Figure 291 (right).
ARMCHAIR ON ROCKERS.
Ash and alder, dark stain. Lancashire, 1830–1900.
A 'nursing armchair', designed for a mother tending her child; the rockers were ideally suited to its purpose and the low arms allowed the elbow room required at just the right height. This example has the added convenience of turned wings attached to the uprights which would probably have supported cushions. Naturally, the type functioned as an ordinary 'easy chair' as well. The rush seat has been replaced and the rear stretcher is missing. 291

was based on the Clissett chairs by Gimson and was probably made by Edward Gardiner, the chairmaker at Daneway House.[25] Gimson was not physically strong and made little furniture himself.

Loudon explained that 'parlour chairs . . . are of various patterns; and, as the characteristic of the kitchen chair was strength and durability, so that of the parlour chair is lightness and elegance'. Among others, he advocated the use of delicate chairs with cane seats, such as that shown in **Figure 302** (left), for 'cottage' parlours, though such chairs served in bedrooms as well. Cane-seated chairs had become reasonably priced in the 19th century and Loudon stated that they were

> sold in London at from 7s. [35p] to 12s. [60p] each. They are usually made of beech . . . Chairs of this sort are made in great numbers in Buckinghamshire, where there are extensive beech woods . . . These chairs are generally painted and varnished; but they are sometimes stained either black mahogany colour, or a rosewood pink.

292

Figure 292.
CHAIR.
Ash with rush seat. Lancashire/Cheshire,
1780–1870.
A 'bar top' ladderback standing on straight turned front legs with pad feet and having slats shaped in an ogee arch to their undersides. This distinctive type with a shaped bar linking the tops of the uprights was apparently not confined to a single town but formed part of the repertoire of many makers throughout the region who produced both ladderback and spindleback turned chairs in a variety of designs.

293

Figure 293.
CHILD'S HIGH CHAIR.
Ash with rush seat. Probably North-West,
1800–60.
The horizontal back rails thicken at the points where they receive the spindles. The front legs, widely splayed for extra stability and tied by a pair of turned stretchers, continue upwards as urn-shaped supports for the thick arms. The arm fronts are pierced to take a restraining rod and a footrest was originally fitted just above the upper front stretcher.

It has been justly said of the English chair that no other piece of furniture can 'serve so usefully as a guide to stylistic changes, for the best chairs have been the first to exhibit the materials and decorative forms dictated by the latest fashion'.[26] The vernacular chair, however, was very often more strongly under the influence of regional trends rather than that of high fashion and it was perhaps one of the most significant and distinctive expressions of local traditions at a time when the cultural regions of England were more sharply defined. While those regions having, or being conveniently near, large urban centres with advanced economies sometimes established extensive chairmaking industries catering to a wide, occasionally almost national, market, some chair types were apparently restricted not only to one county but just to the vicinity of a single village (e.g. **Figures 306–308**) and form an immediately recognisable species. By their very nature, those chairs manufactured for wide markets are now

Figure 294 (right).
CHAIR.
Ash with elm seat. Bosbury, Herefordshire,
1845–1910.
A West Midlands variety of single-row spindleback
with wooden seat, the front legs terminating in turned
feet, which has come to be popularly named 'Clissett'
after the well-known chairmaker who made many of
this kind. It was fairly common practice for the
makers of these chairs to stamp their initials on their
products; this example bears those of Philip Clissett
himself.

295

Figure 295 (above).
CHILD'S ARMCHAIR.
Ash. West Midlands, 1810–60.
A diminutive example which may conceivably have   294
started life as a child's high chair, although short
armchairs of this form were also produced for children
contemporaneously. Unusually, this piece combines a
plain arched top slat with lower ones shaped on their
undersides. The seat rails are grooved to receive a
wooden seat but this has been replaced by pine planks
nailed on top; the front frieze, however, survives. The
front stretcher is missing and the bottom slat damaged.

Figure 294a (right).
(Detail of Figure 294.)
The initials 'PC' stamped on top of the rear uprights
are those of Philip Clissett (1817–1913).[27]   294a

297

298

Figure 296 (opposite, left).
CHAIR.
Ash with elm seat. Shropshire/Staffordshire, 1810–60.
A 'bar top' ladderback similar in general appearance to that in Figure 292, having front legs with pad feet and ogee arches to the slat undersides, but here the seat is wooden with a shaped frieze at the front – a typical feature of the West Midlands, although rush-seated chairs were made in this region as well.

Figure 297 (left).
CHAIR.
Ash with rush seat. North-West, 1800–70.
An example of the 'Dales' variety of single-row spindleback; a simple type of rush-seated chair often made (apart from the occasional arms and rockers) exclusively from turned members. It receives its popular name from the area of the country in which the type was made and widely distributed – a rural region including large parts of Lancashire and West Yorkshire and stretching north into Westmorland and Cumberland. The inconsistency of the spindles on this specimen suggests that one or two may be replacements.

Figure 298 (left).
ARMCHAIR AND SINGLE CHAIR.
Ash with rush seats. Possibly Lincolnshire, 1790–1840.
The graduated slats are a normal and aesthetically pleasing feature of ladderback chairs; here they are shaped with a central point on their lower edges. Both chairs have plain front posts with turned feet and topped by balusters, those of the armchair continuing upwards to support the arms with thinned central sections. The tiny balls topping the rear posts may be regarded as vestigial survivals of the large, elaborate finials on early turned chairs (cf. Figures 20, 88, 172 and 173).

296

299

Figure 299 (above right).

ARMCHAIR.

*Ash with rush seat. Sapperton, Gloucestershire,
1904–09.*

Probably made by Edward Gardiner for Ernest
Gimson and based on chairs produced by Philip
Clissett. The pair of plain front stretchers and the
pegged joints of this chair reflect the regional traditions
of the Clissett prototype. This example is stated to
have been one of a small set bought directly from
Gimson by Eric Gill, the calligrapher, as a gift to his
sister, Gladys Mary Gill, on the occasion of her
marriage in 1909 (cf. Figure 294 and Bernard D.
Cotton, The English Regional Chair, Figure
WM29). Presently owned by a descendant of the
original recipient.

Figure 300 (right).

CHAIR.

*Ash with elm seat. Shropshire/Staffordshire,
1810–60.*

A single-row spindleback exhibiting another back
design of the chairmaking tradition of this region (cf.
Figure 296). The back is similar to those of 'Dales'
chairs (cf. Figure 297) while front legs with pad feet
support a wooden seat with a shaped frieze. Such chairs
were made for use in factories and other public places
as well as in the home.

300

301

302

Figure 301 (left).
'CORNER' CHAIR.
Beech with rush seat, dark brown stain. 1870–1915.

William Morris's company, Morris & Co., produced an inexpensive and highly successful range of simple rush-seated chairs; this chair was probably made by one of the many firms who imitated his products and is similar to an example illustrated in a Morris & Co. catalogue at the end of the century. The designs were said to be based on a chair Morris found in Sussex, though it is possible that this prototype originated elsewhere. The seat rushes of the chair shown here were originally stained alternately green and yellow.

Figure 303 (opposite, left).
WINDSOR ARMCHAIR.
Yew with elm seat. Probably Nottinghamshire, 1820–50.

A short or 'low' bow-back armchair with a pierced splat and turned arm supports, which stands on legs turned in a manner common to many 19th-century Windsors. The front legs are linked by a bowed front stretcher – an archaic feature still in use at a much later date than this example. (cf. Bernard D. Cotton, The English Regional Chair, Figure NE314, which shows a chair stamped 'F. WALKER ROCKLEY'.)

Figure 302 (left).
Left:
CHAIR.
Beech with cane seat, brown over cream paint finish with black patterns and striping. Probably Thames Valley, 1825–60.

A delicate cane-seated chair popular for both parlours and bedrooms at this early period. This example combines the usual feature of front legs splayed at the feet with a bowed front seat rail, curved crest rail and 'willow-twist' decoration in the back – all expressive of the fashionable Grecian style.

Right:
CHAIR.
Beech with cane seat, cream paint finish with maroon striping. 1850–1900.

Again the front legs are splayed but the Grecian trend has been interpreted in a more rectilinear form produced by straight seat rails and crest rail, here chamfered. The paint finish suggests a somewhat later date than that of the chair on its left and the style is very similar to one shown in a pattern book printed by Wyman and Sons of London in 1877. By mid-century, bulkier furniture had become more fashionable in parlours; this example was almost certainly intended purely as a bedroom chair.

303

304

Figure 304 (above right).
WINDSOR ARMCHAIR.
Yew with elm seat. Nottinghamshire/North-East, 1840–80.

Generally described as a 'smoking high' chair in Nottinghamshire and a 'high back smoker' in Yorkshire. Similar chairs were also produced as far south as Buckinghamshire and as far north as Northumberland. Another term for the type is 'broad arm' Windsor, alluding to the distinctive characteristic seen clearly on this example. Although Windsor chairs of this type were also made in a variety of other timbers, yew was regarded as the most prestigious – a factor originally reflected in the comparative prices.

Figure 305 (right).
CHILD'S WINDSOR ARMCHAIR.
Fruitwood with alder seat. Nottinghamshire/North-East, 1850–90.

The upper and lower splats are fretted in a Grecian scroll pattern which curiously leaves a distinctive 'fir tree'-like profile to the central cut-out portions. The Grecian theme is echoed in the concave upper parts of the turned legs tied by H-form stretchers. The use of alder for the seats of Windsor chairs was quite common in the North of England.

305

306

307

Figure 306 (left).
WINDSOR ARMCHAIR.
*Ash with elm seat. Probably Yealmpton area,
Devon, 1810–40.*
The 'continuous-arm' Windsor – in which a single
member is gracefully shaped to form both the back
bow and the arms. On this example the legs are tied by
box-frame stretchers and all turned members,
including the spindles, are fashioned to resemble
bamboo with black painted accents. Branded 'JE' on
the underside of the seat.
The discovery of a number of these chairs in Devon
some years ago caused reverberations in the field of
furniture studies.[29] The 'continuous-arm' Windsor is
a well-known type in New England and was long
thought to be an indigenous type peculiar to North
America. The existence of these versions in England
adds a new dimension to the story.

Figure 307.
WINDSOR ARMCHAIR.
*Ash with elm seat. Probably Yealmpton area,
Devon, 1810–30.*
A small group of chairmakers working in and around
the village of Yealmpton produced a distinctive variety
of Windsor chair styles in the early 19th century.
This example, with arms bent from flattened sections
of ash, is likely to have been one of their products. The
close relationship between Devon and New England
may explain the popularity of 'bamboo'-turned legs
and box-frame stretchers on similar Windsor chairs of
this period from each of these areas.

broadly distributed over large areas of the country and are consequently often the most difficult to trace to their exact source. In these cases, records of recent ownership are frequently of little use in determining origin. Regional identification can be made by other methods however, and occasionally the historian is provided with evidence on the chair itself; two such examples are shown in **Figure 311**.

Windsor chairs are often stamped with the initials or surname of their maker. 'NORTHAMPTON / C. POWELL' was found on the rear seat edge of the chair shown on the left in **Figure 311**. This probably refers to Charles Powell, mentioned as a chairmaker in Bridge Street, Northampton, in Pigot's *Directory* of 1830.[28] Certainly, the ability to identify pieces in this way adds a personal dimension – setting the article within its correct context, at

Figure 308.
WINDSOR ARMCHAIR.

Fruitwood with elm seat. Mendlesham area, Suffolk, 1800–60.

A distinctive variety of Windsor chair, with 'Sheraton' back, which appears to have been peculiar to the immediate area of Mendlesham. The style may have been invented by Richard Day (1783–1838), a chairmaker living in the village. A recent intensive study of the type has shown that, contrary to popular belief, Day was by no means the sole producer. Rather, there were several makers working within the same tradition, occasionally adding slight variations of their own. These attractive chairs were considered more as special, rather than as everyday, pieces and they are seldom found without arms[30]. This example is one of twelve formerly belonging to Sir Anthony Eden.

308

Figure 309.
WINDSOR SETTEE.

Elm with beech legs. West Country, 1800–35.

A bench with back and arms, or 'settee', of Windsor form is very rare within the English furniture tradition; this example displays several West Country features, among them the arm bow construction and the square-fronted slab seat, here supported by robust legs which are not tied by stretchers. The front legs are turned with multiple rings, graduated at the top and more even on the feet. The arm supports are also decorated with multiple ring-turnings, but spaced between concaves.

309

Figure 310.
WINDSOR ARMCHAIR.

Beech with elm seat. Buckinghamshire/Oxford-shire, 1830–1900.

The archetypal Grecian back of joined chairs has been applied to the Windsor form where it is termed the 'scroll-back'; scrolled and round-fronted rear uprights are linked by a plain crest rail and, on this example, by a central rail embellished with the Classical tablet motif. In a variation of this style, the arms curve downwards into the supports.

Figure 311.
Left:
WINDSOR CHAIR.

310 Fruitwood back, ash legs and stretchers with elm seat. Northampton, 1820–50.

A scroll-back Windsor with unusual bands of demi-ring decoration on the back rails and three ornately turned spindles linking the two central rails. The overall style suggests a strong influence from the Buckinghamshire Windsor tradition to the south. This example is stamped 'NORTHAMPTON/C. POWELL' on the rear seat edge and retains the dark stain which concealed the diversity of timbers used in its construction.

Right:
CHILD'S WINDSOR HIGH CHAIR.

Beech with elm seat. West Wycombe, Buck-inghamshire, 1910–23.

A child's chair at normal adult height for seating at a dining table; it was originally provided with arms and a footrest, now missing. Chairs with this style of broad shaped crest rail overlapping the back uprights and a series of ornately turned spindles were classified as 'Roman'; here the uprights are topped by ball turnings and flank three curved laths. This example has been dated and its place of origin identified by a railway label under the seat.

311

Figure 312.
WINDSOR ARMCHAIR.
Beech with elm seat. 1850–1920.
A variety often described as an 'office' chair or 'low back smoker' in the 19th century; today it is normally referred to as a 'smoker's bow' – an allusion to the dominant characteristic of an arm bow usually topped by a heavy scrolled cresting. The type was commonly used in offices, libraries, restaurants, pubs and other public places. It is possibly related to earlier joined 'corner' chairs (e.g. Figures 161 and 166).

312

313

Figure 313.
WINDSOR CHAIR.
Beech with elm seat. Buckinghamshire, 1830–80.
As usual with this type of chair, the timber has been darkly stained to resemble mahogany. National pride in British naval achievements was high during the 19th century and the rope-twist turning to the central rail on this chair had intentional nautical connotations. Rope-form mouldings on all types of English furniture had been particularly popular in the Regency period – in the decades after Trafalgar. The motif occurs in the repertoires of other nations as well.

least of initial manufacture if not of subsequent use – and also helps to establish an overall chart of distinctive regional varieties by which other, unstamped, chairs can be recognised.

Source evidence of a different kind was found on the chair beside the Powell example (**Figure 311, right**), in the form of two 'prepaid parcel' labels still glued underneath the seat. These read: 'G.W. & G.C. RAILWAYS . . . West Wycombe to [blank]'. Furniture was often labelled during house removal by later owners and usually such tickets serve as no indication of origin; nevertheless, in this case, West Wycombe was a well-known centre for the production of this kind of chair and it is reasonable to suppose that these labels were used by the actual manufacturer to send his goods on their way. If so, then we are also provided with a date range for this particular chair since the Great Western and Great Central Railways operated this joint line only from 1910 until 1923.

314

314a

315

Figure 315 (left).
WINGED SETTLE.
Pine, dark over medium red-brown scumble finish
imitating mahogany. South Somerset, 1840–90.
This curved settle with winged slab ends was removed
in 1963 from a farmhouse kitchen in Chard,
Somerset, where it stood near the fireplace. The
cupboard space in the back, enclosed by three pairs of
panelled doors affixed by iron butt hinges, was used for
hanging bacon. Tools were kept in the storage space
under the three lids in the seat. The back and the front
of the base are enclosed by narrow parallel boards or
'matchboarding'.

Figure 314 (opposite, left).
SETTLE.
Pine and elm, original finish removed. Devon,
1810–40.
Enormous settles of this kind were theoretically
moveable although their very size and weight made
moving them impracticable. They were usually
regarded as fixtures, very often being built-in as
internal room partitions. This panelled example
standing on 'sledge' feet, found in the Dartmoor region
of Devon, conforms to the curved shape common in
West Country settles and would have been situated
close to the fireplace. In order to benefit from the
warmth of the fire, the back is made as cupboard
space, accessible from the rear, and used to hang bacon
when curing it, a process sometimes taking several
weeks. The three drawers in the base were convenient
for storing firewood, tools and other items. The
scrolled arms are suported by turned balusters. The
brass handles are modern.

Figure 314a (opposite, right).
(Rear view of Figure 314.)
Rear view showing the doors to the cupboard space.
The hand-forged iron hooks for hanging bacon survive
inside.

316

Figure 316 (above right).
WINGED SETTLE.
Pine with elm sides and top rail, original finish
removed. 1810–50.
The large fireplaces still common in the 19th century
required a strong flow of air to keep them working
satisfactorily, and the high-backed settles near them
afforded their warmth-seeking occupants some protection from draughts, particularly when provided with
winged ends. On this curved example, shaped slab ends
flank a seat partly supported by a central strut and the
matchboarded back is topped by a moulded cornice. In
order to exclude draughts as much as possible, the
space under the seat is also backed by further
matchboarding.

Figure 316a (right).
(Rear view of Figure 316.)
Loudon suggested that the back of a settle 'might be
ornamented with prints or maps, in the manner of a
screen'.

316a

317

318

Figure 317.
SETTLE.

Pine, dark brown paint and stain. 1830–90.
A long low settle form frequently found in inns and pubs; this curved example standing on short tapered legs includes some crude nailed construction and has the back and ends enclosed by thin wooden sheets. The matchboarded seat and back covering are possibly later replacements.

Figure 318.
STOOL.

Pine, red paint finish. 1810–70.
A low stool, or 'cricket', which would have served equally well as a footstool, milking stool, child's stool or for any other purpose. On this boarded example, the shaped slab ends are rebated at the top to receive the side members and tenoned into the seat. The similarity of both this and the stool in Figure 320 to their distant ancestors (see Figures 34 and 33 respectively) is obvious and it is interesting to note how little these basic items of furniture have changed over the centuries.

Figure 319 (right).
SMALL STOOL.
Yew. Probably Worksop, Nottinghamshire,
1850–80.
A distinctive type of almost miniature stool which was
probably made by chairmakers for their own use
rather than for sale and intended either to be purely
ornamental or as a stand for displaying a piece of
pottery on a dresser or sideboard. The concave-sided
top of this example is only 7½ inches long.

319

320

Figure 320 (above).
STOOL.
Ash. West Country, 1780–1840.
A stool of 'primitive' construction; the end edges of the
seat bear the notched decoration which survived in the
West Country until a particularly late date. The
wedges securing the tops of the stake-legs on this
example are clearly visible as they have been forced to
protrude above seat-level by the contraction of the
timber over the years.

OTHER TYPES

When Loudon illustrated the 'tent' bed shown in **Figure 199**, he stated that they 'are in universal use, and scarcely require description'. He also illustrated or mentioned several other forms of wooden bedsteads, including folding 'sofa beds' (not a 20th-century invention!) and 'press bedsteads' which could be compacted into what looked like a cupboard or a

Figure 321.
CRADLE ON ROCKERS.
Pine with elm ends, paint finish: red exterior, blue-
green interior. 1810–50.
Formed from thin pine boards nailed to polygonal elm
ends, this light cradle incorporates a hood with shaped
sides to protect its occupant from draughts and pierced
hand-grips for easy transportation from the parlour to
the parents' bedroom at night.
321

322

Figure 322.
PRESS BEDSTEAD.

Pine, brown paint. Probably North-East, 1830–90.

Press bedsteads, in which the bedstead folds away into a cupboard, were apparently common before the turn of the century and were particularly useful in downstairs rooms given over to daytime priorities. Loudon described them as 'very common in kitchens, and, sometimes, in parlours where there is a deficiency of bed-rooms; but they are objectionable, as harbouring vermin, and being apt soon to get out of order when in daily use. They have, however, one advantage, which is, that persons sleeping in them are generally obliged to get up betimes in the morning . . .' and, perhaps not surprisingly, added that 'beds of this kind are not held in much repute'. It is that lack of esteem which must account for a very low survival rate; the present example was acquired in 1967 from a cottage in Little Kildale, North Yorkshire, and is similar to one shown in the 1850 catalogue of W. Smee & Sons. In the photograph, one of the panelled doors opens to reveal the conventional laced canvas bottom of the bed. Part of the swivelling foot member, with one of the plain feet, can also be seen. (The cupboard stands on turned feet which are not shown in position here.)

chest of drawers by day (Figure 322). However, by this time (1833) iron was rapidly superseding timber as the most popular material in the construction of bedsteads, partly because those made of wood (which generally had 'sacking bottoms') were thought 'apt to harbour vermin'. Iron bedsteads were also generally cheaper and they were produced in all the current varieties of their wooden counterparts: four-poster, tent, half-tester, folding and plain.

The modern bathroom, with bath, wash basin, toilet and hot and cold running water, did not become general in ordinary houses until the 20th

Figure 323.
CRADLE ON STAND.

Pine cradle, beech stand. 1860–1900.

Simple box-like cradles without a hood were made from at least the 15th century onwards and either stood on rockers or hung on a frame, as here. On this piece, a boarded cradle with slatted bottom is suspended by iron fittings from a stand with each upright on a T-form base on bun feet. The stand may be dismantled by removing long bolts which keep the turned central rail in position, a convenient technique used on much earlier examples.

This specimen came from a farmhouse at Stoke, near Andover, Hampshire, in 1955 and the presence of the apparently superfluous rockers on the cradle base was explained by a member of the household. It was found that the other children rocked the cradle so vigorously that it fell off the stand and tipped the baby out. The father, presumably somewhat alarmed, added rockers to the base of the cradle allowing it to rock more safely on the floor by itself. Fortunately, the stand was preserved as well[31].

323

century. For most people in the 19th century, the toilet was usually a chamber pot in the bedroom and an outhouse in the yard or garden. The bath (if any) was a portable metal tub kept hanging on a wall and set up in the kitchen or a bedroom to be laboriously filled with water by hand when required. All personal washing was either performed at the scullery sink, if there was one, or at a ceramic jug and basin on a table in the bedroom. By the mid-18th century purpose-made tables or stands to hold the jug and basin had come into use and these were called 'basin' or 'wash-hand' stands – nowadays normally abbreviated to 'washstands' (Figures 324–327). Washstands often have a splash-board, or wooden screen, around the top to protect the wall from splashes and occasionally the top itself is pierced to receive the basin.

By the early 1770s, a new form of dial was being marketed for clockmakers to attach to their movements – the first recorded suppliers being the partnership of Thomas Osborne and James Wilson.[33] These factory-made dials were made of iron with the painted decoration japanned on the surface and, because of the cream-white colour normally used for the ground, are known simply as 'white dials'. As they could be supplied with the clockmaker's own name and town already inscribed, all the clockmaker had to do was mount one on his movement. White dials were not necessarily cheaper than the earlier brass type, which itself had often been engraved by a specialist rather than the clockmaker himself, but gradually overtook them in popularity. By the 1820s, the movements themselves were also increasingly likely to be bought from large

324

325

Figure 324.
WASHSTAND.
Oak. 1790–1835.

Typical of thousands made during the very late 18th and early part of the 19th century, this square style of washstand was not usually provided with a splash-board. The top is pierced to take a basin and accompanying small bowls for soap and so on. The jug was kept on the flattened stretchers at the base. The dovetailed drawer retains the original brass knob.

Figure 325.
WASHSTAND.
Pine, greyish blue-green paint overall with striping in blue, white and black; paint finish on top surface imitating marble. 1800–1825.

A piece made in the newest fashion of its day; an early stage of Grecian development from the Neoclassical is indicated by the combination of scrolled splash-board, bow-fronted 'marble' top and thin tapered legs. Both the drawer, with original brass knobs, and the splash-board are finely dovetailed. Painted pine furniture of this quality was aimed predominantly at the middle classes rather than the poor; painted furniture was immensely fashionable at this time and was used with dramatic effect in the Royal Pavilion, Brighton.[32]

326

327

Figure 326 (left).
WASHSTAND.
Pine, later dark blue paint finish. Probably North Midlands, 1845–90.
Although features of this example suggest a 19th-century date, this basic form was still being produced as late as the 1930s. The ring-turned legs are linked by stretchers upon which rests a shelf shaped in the ogee arch familiar from earlier times. The mortise-and-tenon joints of the underframe are pegged but the overall design is extremely simple.

Figure 327 (above).
WASHSTAND.
Pine, brown over yellow paint finish imitating curly maple, white paint finish on top surface imitating marble. 1850–1900.
Probably once forming part of a bedroom suite, with matching semicircular dressing table, this washstand combines plain Grecian geometric styling with French influence. Carving is confined to the single front support with acanthus ornament. This is a rather grand design which, in this case, overlooks the useful inclusion of a drawer. A very similar washstand was illustrated in the store catalogue of George Maddox, a London retailer, in 1882.

328

Figure 328 (left).
WASHSTAND.
Pine, brown over yellow scumble finish imitating satinwood, dark over pale brown scumble 'panels' on drawer fronts imitating mahogany. 1900–25.
Also described as a 'toilet chest of drawers', this is basically a chest of drawers with a washstand top. All the dovetails are still cut by hand but the use of plywood (apparently original) for the back and the drawer bottoms suggests a date after 1900. The knobs are of the type secured by a domed wooden screw inside the drawer. There are no locks.

329

manufacturers, sometimes in kit-form, and the heyday of individual clockmaking in small towns was slowly drawing to a close. Despite the wide-scale adoption of factory methods, however, English clock manufacturers insisted on maintaining a high standard – a factor which was naturally reflected in the price – and as the 19th century progressed, native longcase clocks found it increasingly difficult to compete for sales against the cheaper mass-produced clocks imported from Germany and the United States.

The kneading-trough or dough bin (**Figures 195 and 336**), an essential article in the bread-making process, is best described by Loudon:

> The cover, which, when on the trough, serves as a table or ironing-board, either lifts off, or, being hinged, is placed so as when opened it may lean against a wall, when the trough is wanted to be used. Frequently a division is made in the centre of the trough, so that the dry flour can be kept in one compartment, and the dough made in the other. Sometimes

Figure 329.

TOWEL STAND.

Pine, original red-brown paint. 1840–1915.
Washstands sometimes had one or two rails on which to hang towels. Alternatively, a separate towel stand, or 'horse', with three or more rails, was placed nearby. This example, with four rails between scroll-topped uprights, is similar to one shown by Loudon in 1833 but the style was long-lived. The pair of rails at the top were intended not only for hanging individual towels but for drying a wet towel thrown across both of them. On this stand, each upright is supported on a T-form base with tiny turned feet.

Figure 330.

BEDSIDE CUPBOARD.

Pine, brown over yellow paint finish imitating satinwood. 1860–1910.

A 'night', or 'pot', cupboard made as part of a matching bedroom suite and intended to stand beside the bed to contain a chamber pot was an alternative to the commode chair (Figure 167). Topped by a low pediment and standing on a plinth base, this example has a single shelf behind the panelled door. The wide painted bands and narrow striping decorating the top surface and door are enlivened by freehand (not stencilled) patterns. The door latch with white ceramic knob appears to be original.

330

331

333

Figure 331.
LONGCASE CLOCK.
Oak with mahogany crossbanding. Reading, Berkshire, 1830–45.

This example of a white-dial clock is housed in a case
with scrolled cresting to the hood and fretting to the
plinth. There are parquetry lozenges above and below
the crossbanded trunk door and bands of simple
parquetry to the narrow mahogany-veneered frieze
above the hood door, on the door itself and on the
chamfered corners of the trunk. (Thirty-hour 'plate'
movement made by John Player (fl. 1830–77) of
Chain Street, Reading.)

332

Figure 332.
PLATE RACK.
Pine, traces of old green paint. 1850–1920.

Although shown hanging, this rack for drying washed
plates was meant to stand on a surface and is provided
with projecting 'sledge' feet. It is mortise-and-tenon
joined and, although it is only a functional item of
furniture, careful attention has been paid to good
proportions. While most space has naturally been
allocated to ordinary plates, full-height slots have been
provided on the right for large dishes or platters. One
rear spindle is missing.

Figure 333.
CUTLERY TRAY.
Oak. 1760–1850.

Of simple boarded construction, this tray has inclined
sides to facilitate usage. The central division is
extended upwards and pierced for a handle, the shaped
bottom edge of the cavity faintly echoing the inverted
ogee arch profile of the division sides. It is interesting to
note the universality of the ogee arch motif affecting
even minor objects in this way. This piece was
probably intended for knives and forks only, spoons
being kept elsewhere.

Figure 334.
SHELVES.
Pine, black over red-brown scumble finish. 1820–50.

Loudon optimistically predicted that 'book-shelves will shortly become as necessary as chairs or tables, for the cottage of even the humblest labourer'. He gave two designs, both of which could either be hung on a wall or stood on a convenient piece of furniture. In practice, particularly in 'cottages' where literacy was non-existent or where the 'humblest labourer' was more inclined to less refined interests, such shelves would often be gainfully employed in displaying the owner's prized china ornaments and other items. The shelves shown here are flat-based, allowing them to stand on a surface if desired, and each of the upper shelves is tenoned into the shaped ends. The paint finish is probably intended to represent mahogany.

334

Figure 335.
Left:
SPOON RACK WITH CUTLERY TRAY.
Fruitwood and beech. 1830–80.

To protect spoons from possible damage caused by being loosely packed among heavy knives and forks, they were often kept separately in special racks. On this wall-hanging example, two battens across the back are pierced to receive the spoons while other cutlery could be stored in the base tray.

Right:
HANGING SHELVES.
Pine, green over red base paint. 1820–60.

A small set of shelves with ornately shaped sides and ends which was probably intended to display china ornaments. It is pierced at both ends and could hang either way.

335

335

336

Figure 336.
DOUGH BIN.
Elm and oak. 1790–1860.

A boarded box on square-section legs, this functional piece lacks the quality of dovetailing and turning seen on the previous example (Figure 195). The canted sides aid its purpose but, contrary to Loudon's recommendation, the lid is relatively thin and not entirely made from one board. The stretchers are missing.

there are three compartments, in order to keep separate two different kinds of flour or meal. The board forming the cover ought to be an inch and a half thick, and always in one piece, in order that neither dirt nor dust may drop through the joints . . . No part of them should be painted, because both the trough and cover, when used for making bread, will require frequent scouring to keep them clean; and, if the board should be used for an ironing-board, the heat of the irons would blister the paint, and make it stick to the cloth or blanket used to cover it.

In practice, the use of this piece of furniture was really a matter of personal choice. In some cases, the dough would be kneaded either on the lid or inside and left within to rise; in others, the piece was employed solely

Figure 337.
HANGING BOX.
Mahogany. 1800–60.

A utilitarian box in mahogany with finely dovetailed corners. The front slides upwards in grooves and the shape of the grip on the front cover is identical to that of the pierced extension for hanging the box on a wall. Boxes of this type were used either for cutlery or candles, the opening method being well-suited to the latter since it allowed candles to be removed without damaging their wicks. Occasionally, boxes of this form have extra compartments inside to contain tinder, steel and flint; smaller boxes altogether were often intended purely for that purpose, candles being stored elsewhere.

CUTLERY TRAY.
Oak. 1820–90.

A sophisticated form of cutlery tray with mitred, dovetailed corners and a brass loop handle affixed by screws. The two divisions were presumably intended to allow the inclusion of spoons along with the usual knives and forks.

337

Figure 338.
CUTLERY BOX.
*Oak with inlay. Probably Midlands,
1790–1850.*
A commonly encountered type of hanging box with long sloped sides and hinged lid (cf. Figure 197) which is often incorrectly described today as a 'candle box'. The inlaid motif of knife and fork on this example makes the true purpose of these boxes abundantly clear. The inclined sides helped to keep the knives and forks strictly upright, with the large handles uppermost. This specimen was bought in Retford, Nottinghamshire, not long after the turn of the century and it was quite possibly made in that area. The simple butt hinges are consistent with the date range given and probably original; the lids on these boxes were very often hinged merely with a strip of leather.

338

Figure 339.
HANGING BOX.
*Oak with mahogany inlay and crossbanding.
Possibly Midlands, 1790–1850.*
Wall-hanging boxes with sloped lids had various uses; this example was probably intended for the storage of salt, although it is not partitioned for different grades. The front is decorated with a mahogany lozenge inlay and both the front and lid are crossbanded — the unmitred corners reminiscent of the crossbanding on the lowboy in Figure 148. This box has lost the upper part of the pierced extension for hanging and a fresh hole has been made further down. The base is of beech and the brass butt hinges of the lid are original.

339

340

Figure 340.
NEST OF DRAWERS.
Mahogany. 1840–90.

Intended for use in a chemist's shop, for storing the various ingredients used in prescriptions of the day. Many of the items named on the labels were recommended in early herbals. John Gerard (1545–1612) stated that 'the decoction of the root of Madder [second row down, second drawer from right] is every where commended for those that are bursten, brused, wounded, and that are fallen from high places'³⁷. Its basic medicinal properties are still recognised today.

for storing dry flour – in which case it would be more correctly called a flour bin.³⁴ As it became increasingly common to buy ready-made bread from the local baker, these domestic articles gradually fell out of use.

A host of small wooden objects for specialised domestic use had developed by the 19th century and a limited selection of those for cutlery, candle and salt storage are shown here. In addition to, or instead of, the storage facility offered by the drawers in a dresser or kitchen table, cutlery could be stored in divided trays (Figures 333 and 337, left), in wall-hanging trays or in tall wall-hanging boxes with sloped sides and hinged lids (Figures 197 and 338) – this last type often erroneously termed 'candle box' today.³⁵ Because of their more fragile nature, spoons would sometimes be kept separately in a special rack (Figure 335).

Candles were frequently stored in boxes with sliding covers, the boxes either lying flat or provided with a pierced extension to hang on the wall (Figure 337, left). Candle boxes were often kept near the foot of the staircase, with one or two candlesticks, a convenient location when bedtime came around.³⁶ Salt was an abundant commodity in most parts of England and was normally contained in a fairly large, lidded box, either wall-hanging or standing, which was sometimes partitioned so as to divide coarse and fine varieties (Figure 339). Occasionally an example still shows a whitish stain or deposit which betrays the mineral's former presence. Such boxes were naturally located near the kitchen fireplace, both for convenience and for the necessity of preserving the contents from the effects of damp.

6 THE HERITAGE

V ERNACULAR FURNITURE DEVELOPED AS A FUNCTIONAL RESPONSE TO THE immediate and perennial needs of daily life throughout the ages and throughout the Western world. In order to view the English variety in its proper perspective it must be recognised as only one part of that wider tapestry, deriving its inspiration, both stylistic and constructional, not only from the fine or ordinary products of its own culture but from those of other countries as well. Thus, while some distinctive types of English vernacular furniture may have no obvious relation to that made for the English upper classes and may, on the surface, appear to be the products of an isolated culture, their counterparts may well exist in the vernacular traditions of other countries; an international link is suggested which bypassed the echelons of more opulent furniture.

The insularity with which English vernacular furniture has often been regarded in the past has contributed to a native mythology and, in order to achieve an objective understanding of such furniture, it is imperative to rectify at least some of the popular misconceptions that tend to surround it.

Firstly, as stated in the Preface, a literal acceptance of its colloquial name 'country' is to be discouraged. Secondly, the popular notion that vernacular furniture as a recognisably separate entity came into being only after the fashionable adoption of veneered and walnut cabinetmade furniture around 1660 calls for reassessment. The development of cabinetmaking that occurred in the late 17th century has possibly been slightly overrated as a watershed in the evolution of English furniture as a whole. Although perhaps constituting the single most important advance (arguably, the earlier introduction of joinery was of even greater consequence), it was only one in a series of refinements made to fashionable furniture through the ages. Also of significance were the introduction of 'clamped-front' construction in the 13th century, joined and panelled construction in the 15th century, the adoption of parquetry and turning for joined pieces in the 16th century, the increasing use of fixed upholstery in the early 17th century, and so on. To regard 1660 as the start of a divergence between 'fine' and vernacular furniture is not justifiable. The distinction between walnut cabinet furniture and oak joined furniture in, say, 1700 is really no more significant than the discrepancy between inlaid and carved panelled

Figure 341.

HIGH DRESSER.

Oak. Probably North Yorkshire, 1750–90.
An impressive breakfront dresser which shares a similar overall configuration to that shown in Figure 123. Here, the superstructure is flanked by fluted pilasters which stand slightly proud of the main structure and the shelves of the central section are embellished with shaped friezes. The back boards are probably later. All the panels of the base are fielded; those on the ends are plain rectangles while that on the recessed cupboard door has quadrant spandrels at the top. The two banks of lip-moulded drawers have simple bead-moulded corners. The base moulding is missing and there are likely to have been bracket feet originally. All the brassware has been replaced.

types and plain boarded or 'primitive' types in 1550 or the enormous distance separating the finest ebony-strung and gilt-mounted rosewood piece of the early 19th century from the cheapest painted pine cabinet furniture mass-produced for the working class at the same period. The point is that a cheaper form of furniture had always been available to the lower classes from at least the Middle Ages up to the present day and, often, it was easily distinguishable from that belonging to the rich.

Nor can 1660 be regarded (as it often still is) as the point from which the motifs of 'fine' furniture began to be copied on lesser pieces and incorporated in a hybrid manner with traditional construction; for example, the creation of flush surfaces on joined furniture to imitate dovetailed pieces, or the combination of a fashionable vasiform splat with an archaic turned-leg base. Earlier examples of boarded furniture attempting to simulate more expensive joined pieces (e.g. **Figure 342**) soon destroy such an hypothesis. It is in human nature to simulate the more distinctive characteristics of something fine but unattainable and graft them onto an inferior article; it is a trait discernible in even the most ancient civilisations (for instance, the copying of gold and silver objects in pottery) and was evidently prevalent in European furniture long before the end of the 17th century.

Yet another topic demanding of closer scrutiny is the popular conception that, until the beginning of the Victorian period, 'country' furniture was nearly always highly individual and unconventional. In fact, the reverse is generally true. Because of the very nature of its market, vernacular furniture was compelled to fulfil the demands of both economic viability and provincial conservatism, so that, from the earliest times, much of it tended to be especially repetitive and conformable to traditional

342

Figure 342.

CUPBOARD.

Oak. Northern Europe, possibly Flemish, 16th century.

The simulation of more expensive furniture types began long before the widespread adoption of cabinetmaking in the 17th century. This late medieval example of boarded furniture has been decorated in such a manner as to give the impression that it is of superior joined construction. The ostensible 'panels', complete with linenfold ornament, are in fact merely carved on the surface of solid boards.

models. Basic variations were more often of a wider workshop or regional type than truly individual; genuinely unique variations were more likely to be expressed in comparatively minor details, such as surface decoration or inscriptions. Much apparent rarity has been conferred on furniture merely by the naturally decimating process of time. The older an item is, the fewer comparable survivals are extant, and the piece can easily give an impression of uniqueness which was far from being the case in the period and region of its manufacture. The pieces most likely to be genuinely unconventional are those made not by professionals but by general carpenters retained on large estates or by laymen for their own household use.

It should also be borne in mind that when vernacular furniture is described as not being 'fashionable', the term is used only in a general, *national*, sense to indicate top market trends, normally generated by affluent London society. Fashion is a complex social code and it also operated in many other planes defined by economic and regional pressures. Within those levels and groups, furniture style was influenced by the relevant mores and vogues of its environment and generally conformed to the prevalent taste. Thus, vernacular furniture was usually 'fashionable', not perhaps by 'designer' standards, but within its own social context.

While the opposite extremes of superior and inferior furniture are manifestly distinct, the exact parameters of a class of furniture that may be called 'vernacular' are by no means easy to define. The development of

343

cheap furniture frequently paralleled (albeit normally at a distance) that of expensive, fashionable furniture and the boundaries between the one and the other are naturally blurred. While vernacular furniture is usually derivative, influence occasionally flowed in the opposite direction and some forms of 'fine' furniture were directly inspired by 'peasant' traditions.

Classifying furniture purely on the basis of timber (e.g. oak and pine as opposed to walnut and mahogany), as perforce has occurred to some extent in the selection of pieces illustrating this book, is patently open to the dangers of oversimplification. The choice of timber could be governed by many factors – such as personal or regional preference, availability and suitability – other than expense. Indeed, the best examples of oak furniture, for instance, must often have been more costly than contemporary mahogany pieces of similar type but inferior quality. Neither, in the case of furniture at least, can 'vernacular' be restricted only to its narrower sense of describing articles made exclusively from indigenous material; oak and pine were imported in vast quantities ever since the Middle Ages and were commonly used for humble pieces conforming to local and traditional idioms.

Nor, in many cases, is vernacular furniture to be defined solely according to either its ostensible function or its constructional type. Any definition of vernacular furniture as a whole must be far more loosely determined and broadly set. Perhaps the only acceptable criterion is that vernacular furniture formed that category which was used, if not always owned, by ordinary members of the working population; it was the everyday furniture of its period or, to fall back on the usual term current in the 18th century, that which was simply 'common'.

Figure 343.

CHEST WITH DRAWERS.

Oak with mahogany crossbanding. Lancashire/ Cheshire, 1770–1810.

Of the same typological group as the chest shown in Figure 95, this example also contains a storage compartment under the hinged top and disguised behind dummy drawer fronts, but here only the bottom three drawers are real. This furniture type, intended to function primarily as a low dresser[1], appears to have been an established form in the North-West and must have been produced in enormous numbers at the time. Though certainly not representative of London fashion, this piece was nevertheless obviously very fashionable within its own region; it conforms almost rigidly to set local conventions and includes all the standard features – mahogany crossbanding, reeded quarter-columns and ogee bracket feet – which were highly esteemed in that area. Far from being invariably individual, it is the conformity of so much vernacular furniture which allows a large number of pieces to be regionally identifiable. The handles are modern.

DOMESTIC CONTEXT

In a brief study of furniture such as this, where pieces have necessarily been selected largely at random, treated as separate entities and classified individually, the subject has unavoidably been divorced from its environment. There is a tendency to lose sight of the very meaning of the word 'furniture' – that which equips a larger whole. Since this book has for the most part dealt with furniture that was primarily domestic, our main concern is with the homes of the past. Although the enormous economic and regional diversity of English vernacular dwellings cannot be adequately described here, a very rough sketch of the interior arrangements common to at least a large proportion of lesser houses throughout many parts of England in the 18th and 19th centuries is called for.

While recognising that among the ordinary working population those better off inhabited fairly large town houses and farmhouses on the one hand and those less fortunate might be consigned to sharing single-roomed garrets or cellars on the other, the home we can accept as typical, and for our purposes representative, was a cottage, urban or rural, generally having two rooms downstairs and one or two further rooms above. The main downstairs room was sometimes set aside as a more or less formal reception area in imitation of the drawing rooms of grander houses and referred to as a 'parlour' or 'front room'. In most cases, however, it fulfilled the less exalted function of a kitchen/living room, a primary communal space in which all family life was centred. Here was the main fireplace in which food was cooked,[2] here the meals were prepared and eaten, here was pursued the occupation of those who worked from home and here, circumstances permitting in the often harsh life of the past, the family could relax and entertain friends. Since such a room combined the functions of kitchen and parlour, furniture suitable to both uses would be found together. As a kitchen, the room required a general-purpose table, stools, chairs and, perhaps, a dresser or corner cupboard, or both. Its subordinate role as parlour might call for one or two armchairs, a settle and such comparative luxuries as a longcase clock, a bureau and a chest. It is worth noting that a chest of drawers might well be included; such pieces were not invariably banished to a bedroom as is the modern custom.

The secondary downstairs room, that usually at the back of the house, normally served as a 'back kitchen' or 'wash-house' intended for laundering and for storing foodstuffs and fuel.[3] Typically, during the 19th century, it was here that the sink and tap (if any) were located and water needed for personal and clothes washing heated, often in a large built-in metal pot or 'copper'. It was a functional, frequently austere, room and furniture was likely to be confined to a dough bin, a kneading trough, a washing trough and perhaps a rough bench/table and stools.

The room or rooms upstairs were reserved for sleeping, although the overcrowded conditions in many such small houses in an era of large families meant that children often slept three or four to a bed and some members of the household frequently had to sleep downstairs in the kitchen/living room. In addition to bedsteads, the items of furniture which might typically be found in 19th-century bedrooms were dressing tables, chests or boxes, chests of drawers, wardrobes, washstands and their attendant towel stands, and pot cupboards or commode chairs. Since bedroom furniture was not on display to visitors, it was an aspect where the householder could most afford to be frugal; thus bedroom furniture was generally of a lower quality than those pieces in the main room downstairs.

IDENTIFICATION

A full understanding of any piece of furniture depends on a knowledge not only of its function and place in its immediate environment but also of its wider context – its region and its period – which in turn may tell us more of the specific socio-economic climate which engendered it.

Even the limited selection of furniture shown in this book reveals a few of the more obvious characteristics which can be attributed to some regions. Research is as yet still in its infancy and in the course of time a great deal more information will certainly emerge, allowing the identification of local 'signatures' which have yet to be recognised. Evidence is uncovered by a variety of methods and from a variety of sources. The most immediate source of regional identification is that occasionally provided by an item of furniture itself – in such forms as a maker's stamp or label (e.g. **Figures 2, 105, 294 or 311, left**), handwritten inscriptions normally in inconspicuous places or 'unwitting testimony' (e.g. **Figures 204 and 311, right**). All these clues must

Figure 344.
WINGED ARMCHAIR.
Oak. Lancashire/Yorkshire Dales, 1760–1810. Even the most seemingly minor idiosyncrasies occasionally survived within regional traditions over a very long time. Here, pyramidal finials, features associated with much earlier furniture from the North-West (cf. Figures 79 and 188), adorn the rear uprights of a late Georgian armchair from the same region. It would, however, be unwise to assign a regional provenance on the basis of one characteristic like this alone; pyramidal finials by themselves are not exclusive to the North-West (cf. the East Anglian chair in Figure 277).
This oak winged armchair is regionally related to those in Figures 156, 275 and 276. On this example, a drawer is mounted at the side beneath a rope-webbed seat. The crest rail is shaped in an inverted ogee arch. The feet have been re-tipped[4].

of course be treated with caution until their true significance is established beyond doubt; stamps, labels and inscriptions were often nothing to do with the maker but were added by retailers or owners after the piece had left its place of origin. Other direct evidence is that of provenance – either a precise connection with a person (e.g. **Figures 3, 102 and 215**) or an association with a family, building or locality (e.g. **Figures 4, 21, 28, 37, 39 and 121**). Although much furniture is now widely dispersed and lacks any obvious indication of its origin, at least a rough attribution to both region and period can often be made by visual comparison not only with other similar yet firmly identified examples of furniture but also with the details of fixed architectural woodwork. The latter comparison is particularly suited to earlier pieces with carved decoration, although significant stylistic and constructional details relevant to any period may also be observed in this way and even seemingly minor points may prove invaluable in reaching tentative conclusions. It is important, of course, to distinguish between a style or practice general to a whole town or region and that exclusive to an individual workshop, whose products may be quite different from those of other makers in the same district and not necessarily indicative of a regional code. Such workshop idiosyncrasies would be particularly misleading when they resemble styles or construction methods characteristic of regions other than their own.

It should also be borne in mind that even a very long association with a certain place is by no means indisputable proof of origin. Although it is probably true to say that in times gone by ordinary members of the population were not as mobile as at present, that is not to imply that it was entirely static. Changing economic climates and other factors have caused large migrations through the ages and, when families moved, their furniture often went with them. It is evident too that the furniture trade of large metropolitan centres, particularly that of London, served a broad geographical clientele from an early date and that even 'common' furniture intended for relatively humble households (e.g. **Figure 2**) reached a surprisingly wide market. As long ago as 1726, Daniel Defoe observed of

Figure 345.
WINDSOR CHAIR.
Elm and other timber, later green over old cream and brick-red paint. Stanhope area, County Durham, 1860–1900.

STOOL.
Elm and other timber, with horsehair, ticking and leathercloth upholstery, later green paint over old dark brown varnish. County Durham, 1860–1900.

Both these simple pieces came from Snowfield Farm, near Stanhope, County Durham. The home-made chair, its members shaped by a spokeshave or draw-knife instead of being turned on a lathe, may be classified as 'primitive' rather than as a true Windsor. According to family tradition, the chair was made during inclement weather by an itinerant worker hired by the farm for the haymaking season. One might reasonably expect such a piece to be entirely individual; in fact, it shows the possible influence of traditions far beyond the region in which it was made. The 'bobtail' bracing was a standard feature of many English Windsors (cf. Figure 182) and a very similar chair to this has been noted in a mid-18th-century painting by Arthur Devis.[5] Alternatively, the vaguely Celtic appearance of the chair may be explained by the fact that many travelling harvest workers were Irish and that the maker may be following the traditions of his own country. This possibility certainly highlights the difficulties inherent in attributing regional origin purely on the basis of style or construction methods in those cases where a piece has been divorced from its provenance. The transmission of local conventions, even in a casual manner, must have been quite frequent.

345

general commodities that, due to a nationwide trade network based in London, 'all the manufactures of England, and most of them also of foreign countries, are to be found in the meanest village, and in the remotest corner of the whole island of Britain, and are to be bought, as it were, at every body's door'.[6] Defoe went on to demonstrate how this national distribution of goods affected even the furnishings of 'but a mean house', taking as his hypothetical example the dwelling of a grocer and his wife living in Horsham, Sussex,:

> The hangings, suppose them to be ordinary linsey-woolsey, are made at Kidderminster, dyed in the country, and painted, or watered, at London; the chairs, if of cane, are made at London; the ordinary matted [rush seated] chairs, perhaps in the place where they live; tables, chests of drawers, &c., made at London; as also looking-glass; bedding, &c., the curtains, suppose of serge from Taunton and Exeter, or of camblets, from Norwich, or the same with the hangings, as above; the ticking comes from the west country, Somerset and Dorsetshire; the feathers also from the same country; the blankets from Whitney in Oxfordshire; the rugs from Westmoreland and Yorkshire; the sheets, of good linen, from Ireland; kitchen utensils and chimney-furniture, almost all the brass and iron from Birmingham and Sheffield; earthen-ware from Stafford, Nottingham, and Kent; glass ware from Sturbridge in Worcestershire, and London.[7]

So much for the popular notion of complete rural isolation and self-sufficiency in the 18th century! Even allowing for the possibility that Defoe was exaggerating (most everyday furniture was in fact made locally) and that his 'mean house' was situated within fairly easy reach of London, it is clear that the transportation of goods was well organised over many parts of England by this early period and that inter-regional trading links were firmly established. It is likely that the furniture industries of most large towns apart from London similarly catered for a wide market within their region and sometimes well beyond it.

While two or three examples of a type of furniture found within one region may lead to tentative suppositions, a truly valid hypothesis must be based on pieces with distinctive stylistic, decorative and constructional features that recur in fairly large numbers and are likely to be exclusive to that region. Furniture-makers, like any other members of the population, sometimes moved to new locations, carrying their old styles and practices with them. Thus many specific furniture-making traditions, which may originally have been peculiar to one region of England, have been transported not only to other regions but even to other countries (such as Canada and the United States) to which the British migrated. Nevertheless, many patterns of regional differentiation which can be identified with some measure of confidence are known or are still coming to light. Collateral research into documentary sources is also providing other fundamental data on the distribution, the organisation and, in some cases, the individual lives of craftsmen and existence of workshops, and the types, varieties and significance of furniture in different kinds of homes, shops and institutions. In this respect, the study of furniture history is not merely an end in itself but a part of the broader spectrum of social history.

ASSESSMENT

The single most important criterion in judging both the academic and monetary value of any piece of antique furniture is its degree of originality. It is inevitable that an item of furniture some two or three hundred years old should show signs of usage and, in fact, these dents, knocks and stains form part of its natural appeal – a desirable testimony of its passage through time. Unfortunately, however, a great deal of old furniture has received somewhat more than a superficial patina and is far from being what it may seem at first glance.

Excavated artefacts which can be accepted at face value, such as those from the *Mary Rose*, are a rare boon in the field of furniture studies. Research must rely almost entirely on pieces which have survived the vicissitudes of daily usage during a normal existence; not only have many pieces been subject to the often inevitable repairs and alterations inherent in such a mode of preservation but also, due to market forces, to deliberate forging and reproduction. Since scientific methods of determining authenticity, such as radiocarbon dating or dendrochronology, are largely inapplicable, impractical or, indeed, ultimately of limited use in the study of comparatively recent furniture, assessment must normally depend on the conventional methods of empirical examination – those based on experience, observation and, essentially, common sense.

Procedure

It is a sensible and invariable rule that an antique be dated from the period of its very latest original feature. That feature may not be obvious and may be incorporated in its style, material, method of construction or just a tiny part of its decoration. The object may be more recent but cannot be older than that original detail.

The first step in judging the age of a piece of furniture is to look at its style. Fashion in 'cottage' furniture was regionally influenced and normally slow to change but, by comparing the piece with other firmly dated ones, we should be able to arrive at some approximation of when its style was current. Styles have been reproduced, of course, all through the ages, but at least it provides a starting point.

Let us take a hypothetical chest of drawers. It has two short drawers above three full-width graduated ones (the usual arrangement), all with cock beading (which first appeared around 1725) round the edges, and stands on simple bracket feet (popular from 1700 onwards). There is a wide triple-reeded moulding applied around the top. This style of moulding did not come into widespread use until about 1800. Though never entirely abandoned, both bracket feet and triple-reeded mouldings had fallen out of general fashion by 1850; thus we can assume that the chest of drawers may well have been made sometime between 1800 and 1850. The piece is made of oak with pine interior – perfectly consistent with the suggested date.

Next to be examined is the construction. The carcase is of flush, dovetailed construction and the back consists of several vertical planks of pine nailed (with rough, hand-made nails) onto a rebate on the rear of the sides and top of the chest. That is quite in keeping with the period.

On removing one of the drawers, we note that, while the front is of solid oak, the rest is pine. The sides of the drawer are fixed to the front and back by dovetailed joints. The dovetails vary just slightly from each other in their size, their angles and the spaces between them. There is a scribed line to indicate to the maker how far to cut and in one or two places the angles have gone a little beyond this line. A scribed mark is not always visible on every chest but, here at any rate, the dovetails were undoubtedly made by hand. This is certainly to be expected on furniture thought to have been made

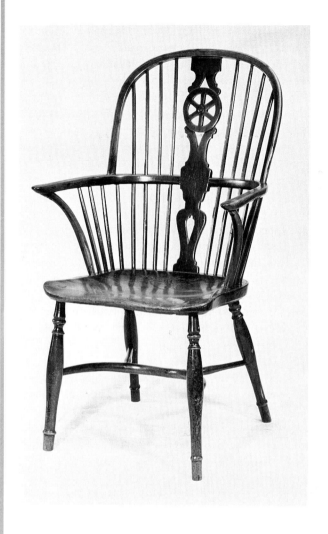

346

before about 1860, when perfect, regular dovetails were increasingly often being cut by machine in factories.

The drawer is turned upside down. Three edges of the bottom are roughly bevelled to fit the grooves in the front and sides of the drawer and the other edge overlaps the drawer back being nailed to it by three or four small, square-headed, handmade nails. Old nails will have rusted and left marks on the surrounding wood. The bottom is rough and unplaned. This is quite normal even on some 'fine' furniture although, when the drawer bottom (or any other interior surface) has been planed, the plane marks should be just perceptibly concave rather than flat. (Early planes used for unimportant surfaces had blades ground with a slightly curved, rather than absolutely, straight edge).

On the underside of the drawer the faint, irregular and roughly parallel marks of a saw are discernible. That is encouraging. The regular, curved marks left by a circular saw would be unusual on a drawer bottom supposedly made before 1850; although the mechanical circular saw was in use in the early 19th century, its signs are only occasionally encountered on furniture of that period.

As to the handles, these are so often changed that they are of no value in dating furniture unless they are demonstrably original. Our chest of drawers is furnished with black, broad, flat wooden knobs fixed by inside

Figure 346.
Left:
WINDSOR ARMCHAIR.
Yew with elm seat. Probably Buckinghamshire, 1770–1820.
Bowed front stretcher.

Right:
WINDSOR ARMCHAIR.
Ash and beech with fruitwood splat and elm seat. Probably Buckinghamshire, 1790–1840.
H-form stretchers.
Stylistic features on vernacular furniture seldom abide by rigid cut-off dates. Apart from the timber, the only obvious difference between these chairs lies in the formation of their stretchers. The bowed front stretcher is generally earlier than the H-form on 'wheel-splat' Windsors but the two types overlapped and the chair on the left may actually have been made long after that on the right. In fact, the use of bowed front stretchers continued until the late 19th century in some areas.

metal screws. The area around the knob, both inside and out, can be examined for any signs of previous handles. Handles that have been attached to a piece of wood for any length of time invariably leave a mark on the front where they have bruised the wood or where the surrounding surface has been polished, leaving the part under the handle untouched. The brass drop pulls popular in the late 17th and early 18th centuries leave a hole with two straight, shallow grooves (caused by the split-pin fastening) visible inside the drawer front. Later bail pulls would, of course, leave two holes which would be visible even if subsequently plugged. There are no signs on this drawer and, as broad flat knobs fixed by inside metal screws were in fashion from 1810 onwards, we can safely assume that they are likely to be original.

We would also expect to find keyhole escutcheons or inserts with curved bases to the cavity at this period; cavities with straight bases were superseded during the 18th century and were not re-adopted as an alternative to the curved-based type until later than the apparent date of our chest of drawers. Although 'Bramah locks', with the keyhole on a circular brass boss, had been patented by Joseph Bramah in 1784, they did not come into general use on furniture until the mid-19th century and are not often likely to be encountered on cheaper categories of vernacular furniture.

The details we have so far examined indicate that the chest of drawers was made probably between about 1810 and 1850, but we must look for the signs of wear that furniture of this supposed age should be expected to have acquired over time. The feet and drawer runners would have worn considerably. In fact, the runners may well have been replaced, eventually an unavoidable repair if a chest is to remain in use. There may be slight

Figure 347.

SETTLE.

Oak. Cheshire/South Lancashire, 1760–1810. When dating a piece on the basis of its stylistic features, it is vital to take into account its likely regional idiosyncrasies. Certain archaic features persisted in some regional traditions much longer than in others (e.g. the notched ends on boarded furniture in the West Country and the Renaissance-style carving in the Lake District). To judge this settle from the North-West by the stylistic standards of London furniture would lead to a wildly inaccurate date — certainly a much earlier one than is likely to be case. If, however, this piece is considered within its appropriate regional context, where features such as panelled backs, slab arms and cabriole legs survived as fashionable for an exceptionally long period, then a more realistic date is suggested.[8]

depressions on the fronts of divisions underneath drawers where the runners have scraped against them. Certainly there are unlikely to be any sharp edges on the polished outer surface of the chest, which will be marked by occasional dents and abrasions.

Another point to bear in mind is wood behaviour. As wood ages, it loses some of its moisture and shrinks. While shrinkage along the grain is minimal, contraction across it is quite perceptible. Timber that is contrained rigidly across the grain, like cleated table tops and fixed panels, will eventually crack with the strain. Old circular table tops will not be completely true but will be slightly wider along the grain than across it. The same applies to turned legs and posts. The contraction caused by ageing will make the turning elliptical in section, detectable by calipers if not by the human eye. Another effect of shrinkage is to force the pegs fixing table tops or mortise-and-tenon joints to stand proud of the surrounding surface. Original pegs are roughly square or oval, seldom perfectly circular.

Last, but far from least, is the colour and condition of the wood, inside and out. Outside, assuming the piece has not been stripped and refinished, the surface of the wood will have acquired a deep, lustrous patina caused by the original varnish, years of polishing, the accumulation of grease and dirt, and the inevitable nicks and scratches that display its pedigree. It is this patina which is traditionally one of the best indications of authenticity and, providing the piece of furniture has not been 'cut down' or made up from old wood, patina can be a reliable guide provided that it is taken into consideration with all other factors. It is very difficult to fake convincingly. When examined closely, the scratch marks and grain will be seen to stand slightly proud of the surface where over a very long period the wax and dirt have become caught and formed small, hard ridges.

Inside, the colour and condition of the unpolished wood are equally important. In fact, it is the state of the bare wood which can best betray alterations, repairs and downright fakes. Bare wood darkens with time, usually to a dirty, greyish-brown, a process called 'air burn'. While the shade will vary according to how long each part has been exposed to air and light (the outer back of a chest will be much darker than the interior), the colour of similar parts should be consistent. Since genuine 'air burn' is extremely hard to imitate, any new wood will be obvious. Re-used old timber from another article will not match the original parts either and fresh saw marks will show. We should also expect to find darker patches caused by the natural oils of human hands on the sides of drawers which will have been handled over the years. The underside of seat rails on chairs and of friezes on tables will show similar signs of human touch where the furniture has been held when being lifted and moved.

All indications of age must be considered in conjunction. After examining the entire piece, inside and out (noting plane and saw marks), and establishing that all parts are original (including the feet), if the signs of wear, degree of patina and colour of 'air burn' all support the dating suggested by the details of style, construction and decoration, then we can confidently date our chest of drawers. In practice and with experience, this procedure is not nearly as laborious as this account may suggest.

Of course, not all vernacular furniture can be dated as closely as this hypothetical chest of drawers. As already mentioned, some styles persisted for a very long time. The most primitive pieces are so simple and ageless in design that it can be difficult to be certain which century they were made in – let alone the decade.

Condition

Vernacular furniture was essentially utilitarian. It was built to withstand everyday, rough usage in ordinary homes and its makers often used heavier widths of timber and stronger methods of construction than would be considered necessary for 'fine' furniture designed for genteel use. Nevertheless, after years of use and abuse, it is inevitable that much workaday furniture should have been damaged, either ending up as firewood or being repaired to prolong its useful life. These repairs need not detract greatly from the value of a piece, and may indeed constitute an interesting part of its history, but it is vital that we are able to detect them and to determine precisely their extent.

The parts of a piece of furniture that are subject to the greatest strain or friction are obviously those most likely to have received attention over the years. It is normal for the blocks under the tops of tripod tables to have been repaired, chair backs to have been strengthened and drawer runners on case furniture to have been replaced. The rule joints on drop-leaf tables are particularly susceptible to damage and a close examination of the stretchers on tables and chairs will occasionally reveal one or more of them to be replacements. Rush seats have a limited life and may have been renewed several times. Small parts of mouldings and minor pieces of decoration may have broken off and been replaced by new wood.

More insidious are those ostensibly minor alterations to a piece of

Figure 348.
FRANCIS WHEATLEY (1747–1801).
Old Chairs to Mend, *a stipple engraving from the 'Cries of London' series, circa 1795.*
Turned chairs with rush seats were undoubtedly common enough within urban London itself, although Wheatley has chosen a more rural setting with only the silhouette of St Paul's Cathedral in the distance to remind us of the vicinity. Such pastoral areas existed considerably closer to the heart of the capital in the late 18th century.
Rush seats naturally had a limited lifespan and an itinerant chairmender is actively engaged in renewing one from the large bundle of new rushes beside him. The task required considerable strength as well as skill and each seat might take up to three hours to replace properly.

348

furniture which may have significantly altered its appearance. In this connection, it is particularly unwise to rely on hardware as a dating criterion unless originality is confirmed beyond doubt. All metal fittings, including hinges, locks, hasps and escutcheons, were especially vulnerable to damage and naturally subject to replacement. Handles were changed because they broke or because they went out of fashion. In Victorian times brass fittings on Georgian drawers were often replaced by wooden knobs to bring the piece up to date.

Nowadays, original wooden knobs on Victorian furniture are frequently replaced by brass handles in an effort to give the piece a Georgian appearance, thereby making it more desirable by today's taste. Even the original wooden knobs on genuine late Georgian furniture are ruthlessly removed and modern brass handles substituted because the general public is convinced that Georgian drawers always had brass hardware and that all knobs must be Victorian.

Much cottage and farmhouse furniture stood on damp flagstone floors which were made still wetter when washed by the usual method of swilling. Naturally enough in many instances, the feet rotted away and were replaced, or the legs were simply cut down and left short. Occasionally, the legs of chairs were deliberately shortened to make them more convenient for children, older people or for mothers nursing infants, rockers sometimes being added to the stumps for extra comfort. A low chair also enabled the occupant to escape at least the worst of the dense

Figure 349.
ARMCHAIR.
Oak. South Lancashire/South-West Yorkshire, 1660–1710.

In the days when old oak furniture had little monetary value, its survival often depended solely on whether it could be adapted to continue fulfilling a useful function. Such a ruthless attitude sometimes led to incongruous absurdities like the 19th-century rockers on this 17th-century armchair. Other alterations include the upper section of the right-hand rear upright, the left-hand seat rail, and the seat itself. The chair must be regarded as severely debased but need not be rejected as valueless; providing all later changes and their extent can be precisely identified, the historical integrity of the basic object remains intact. Significantly, all the carving is original and this highlights the artificiality of county borders as a means of regional definition: a chair type usually found in Lancashire incorporates a panel design normally associated with Yorkshire.

349

Figure 350.

CHEST ON CHEST.

Oak. North, 1760–1800.

The two sections of a chest on chest have often become separated over the years and each part sold as a complete chest of drawers in its own right. The products of this amoeba-like fission can normally be detected fairly easily. Like those of a purpose-built chest of drawers, the proportions of a complete chest on chest conform to sound principles of design and are pleasing to the eye. The proportions are ruined, however, if one section is separated from the other; the resulting 'chest of drawers' will tend to look heavy and awkward.

A new top on a chest must be viewed with suspicion. The top surface of the upper section of a chest on chest or a chest on stand was seldom finished originally, as it was above eye level; the top surface of the lower section was not finished either, as it was covered. Thus, a chest of drawers made from either section must have a new top. (The upper section would have to be provided with new feet as well.)

350

smoke which usually hung in the air in low-ceilinged cottages with inefficient fireplaces.

Authenticity

The detection of major alterations and faking in the field of antique furniture has become a science in itself (replete with its own specialised literature). Although this is not the place to discuss such matters at length, mention may be made of some of the most commonly encountered types of faking and alteration.

The union of one incomplete piece of furniture with the remnants of another to make a whole is popularly called a 'marriage'. Table tops and bases, dresser shelves and bases, bookcases and bureaux may have been 'married' simply and honestly for the sake of convenience when the originals were lost or damaged. Nevertheless, the temptation to disguise such a union, passing the piece off as original, is often irresistible when a much higher price can be obtained by so doing. It has to be accepted that the vast majority of 'marriages' were actually created with dishonest intentions in mind. It is usually possible to distinguish between a genuine piece and one in which two parts have been combined.

Often the differences between the two parts are obvious enough if the piece is inspected closely. If they are original, both parts should be in proportion to each other and should match perfectly in style, details of construction (dovetails, hinges, locks, nails, screws and so on), patina and 'air burn' colour. As the tops of tables have often been replaced, one should compare the underside to see that it matches the unpolished inside surfaces of the frame. The underside of that part of the top which overlaps the frame will usually be darker (because of handling) than the area within it. The top of a tripod table should be in proportion to the base and, if a tilt-top, the top normally folds down above two of the legs with the other leg behind it. On original tilt-tops, the two bearers are unlikely to have been moved and, due to reduced exposure to air, the area of the top underside in contact with the block will be of a slightly lighter colour than the surrounding surface.

Old furniture has been subject not only to later replacements or additions but also to the danger of later subtractions. As furniture became old-fashioned it was no longer wanted in grander houses and was either stored in attics or relegated to the homes of poorer people who could not afford to be fastidious. Many items have had parts removed or have been reduced in size in order for them to be accommodated in humbler and smaller surroundings than those for which they were designed. The usual motive for reduction today, however, is one of commercial expediency; small furniture, with the exception of dining tables, generally fetches a higher price. On a 'cut-down' piece the proportions will have been affected and fresh dovetails or other saw marks (possibly disguised by stain) will normally be evident.

While stain was commonly employed on vernacular furniture, it was confined to those areas which would be visible and very seldom applied to interior surfaces, the backs of furniture intended to stand against a wall or

351

Figure 351.
DESK.
Walnut. 1750–80.

Oak furniture was not the only victim of 19th and early 20th-century 'improvers'; this piece started life as a pleasant, if plain, Georgian desk or dressing table – in walnut. The later wholesale decoration of carved kings and wizards (Arthur and Merlin ?) on almost every surface would have appealed irresistibly to the Victorian romantic – but, as an historic artefact, its appearance has been irredeemably spoilt.

The late date of the carving on this example is readily apparent; unfortunately, a great deal was far more faithful to genuine period styles and, when encountered on suitable period pieces, may be quite difficult to expose as fraudulent. (The feet are later.)

the undersides of table tops or chair seats. The presence of stain in these places should be treated with the greatest suspicion since, in all probability, it has been used as a means of disguising alteration. People expect to see dark marks around old nail heads where the nails have rusted over the years and discoloured the surrounding timber. Fakers anticipate such scrutiny by obligingly adding blotches of stain around the modern nail heads.

There has long been a strong temptation to 'enhance' a genuine but plain piece of antique oak furniture by adding modern carved decoration. This act of vandalism was not invariably perpetrated by those seeking to increase monetary value. In Victorian days it was considered genteel for amateurs of the leisured classes to take up wood carving as a hobby and practise this art upon any neglected old furniture that came to hand. Furniture undergoing this treatment would have been thought of by most people as vastly improved at the time; present-day academics, dealers and collectors take a somewhat different view. Much early oak furniture has been defaced forever. Some of this Victorian carving, whether by amateurs or professionals, was very competently executed in the correct period style and, after the passage of a century or more, it can be difficult to discern as being unoriginal to the article. Human beings have a habit of conforming, even unconsciously, to the subtle nuances of the general art form of their own generation however, and usually the difference between 17th-century carving and 17th-century-*style* carving can be seen after a little experience of both. Certainly, it is not enough to rely purely on the relative sharpness of the carving as an indication of age. Much recent carving has been deliberately smoothed and polished while a great deal of genuinely early carved decoration remains astonishingly crisp even after the passage of three or four centuries.

It is hardly surprising that carved dates on furniture arouse particular suspicion. It is the easiest thing in the world to incise an early date on a wooden object and thus enhance its interest. Even the famous (and obviously Elizabethan) Great Bed of Ware, now in the Victoria & Albert Museum, has been inscribed at some time with the impossible date of '1463'. In today's more informed climate, such a patent anachronism as this is immediately obvious but, when an inscribed date is more plausible, it must be examined carefully since the matter of its authenticity can be very important. One or two genuinely dated pieces of furniture can be extremely useful in helping to place similar but undated items within their correct period (for instance, the chairs in **Figure 174**). Like decorative carving, inscribed initials and dates tend to reflect the stylistic idiosyncrasies of the period in which they were carved, conforming to calligraphic conventions and proportions which are difficult (though unfortunately not impossible) to mimic successfully. Again, familiarisation with undoubted genuine examples and contemporary written, carved or engraved calligraphy (such as that found on old gravestones and monuments) is of the utmost importance in learning to distinguish period from later inscriptions.

There is a common tendency automatically to dismiss inscribed dates on furniture as being false. While it would indeed be naïve always to accept dates at face value, it is equally blind constantly to reject them as being inherently spurious. Past generations appear to have had quite a fondness for displaying dates on furniture, particularly during the 17th and early 18th centuries; a great deal of this furniture has survived and need give no grounds for suspicion. Of course, a carved date may not necessarily indicate the year in which a piece was actually made, and there must be many instances where an article was inscribed to commemorate some other event. It is only by dating the calligraphy that conclusions may, with reasonable certainty, be drawn.

It was relatively common practice in the past to incorporate re-used timber from scrapped furniture in the construction of a new piece (e.g. Figures 65 and 96), thus making the most of cheap, well-seasoned wood. When selecting scrapped timber, the furniture-maker would have been discriminating and would have rejected any damaged, rotten or otherwise unsuitable material. In particular, he is unlikely to have knowingly re-used wood that showed the slightest signs of woodworm. The presence of a piece of re-used timber with evidence of infestation predating its use in an item of furniture (woodworm channels not matching up on adjacent wood etc.) must normally be regarded as proof that it cannot be an original component of that item.[9] It should also be stressed that re-used timber which is original to the article of which it now forms part should, after a long period of coexistence, show a degree of patina and 'air burn' consistent with the rest of the piece.

Most fakes are made up from pieces of old wood and it must be said that, perhaps more often than not, the presence of re-used timber in an item of furniture is evidence of forgery. Holes for pegs or nails where they serve no purpose or, conversely, blank spaces where there should be pegs must be viewed sceptically. One of the best sources of antique timber available in broad widths, and thus ideal for faked backboards and table or other tops, is old floorboards. However, floorboards were generally nailed to joists at roughly 15-inch (38-cm) intervals and, even if the faker has taken the trouble to plane away the telltale 'air burn' marks left by the joists on the underside, the old nail holes are not as easily concealed.

Veneer, apart from crossbanding and inlay, is seldom encountered on the items described in this book, but mention should perhaps be made that, until the second half of the 19th century, when it could be cut paper-thin by machine, genuine veneer on early furniture was seldom less than $\frac{1}{16}$ inch (just under 2mm) thick.

It is vital to be fully familiar with the signs of genuine wear. Bad fakes often give themselves away by showing too much wear, wear too evenly distributed or wear in places where it could not be expected to have occurred naturally. Unfortunately, not all faked furniture will be so readily detectable. The best fakes are made by people who have a thorough knowledge of the genuine article. They know exactly where wear should come and precisely what other points prying dealers and collectors will be looking for. Their products can be extremely convincing. Experience is the only real teacher and eventually, to some extent, one can develop an almost instinctive 'feel' for what is right and what is not. It is probably safe to say that the majority of examples in all classes of furniture are basically old, even if later altered or repaired. In the less coveted realm of later vernacular furniture, outright fakes are in a small minority; it is generally the more subtle changes that we must watch out for.

Reproductions are not fakes, as they were never intended to deceive, but, if made many years ago, they may naturally have acquired some convincing wear and may easily be mistaken for period pieces even at more than first glance. If made by hand in a traditional way, then it is the relatively fresh appearance of the unpolished surfaces, the lack of 'air burn', that most readily reveals what they really are.

352

Figure 352.
PEDESTAL TABLE.
Elm with burr elm top. 1790–1840.
An eccentric one-off piece; the column and legs of this small table, or 'candlestand', were formed in one piece from the root of a young elm tree and the top from a slab of burr elm, centrally bored to receive the end of the column but left free to swivel. The shaped rectangular top and simple arched root-legs with a downward turn echo their sophisticated counterparts on fine 'candlestands' of the same period.

Figure 353.

Illustration of a cottage interior near Blandford, Dorset, from The Illustrated London News, 5 September 1846.

The furniture in this simple kitchen/living room is described in the accompanying text as 'poor and scanty'. Seating consists of three turned chairs and the girl engaged in needlework rests one foot on a 'primitive' cricket. Behind her, a tripod table has been stored with its top tilted in the vertical position. A corner cupboard hangs above the table and further storage is provided by the rudimentary high dresser dominating the left-hand wall. The baby sleeps in a simple box-like cradle (described in the text as being 'of rough boards, clumsily nailed together') with rockers fixed to its base. Behind the mother tending her son, a crude table supports a large pot. Outdoor clothing is merely hung on wall pegs or nails. The chimney-cloth mounted along the mantel was an expedient commonly resorted to in an attempt to reduce the smoke which inevitably escaped from large open fireplaces. This is a wood-burning hearth; cast iron hob grates for burning coal were common in many houses by this period.

353

CONCLUSION

Although a need for the serious study of 'cottage furniture' was enthusiastically expressed by a few people early in the present century, the prevalent attitude of that time, that only the finest furniture was worth preserving, was even shared by many museum curators. It was perhaps a hangover from a common Victorian perception of museums as showcases in which the objects displayed would act as ideal models to edify and stimulate the masses; the selection of artefacts was very often based on a purely qualitative rather than a broadly representative assessment and the collections were consequently of limited use to the social historian seeking a more general, unblinkered view of life in times gone by. Fortunately for the future security of our heritage of vernacular furniture, such an approach is now seen as too narrow; the ordinary pieces from the past have since become more widely treasured and their significance generally recognised. Nevertheless, the sheer quantity of surviving material precludes its comprehensive preservation within the sanctuary of museums and other institutions. The task of conserving the vast bulk of antique vernacular furniture must then remain for the most part in the hands of private owners, and this is a responsibility which should prove an enduring source of pleasure and interest. Most old furniture not only continues to perform consummately the useful function it was designed for but, by association, is a direct link with the remote world which created it.

Furniture is inanimate; the social history that it represents is not. It is the history of the people who made it and of the generations it has served. Every piece, however humble, has something to add. While we must accept that most items of vernacular furniture will forever remain individually anonymous, each article contributes to our understanding of the whole and, placed as accurately as possible within the likely context of its makers and users, constitutes part of the wider narrative of English social history.

NOTES

INTRODUCTION

1. Geoffrey Beard and Christopher Gilbert (editors), *Dictionary of English Furniture Makers 1660–1840*, The Furniture History Society and W.S. Maney and Son Ltd, 1986.

CHAPTER 1: CONSTRUCTION

1. 'Burr' and 'burl' are synonymous. 'Burl' is the preferred term in North America.

2. The English preference for pit-saws is dealt with at some length in W.C. Goodman, *The History of Woodworking Tools*, London, 1964 (reprinted 1976).

3. E.F. Carter, *Dictionary of Inventions and Discoveries*, Frederick Muller, London, 1974 (first published 1966), p.159.

4. Bryan Latham, *Timber. A Historical Survey*, George G. Harrap & Co. Ltd, London, 1957.

5. Bennet Woodcroft, *Alphabetical Index of Patentees of Inventions*, Evelyn, Adams and Mackay Ltd, London, 1969 (first published 1854).

6. A circular saw is mentioned in the 1815 deposition of Mark Chippindale, a chairmaker working in Lancashire. See Bernard D. Cotton, *The English Regional Chair*, Antique Collectors' Club Ltd, Woodbridge, 1990, p.322. Circular saws are also included in the 1827 inventory of Cust and Co., a sawmill in Barnard Castle, Co. Durham. See Sarah Medlam, *Parts and Materials: A Sawmill in the 1820s*, Journal of the Regional Furniture Society, Vol. V, 1991.

7. Woodcroft, op. cit.

8. Sir Thomas Thynne, first Viscount Weymouth (1640–1714). There is a reference to 'Lord Weymouth's Pine' in 1731 and in 1781 it was noted that the 'Weymouth-pine has been long naturalised here; the patriarch plant still existing at Longleat'. (*Oxford English Dictionary*)

9. 'Wainscot' is generally thought to be a corruption either of *wagenschot*, a wagon shaft, or of the compound *waeg*, a wall, and *schot*, a covering. In fact, many other words and permutations have been suggested, with varying plausibility, ever since the 16th century. It is unlikely that we shall ever be certain of the true origin of the word. See Latham, op. cit.; Victor Chinnery, *Oak Furniture. The British Tradition*, Antique Collectors' Club Ltd, Woodbridge, 1979, p.155; Christopher Gilbert, *English Vernacular Furniture 1750–1900*, Yale University Press, New Haven & London, 1991, p.11; and *The Oxford English Dictionary*, where the earliest example quoted (1352–3) implies imported timber.

10. Goodman, op. cit.

11. Woodcroft, op. cit.

12. Chinnery, op. cit., p.71.

13. e.g. Moreton Marsh, *The Easy Expert in American Antiques*, Lippincott, New York, 1978, p.123. The author gives an instance of twenty years.

14. An early example of multiple dovetailed construction is the medieval chest which has survived at Haddon Hall, Bakewell, Derbyshire. This bears the arms of Vernon and Pembrigge carved on the front. Since Sir Richard de Vernon and Juliana de Pembrigge were married c.1376, it is likely that the chest dates from around that time or shortly after. The corners of the chest are dovetailed and, while the presence of English coats of arms does not necessarily mean that the chest was itself made in England, the technique was presumably not entirely unfamiliar to English craftsmen at that time. The chest is illustrated in Keith H. Mantell, *Haddon Hall*, guide booklet, 1990, p.25.

15. Strictly speaking, simulation is also a kind of polychrome finish since more than one colour is employed; the term 'polychrome' as normally applied to painted furniture, however, has a more restricted sense and implies the use of pure, defined colours to create contrasts or to delineate clear designs. The subject of paint finishes on furniture is discussed at some length by Robert Young in 'Early Painted Furniture', *Antique Collecting*, Vol.24, No.4, September 1989.

16. Woodcroft, op. cit.

17. Ibid.

18. The standardisation of screw threads was suggested by Sir Joseph Whitworth, a mechanical engineer, in 1841 and his system was widely adopted within twenty years.

19. *The Maple Story*. Maples International, photocopied company history, undated.

CHAPTER 2: MEDIEVAL AND SIXTEENTH CENTURY

1. Bayleaf was originally built at Chiddingstone, Kent, and the main section has been dated by dendrochronology to about 1400–5.

2. Anthony Quiney, *House and Home*, BBC, London, 1986, p.33.

3. Margaret Rule, *The Mary Rose. The Excavation and Raising of Henry VIII's Flagship*, Windward, 1983 (first published 1982).

4. Anthony Wells-Cole, 'Classical Inspiration in English Oak' *Antique Dealer & Collectors' Guide*, February 1984, and 'Oak Furniture in Norfolk, 1530–1640', *Journal of the Regional Furniture Society*, Vol. IV, 1990.

5. F. Gordon Roe, *English Period Furniture*, Tiranti, London, 1946, p.5, and Gabriel Olive, 'West Country Chests, Coffers and Boxes', *Journal of the Regional Furniture Society*, Vol. IV, 1990.

6. The paint on the Chichester chest has not been *proven* to be original. There exists the possibility that it was added sometime later.

7. Chinnery, op. cit., p.110.

8. Ibid. p.111.

9. Ibid. p.336.

10. Before the widespread adoption of chimneys the custom of sitting at only one side of a dining table was common but not invariable. There exist early illustrations of people being seated all round a dining table situated near the open hearth in the centre of a hall.

11. The absence of incised markings on the table-top itself does not disprove this use; most often a marked table cloth was probably employed.

12. Victor Chinnery (op. cit., p.276) quotes the 1436 reference to a 'bacstowyll' noted by R.W. Symonds in 'Coffer-makers and Upholsterers' Chairs', *The Antique Collector*, January-February 1950.

13. William Warner, *Albion's England*, London, 1592. 8th book, Chapter 42. This is the third edition; the earlier editions do not include the 8th book.

14. It is possible that the woodcut artist was a Continental immigrant, but there can be little doubt that he was depicting a type of chair common in England.

CHAPTER 3: SEVENTEENTH CENTURY

1. Quiney, op. cit., p.53. Gregory King (herald and statistician, 1648–1712), *Scheme of the Income and Expense of the Several Families of England*, 1690s.

2. I am talking here only of the furniture of the rich and that of the lesser tradesmen and farmers. There was hardly any more distinction between the very opposite extremes in the quality of furniture after 1660 than there had been before. The urban and rural poor had always made do with crude forms of 'primitive', turned or boarded furniture and their situation remained unaffected.

3. 'Hall' or 'parlour' cupboard, although contemporary inventory descriptions, are perhaps too restrictive of location to be used as generic terms. These pieces were used in either room

4. c.f. Chinnery, op. cit., figs.4:158 and 4:163.

5. John Earle, *Micro-cosmographie*, London, 1628. (*Microcosmography* (Harold Osborne, editor), University Tutorial Press, London, 1933, p.87.)

6. Randle Cotgrave, *Dictionary*, 1611. Quoted in Ralph Edwards, *The Shorter Dictionary of English Furniture*, Country Life Books, 1983 (first published 1964).

7. Indeed, such words as 'dresser', 'sideboard' and 'cupboard' were not as rigidly defined in the 17th century as they are today; they were descriptive of usage rather than of type and appear to have been fairly interchangeable.

8. On close inspection, most high dressers purporting to be 17th-century turn out to have later superstructures. Nevertheless, genuine 'formal dressers' with integral superstructures dating from the late 17th century are not unkown. A rare Westmorland example of about 1690 is illustrated by Victor Chinnery in 'Regional Oak Furniture', *Antique Collector*, October 1985. This was open-based with a potboard.

9. 'Joint' occurs frequently in English literature, including Shakespeare. Among quotations in the present book, it appears in both Spershott and Cobbett.

10. Chinnery, op. cit., p.266.

11 The Oxford English Dictionary, Oxford, 1970.

12. Ibid.

13. In more recent times, the word 'buffet' appears to have been confused with 'tuffet' and some authors have explained that 'Little Miss Muffet, (of nursery rhyme fame) was actually sitting on a stool. Nevertheless, there is no evidence of 'tuffet' ever having been used to describe anything other than the generally accepted grassy hillock before the comparatively modern day, and it would seem that, sadly, Miss Muffet was not provided with more refined seating arrangements. See Iona and Peter Opie, *The Oxford Dictionary of Nursery Rhymes*, Oxford, 1952 (first published 1951), p.324.

On a more serious note, there also appears to be no evidence to support the old theory that 'buffet' stools were necessarily upholstered; in fact, Holme asserts the contrary. See Chinnery. op cit., p.273.

14. Arcades of rounded arches were, of course, also part of the Romanesque stylistic repertoire and occasionally appeared as decoration on medieval furniture, but Renaissance Italy seems a more likely design source here. Through pattern books Renaissance designs were disseminated all over Europe.

15. Nicholas Grindley (*The Bended Back Chair*, exhibition catalogue, Barling, London, 1990) quotes a 17th-century petition of the Cane Chair Makers' Company: 'about the year 1664, Cane Chairs & c. came into use in England'. Noted by R.W. Symonds in 'English Cane Chairs', Parts I and II, *The Connoisseur*, March and May 1951. Nicholas Grindley concludes that caning may have been introduced into Europe from the East Indies; this origin seems likely.

16. This chair is included in this chapter as it continues 17th-century traditions. It is likely, however, that the vast majority of chairs conforming to either this slat-back style or the tall panel-back type shown in Figure 83 actually belong to the first half of the 18th century (cf. Figure 6, left).

CHAPTER 4:
EIGHTEENTH CENTURY

1. West Sussex Record Office Add. Ms. 2791. I am indebted to the WSRO and the County Archivist for permission to quote from this manuscript. The complete work has been published as *The Memoirs of James Spershott* (Francis W. Steer, editor), The Chichester City Council, 1962.

2. In fact, depictions were a far more likely design source than actual pieces of Chinese furniture. See Grindley, op. cit.

3. By the time a writer in *The Lounger* of 1786 said of the British gentleman that 'his house is Grecian, his offices Gothic, and his furniture Chinese' (Oliver Brackett, *English Furniture*, Benn, London, 1928, p.23), he was possibly referring only to the more obvious manifestations of *chinoiserie* that still lingered in decorations on furniture. Just how far the 'Chinese Connection' went beyond these superficialities and revolutionised the design even of fundamental elements in the decades around 1700 appears to have been largely unrecognised until the complete picture has been slowly reconstructed during the present century. The cabriole leg with claw-and-ball foot was being acknowledged as a 'Dutch importation from the East' soon after the turn of the century (Arthur Hayden, *Chats on Old Furniture*, London, 1909 (first edition 1905), p.127). (In fact, the claw-and-ball feature appears to have been more of a European elaboration of a Chinese motif that does not occur on native furniture and is less authentic than the cabriole leg itself.) Since then, the splat-back chair and the 'bended-back' chair have also been attributed to China. Gradually, an Oriental source for other factors has likewise become apparent and we are just beginning to appreciate the true scale of an influence that has long been underestimated.

A Chinese origin for the cabriole leg and the bracket foot is perhaps difficult to prove conclusively; curved legs appeared on furniture in Classical times and the use of a bracket foot might seem so simple as not to require any inspiration at all. Nevertheless, the fact that cabriole legs and bracket feet, identical to their Chinese counterparts, emerged in Europe during precisely the same decades that the European adulation of anything Far Eastern had nearly reached fever pitch, and the imitation of Oriental designs on every type of object had become an almost fanatical vogue, is far too opportune to be merely coincidental. The cabriole leg is only vaguely similar to Classical prototypes, whereas, at least in its mature form, its resemblance to Chinese types is exact.

It is also significant that many of the earliest instances of scrolled legs in Europe were as the supports on the stands of imported Oriental cabinets; it is more than likely that such scrolled legs (even in 'broken S-scroll' form) were imperfect European expressions of Chinese design, 'embryonic' cabrioles, intended to complement the cabinets which they supported. The Oriental style shared with Classicism the evolutionary process of initially being imperfectly interpreted and only later being expressed with conscientious exactitude. With the Oriental style, the latter development did not take place until the early 18th century.

4. A mahogany bureau inscribed 'made by Amos Poulsum. January ye 14th 1727' underneath a drawer and exhibiting early use of several features was recently sold in Worcester. There is no well; the carcase is flanked by quarter columns; the drawers are cock beaded and bear 'swan-neck' handles. See Barbara Pearce, 'The Amos Poulsum Bureau – A Useful Benchmark in 18th Century Furniture Analysis', Newsletter of the Regional Furniture Society, No. 14, Summer 1991.

5. With regard to clock cases at least, this form of inset crossbanding appears to be especially typical of South-West Yorkshire, although encountered in other (mainly northern) regions as well. See Brian Loomes, *Grandfather Clocks and their Cases*, David & Charles, Newton Abbot, 1985, p.217.

6. *The Oxford English Dictionary*.

7. Beard and Gilbert, op. cit.

8. A low dresser with double doors to the central cupboard, similar in style to this and the following piece, was shown in the specification book of a Chester cabinetmaking firm working from 1821 to 1849. The dresser was provided with a low 'Back Board' and was evidently not intended to take a superstructure. It was of 'Dantzick [wain-scot] Oak', stood on 'Turned Feet', and was priced at £9. 9. – (£9.45) with £1. 18. 10 (£1.95) as profit. Nicholas Moore, 'A Chester Cabinet Maker's Specification Book', *Journal of the Regional Furniture Society*, Vol. I, 1987.

9. There seems no real justification for the theory that the various regional styles of English dressers derived from those of Wales. The high quality of early 18th-century Welsh dressers is a reflection of their local status rather than an indication of invention. Certainly, North Wales was early to adopt a fixed superstructure (almost a mere modification of the press cupboard) but that alone is insufficient reason to suppose that Wales was an originating hub of high dresser design. The interchange of ideas must have worked in both directions across the border and some designs of Welsh dressers are just as likely to have been influenced by those of English types. Indeed, evidence suggests that Welsh design lagged behind in the second half of the 18th century; it is significant that archaic turned supports for dressers were retained in parts of Wales long after many of their English counterparts had assumed cabriole legs.

10. Bernard D. Cotton, 'Store-piece and Status Symbol', *The Antique Dealer & Collectors' Guide*, February 1986.

11. There are, of course, some corner cupboards extant which were never fitted with doors. These can be identified by the absence of any trace of former hinges, lock mortises, etc.

12. English cabinetmakers' cost books usually followed Sheraton's usage, whereas American cost books followed that of Hepplewhite. See Charles F. Montgomery, *American Furniture, The Federal Period, in the Henry Francis du Pont Winterthur Museum*, Thames & Hudson, London, 1967, p.440.

13. Tables with reversible tops are particularly associated with the West Country. See Peter Philp, 'Country Furniture', *The Antique Dealer & Collectors' Guide*, September 1978, and Gilbert, op. cit., pp.45 and 51.

14. In the 18th century, the word 'cabriole' implied a type of upholstered armchair. The use of the term as a description of a curved leg is of Victorian origin and was possibly suggested by the fact that many cabriole chairs had legs of that type. The earliest mention of 'cabriole' as a description of a curved leg quoted in the *Oxford English Dictionary* is dated 1888. See also Edward T. Joy, *The Country Life Book of Chairs*, Hamlyn, 1967, p.37.

15. These legs also occasionally appear on fine furniture and it is doubtful that the motivation for their use in these cases was invariably one of economy.

16. Throughout this book, the term 'Marlborough' has been used as a conveniently short description of the type of leg discussed here. This is its widely accepted meaning in the present day (e.g. Montgomery, op. cit., p.323); however, its application in the 18th century seems to have been somewhat inconsistent or, at least, less restricted. It frequently appeared in connection with the later fashion for tapered legs, although in other contemporary sources tapering is given as an additional cost, implying that 'Marlborough' was basically untapered. Perhaps it was a term for any leg with straight flat sides, tapered or not, as opposed to turned or cabriole. Certainly, the presence or absence of a block foot appears to have been irrelevant. It has been speculated that the term may have some connection with the fourth Duke of Marlborough, to whom Ince'and Mayhew's pattern book was dedicated in 1762.

17. Strictly speaking, only the base of a pillar or column is the 'pedestal', although the term has been extended to include the whole support when the pillar is of massive proportions (e.g. on some 19th-century circular dining tables).

18. Randle Holme (writing in 1648–49) illustrates an early example of a tripod base on a 'Stand: a little round table . . . used for to set a Bason on whilst washing, or a candle to read by.'

19. Asa Briggs, *A Social History of England*, Book Club Associates, London, 1984, p.224.

20. The cabriole leg in its simple, mature form does not seem to have appeared much before about 1710, even on fine furniture. Nicholas Grindley (op. cit.) suggests an even later introduction.

21. e.g. Grindley, op. cit., plate 13.

22. Traditional styles of furniture survived until a particularly late date in the Lake District. An even more archaic chair than the example shown here, similarly dated 1742, came from Troutbeck, Westmorland, and is illustrated by Christopher Gilbert (op. cit., Plate 4).

23. An oak chair somewhat similar to this one may have been one of a set of thirty-six ordered for the Manor Court at Temple Balsall, Warwickshire, in 1777 at a cost of 3s. 8d. (18p) each. See Gilbert, op. cit., Plate 315.

24. The basic labour cost of 2s. (10p), plus an extra 4d. (2p) for the 'vase back top', is quoted for a chair of this type in an 1801 cost book for Norwich chairmakers. See Gerry Cotton, '"Common" Chairs from the Norwich Chair Makers' Price Book of 1801', *Journal of the Regional Furniture Society*, Vol. II, 1988.

25. Lack of quality is not necessarily indicative of a late date. A cruder example of a crest rail sitting atop the splat and uprights occurs on an elm and oak joined chair which has a solid vasiform splat and which bears the inscription 'William John / Carpenter fecit / October 21 1778' underneath the solid seat. See Gilbert, op. cit., Plate 197.

26. Ivan G. Sparkes, *English Windsor Chairs*, Shire Publications Ltd., Princes Risborough, 1981, p.3.

27. A 1594 record of 'three chairs with bottoms of bullrushes' is cited by Chinnery (op. cit., p.92).

28. Bernard D. Cotton, *The English Regional Chair*, Antique Collectors' Club, Woodbridge, 1990. Figure NW313.

29. As late as 1822, William Cobbett (*Cottage Economy*, 1822) asserted that his 'grandmother, who lived to be nearly ninety, never . . . burnt a candle in her house in her life' and went on to describe how she made rushlights. Indeed, rushlights were in common use much later still.

30. These two chairs were made by John Pitt and Richard Hewett, who died in 1759 and 1777 respectively. See Bernard D. Cotton, *The English Regional Chair*, Antique Collectors' Club Ltd, Woodbridge, 1990, p.44.

31. Windsor chairs without arms are less common than the armchair form at this period.

32. This well-known chair was reputedly given by Oliver Goldsmith (1728–74) to William Hawes, the surgeon who attended Goldsmith on his deathbed; it was presented by the widow of Hawes's grandson to the Victoria & Albert Museum in 1872. See Austin Dobson, *Eighteenth Century Vignettes*, Nelson, London, 1897, p.227. Goldsmith was nearly penniless until the final decade or so of his life. Unless it was acquired second-hand, his chair is unlikely to be older than about 1760.

33. Anthony Wells-Cole, 'A Painted Bed dated 1724', *Journal of the Regional Furniture Society*, Vol. I, 1987.

34. The sheer quantity of this type of Windsor chair at the Bodleian Library suggests that at least some, if not all, are possibly not original. Nevertheless, they may well replicate the original design. (Illustrated by Nancy Goyne Evans, 'A History and Background of English Windsor Furniture', *Journal of the Furniture History Society*, Vol. XV, 1979, Plate 89.) A similar chair also appears in an Edwardian illustration of a kitchen at Weston Patrick, Hampshire (Gertrude Jekyll and Sydney R. Jones, *Old English Household Life*, Batsford, London, 1939 (1945 edition), Figure 50), suggesting a wide distribution.

35. Strictly speaking, tall cases appeared immediately after the application of the pendulum and before the adoption of the anchor escapement. Thus, a long pendulum was not a factor in the development of the tall case in these early intermediate years.

36. Briggs, op. cit., p.263.

CHAPTER 5:
NINETEENTH CENTURY AND LATER

1. John Bly quotes the example of Thomas Seddon, who employed over 300 journeymen in the 1780s. See John Bly, *Discovering English Furniture*, Shire Publications, Princes Risborough, 1976 (reprinted 1981), p.132.

2. The subject of the 19th-century furniture trade in London is dealt with at length in Pat Kirkham, Rodney Mace and Julia Porter, *Furnishing the World*, Journeyman, London, 1987.

3. Briggs, op. cit., p.263.

4. William Cobbett, *Rural Rides*, 1830.

5. John Bly (op. cit., p. 128) mentions the woodcarving machine of T.B. Jordan in 1845.

6. William Cobbett, *Cottage Economy*, 1822.

7. The disruption of regional furniture-making by the advent of machinery is sometimes overrated. In many instances, machinery actually aided the competitive production of traditional types.

8. Mary Comino, *Gimson and the Barnsleys*, Evans Brothers Ltd, London, 1980, p.82 and fig.49.

9. A further example of an internally painted sea chest is provided by Christopher Gilbert, op. cit., Plate 390.

10. 'Eastlake' is used in the same way as 'Chippendale', i.e. merely to indicate a contemporary fashion and not necessarily a direct influence. The style characteristics associated with Charles Lock Eastlake were in existence before the publication of his book in 1868.

11. Isabella Beeton, *Every-Day Cookery*, Ward, Lock & Bowden, London (1893 edition).

12. Brian Loomes (op. cit., p.245) notes this practice on clock cases.

13. The earliest mention of 'linen press', cited in the *Oxford English Dictionary*, is an American one of 1852. The term 'linen press' does not appear to hve been generally applied to this type of furniture until the mid-19th century.

14. Thomas Sheraton, *The Cabinet-makers' and Upholsterers' Drawing Book*, 1791–94.

15. A contemporary housekeeping cupboard inscribed 'Jos Butler 1814' (Gilbert, op. cit., Plate 99) stands on turned feet and has slightly smaller (original?) wooden knobs, but this evinces more of a developing Grecian character rather than the overtly Neoclassical design of the example seen in Figure 239.

16. The rigid belief, sometimes expressed, that examples *without* baize were 'tea tables', whereas those *with* baize were 'card tables', is far too dogmatic. The latter case is true enough, but the former type was undoubtedly used for *either* purpose – occasional *or* games.

17. Beeton, op. cit.

18. Large city firms dealing in ironmongery kept an enormous stock of ready-made iron catches, locks, hinges, spiders, screws, nails and other items for sale to furniture makers all over the country – and even to retailers abroad. Local blacksmiths would be resorted to only if more convenient.

The right-hand bearer here has been replaced in oak at some time and the catch has been slightly moved to allow for the shrinkage and warping of the top – a frequent hazard with fruitwood – but otherwise all is original. Note the extremely narrow slots of the screws securing the left-hand bearer.

19. These flat-sided cabriole legs are identical to those on many North American vernacular tables of the same period (e.g. Donald Blake Webster, *English-Canadian Furniture of the Georgian Period*, McGraw-Hill Ryerson, Toronto, 1979, figures 115 and 279). This table was found in England, although the late use of oak in a vernacular context suggests a possible Welsh origin.

20. Objections to the term 'cricket table' may be raised on account of its modern origin. Nevertheless, it has the merit of being an instantly recognisable description of a distinctive type of furniture and, since it is descriptive of form rather than usage, it is not misleadingly picturesque. Labels such as 'centre', 'circular' or 'drinking', although contemporary, lack the virtue of precision and could be equally applied to several other types of table.

21. Legs which taper only below the stretchers were a common form on contemporary vernacular joined chairs from South Wales (see Luke Millar, 'Late Georgian Wooden-bottomed Chairs in South Wales', *Journal of the Regional Furniture Society*, Vol. V, 1991) and this characteristic may suggest a similar origin for the table shown here. However, identical tables are now, at least, widely distributed and it is certainly possible that the leg form was made elsewhere as well.

22. A particularly wide selection of American fancy chairs, several of which are almost indistinguishable from their English counterparts, is illustrated in Zilla Rider Lea (editor), *The Ornamented Chair*, Charles E. Tuttle Co., Vermont, 1960 (reprinted 1966).

23. This chair type has often been described as an 'Essex chair'; however, there seems no reason to attribute it exclusively to one county rather than to East Anglia in general (see Cotton, op. cit., p.228). It is only the dished seat that is specifically regional; turned ball decoration, although common in East Anglia, was a universal motif of the period which appeared on vernacular chairs not only in other parts of England but also in

Scotland, Wales and Canada. The cost of making these turned balls was set at a ½d. each in an 1801 cost book for Norwich chairmakers which scrupulously lists the prices that makers were to be paid for each past of their work. The construction expense of the whole chair would have been under 3s. (15p). (Gerry Cotton, '"Common" Chairs from the Norwich Chair Makers' Price Book of 1801', *Journal of the Regional Furniture Society*, Vol. II, 1988.)

24. Comino, op. cit. I am grateful for the information supplied by the author in correspondence on this specific chair.

25. I am especially indebted to Bernard D. Cotton and Nancy Goyne Evans for their informative opinions on this chair.

26. Edward T. Joy, op. cit., p.10.

27. Clissett conformed to the traditional chairmaking techniques of his region, employing green timber felled in the autumn and turning it on a pole lathe in a small workshop attached to his cottage. He is said to have made a chair a day for 6/6d. (32½p) and the final rushing of rush-seated chair types took place in his kitchen. Clissett sang as he worked: 'According to old Philip Clissett, if you were not singing you were not happy.' Quoted from an account written by Edward Gardiner in 1956. See *Ernest Gimson*, exhibition catalogue, Leicester Museum, 1969, p.34.

28. Cotton, op. cit., p.471.

29. Gabriel Olive, '"American" Windsor Chairs from Devon', *Journal of the Furniture History Society*, Vol. XII, 1976.

30. Cotton, op. cit., pp.241–58. It would appear that the oral tradition of a 'Daniel Day' being Richard's father has no basis in fact.

31. Records of the Museum of English Rural Life, University of Reading. Note from Miss M. Brown, 1955.

32. I refer in particular to two painted washstands branded 'G.R. PAVILION' which were discovered in a Worthing antique shop and subsequently returned to the Royal Pavilion, Brighton. One of these is painted in a similar colour scheme to that on the piece shown in Figure 325 and was apparently intended for the bedroom used by Princess Charlotte (1796–1817). (See *Regency Exhibition*, exhibition catalogue, Royal Pavilion, Brighton, 1960.) Although the base timber of this washstand is mahogany rather than pine, and the piece is of an altogether superior quality to that of the example in Figure 325, it serves to demonstrate the extent to which painted furniture in general was considered socially acceptable.

33. Loomes, op. cit., p.204.

34. Bernard D. Cotton (*Cottage and Farmhouse Furniture in East Anglia*, exhibition catalogue, 1987, p.26) notes an example of this exclusive use in Norfolk.

35. The proper purpose of these boxes is clearly shown by Edward H. Pinto, *Treen and Other Wooden Bygones*, G. Bell & Sons, London, 1969, plate 147D.

36. Ibid. p.115.

37. John Gerard, *The Herball* (Thomas Johnson, editor), London, 1636. (*Gerard's Herball* (Marcus Woodward, editor), Bracken Books, London, 1985.)

CHAPTER 6:
THE HERITAGE

1. A chest of this description is unequivocally named a 'dresser' in the *Bolton Supplement to the London Book of Cabinet Piece Prices* of 1802. Interestingly, in the list of optional extras, the labour cost of converting a mock drawer front on the standard model into a real drawer is given as 2s. (10p) each. (Gilbert, op. cit., p.26.)

2. The supreme importance of the main (and sometimes only) hearth in old houses cannot be

overstated. It was quite literally the focus (the Latin for 'hearth') of the household and, up until recent times the room in which it was located was still known by the ancient name of 'fire-house' in the north of England.

3. In the north of England the secondary downstairs room often functioned either as a parlour or as the main bedroom, the 'back kitchen' being housed in an extension.

4. This local furniture type is also mentioned in the *Bolton Supplement* of 1802 (see note 1) where it is called an 'easy chair'. The basic labour cost of 10s. (50p) for this piece can be compared with that of the dresser (£2.05). (Gilbert, op. cit., p.27.)

5. Arthur Devis (1711–87), *A Married Couple*, oil, 1747, Wimpole Hall, Cambridgeshire. I am grateful to Sarah Medlam for drawing my attention to an illustration of this painting which appeared in an article by Alastair Laing, 'Every Picture tells a Story', *Country Life*, March 21, 1991. (See Sarah Medlam, 'A Harvester's Work', *News-letter of the Regional Furniture Society*, No. 14, Summer 1991.)

6. Daniel Defoe, *The Complete English Tradesman*, 1726 (republished Alan Sutton, Gloucester, 1987 from 1839 edition).

7. Ibid.

8. This kind of settle is another furniture type noted in the *Bolton Supplement* of 1802 (see notes 1 and 4) where it is called a 'couch chair'. The basic labour cost of 13s. (65p) includes 'Marlbro' legs'; optional 'dog [cabriole] legs' cost an extra 1s. 3d.

(6p) each. Further costs are also given for such extras as fielding the panels and shaping their tops. (Gilbert, op. cit., p.27 and Appendix Two.)

9. I refer to vernacular furniture made from cheaper timber which was readily available. The temptation to re-use expensive timber even if it was damaged must have been considerably greater. In 1753 a Scottish cabinetmaker was accused by his client of using 'Rotten worm eaten wood the holes filld up with Saw dust & Glue' to make his walnut chairs (Sebastian Pryke, 'The Extraordinary Billhead of Francis Brodie', *Journal of the Regional Furniture Society*, Vol. IV, 1990.). The accusation may have been unjustified in this case, but it is quite likely that this deceptive practice was not unknown.

BIBLIOGRAPHY

Since it would be impractical to provide an exhaustive list of the works consulted in this study, this bibliography is restricted to books which are widely recognised or which have been particularly useful. Those which are most revelant to vernacular furniture are indicated by an asterisk. Invaluable information has also appeared in articles published in various periodicals of an antiquarian nature (some of which are mentioned in the notes) and, especially, in the learned publications of the Furniture History Society (founded in 1964) and the Regional Furniture Society (founded in 1986).

BRITISH FURNITURE

Agius, Pauline, *British Furniture 1880–1915*, Antique Collectors' Club, Woodbridge, 1978.

*Barder, Richard C.R., *English Country Grandfather Clocks*, Bracken, London, 1983 (first edition 1975).

Bly, John, *Discovering English Furniture*, Shire Publications, Aylesbury, 1981 (first edition 1971–76).

*Chinnery, Victor, *Oak Furniture. The British Tradition*, Antique Collectors' Club, Woodbridge, 1979.

Comino, Mary, *Gimson and the Barnsleys*, Evans, London, 1980.

*Cotton, Bernard D., *The English Regional Chair*, Antique Collectors' Club, Woodbridge, 1990.

Edwards, Ralph, *A History of the English Chair*, HMSO, London, 1951.

*Filbee, Marjorie, *Dictionary of Country Furniture*, The Connoisseur, London, 1977.

*Gilbert, Christopher, *English Vernacular Furniture 1750–1900*, Yale University Press, New Haven & London, 1991.

Gloag, John, *English Furniture*, A. & C. Black, London, 1946 (first edition 1934).

Gordon, Hampden, *Old English Furniture*, John Murray, London, 1962 (first edition 1948).

Hayden, Arthur, *Chats on Old Furniture*, T. Fisher Unwin, London, 1913 (first edition 1905).

*Hayden, Arthur, *Chats on Cottage and Farmhouse Furniture*, Benn, London, 1950 (first edition 1912).

Joy, Edward T., *Antique English Furniture*, Ward Lock, London, 1981 (first edition 1972).

Joy, Edward T., *The Country Life Book of Chairs*, Country Life, London, 1967.

*King, Constance, *Country Pine Furniture*, Apple Press, London, 1989.

*Kirkham, Pat; Mace, Rodney; and Porter, Julia, *Furnishing the World*, Journeyman Press, London, 1987.

*Loomes, Brian, *Grandfather Clocks and their Cases*, David & Charles, Newton Abbot, 1985.

*Loudon, J.C., *Encyclopaedia of Cottage, Farm and Villa Architecture and Furniture*, London, 1833.

Macquoid, Percy & Edwards, Ralph, *The Dictionary of English Furniture*, Antique Collectors' Club, Woodbridge, 1986 (first edition 1924–27, revised 1954).

Pictorial Dictionary of British 18th-Century Furniture Design, (Elizabeth White, editor), Antique Collectors' Club, Woodbridge, 1990.

Pictorial Dictionary of British 19th-Century Furniture Design, Antique Collectors' Club, Woodbridge, 1977.

*Pinto, Edward H., *Treen and Other Wooden Bygones*, G. Bell & Sons, London, 1969.

Price, Bernard, *The Story of English Furniture*, Ariel, London, 1978.

Robinson, Tom, *The Longcase Clock*, Antique Collectors' Club, Woodbridge, 1981.

Roe, F. Gordon, *English Period Furniture*, Tiranti, London, 1946.

*Roe, F. Gordon, *English Cottage Furniture*, Phoenix, London, 1949.

Roe, F. Gordon, *Windsor Chairs*, Phoenix House Ltd, London, 1953.

Rogers, John C. (and Jourdain, Margaret), *English Furniture*, Spring Books, London, 1967 (first edition 1923, revised 1959).

*Sparkes, Ivan, *The English Country Chair*, Spurbooks, 1973.

Sparkes, Ivan, *An Illustrated History of English Domestic Furniture (1100–1837)*, Spurbooks, 1980.

*Toller, Jane, *Country Furniture*, David & Charles, Newton Abbot, 1973.

Tracy, Charles, *English Medieval Furniture and Woodwork*, Victoria & Albert Museum, London, 1988.

*Twiston-Davies, L. and Lloyd-Johnes, H.J., *Welsh Furniture*, University of Wales Press, Cardiff, 1950.

Ward-Jackson, Peter, *English Furniture Designs of the Eighteenth Century*, Victoria & Albert Museum, London, 1984 (first edition 1958).

Wills, Geoffrey, *English Furniture 1550–1760*, Guinness, Enfield, 1971.

GENERAL AND FOREIGN FURNITURE

Aronson, Joseph, *The Encyclopedia of Furniture*, Batsford, London, 1966.

Clunas, Craig, *Chinese Furniture*, Bamboo, London, 1988.

Dampierre, Florence de, *The Best of Painted Furniture*, Weidenfeld & Nicolson, London, 1987.

*Dobson, Henry and Barbara, *The Early Furniture of Ontario & the Atlantic Provinces*, M.F. Feheley, Toronto, 1974.

*Fales, Dean A., Jr, *American Painted Furniture 1660–1880*, Dutton, New York, 1972.

Hayward, Helena (editor), *World Furniture*, Hamlyn, London, 1965.

Jenyns, R. Soame and Watson, William, *Chinese Art* (Chapter VII: Furniture), Phaidon, Oxford, 1980.

*Kovel, Ralph and Terry, *American Country Furniture 1780–1875*, Crown, New York, 1965.

*Loughnan, Nicholas, *Irish Country Furniture*, Eason & Son, Dublin, 1984.

Montgomery, Charles F., *American Furniture, The Federal Period, in the Henry Francis du Pont Winterthur Museum*, Thames and Hudson, London, 1967.

*Oliver, Lucile, *Mobilier Breton*, Massin, Paris, (n.d.)

*Oliver, Lucile, *Mobilier Normand*, Massin, Paris, (n.d.)

*Pain, Howard, *The Heritage of Upper Canadian Furniture*, Van Nostrand Reinhold, Toronto, 1978.

*Shackleton, Philip, *The Furniture of Old Ontario*, Macmillan, Toronto, 1973.

*Shea, John G., *Antique Country Furniture of North America*, Van Nostrand Reinhold, New York, 1975.

HISTORICAL AND ARCHITECTURAL CONTEXT

*Ayres, James, *The Shell Book of the Home in Britain*, Faber & Faber, London, 1981.

Briggs, Asa, *A Social History of England*, Book Club Associates, London, 1983.

Camden, William, *Britannia*, London, 1610.

Cave, Lyndon F., *The Smaller English House. Its History and Development*, Hale, London, 1981.

Cobbett, William, *Cottage Economy*, London, 1822.

Cobbett, William, *Rural Rides*, London, 1830.

Davidson, Caroline, *The World of Mary Ellen Best*, Chatto & Windus, London, 1985.

Defoe, Daniel, *A Tour thro' the Whole Island of Great Britain*, London, 1724–6.

Defoe, Daniel, *The Complete English Tradesman*, Sutton, Gloucester, 1987 (first edition 1726).

Edwards, Ralph & Ramsey, L.G.G. (editors), *The Connoisseur's Complete Period Guides*, The Connoisseur, London, 1968.

*Hughes, Therle, *Cottage Antiques*, Lutterworth Press, London, 1967.

*Jekyll, Gertrude and Jones, Sydney R., *Old English Household Life*, Batsford, London, 1945 (first edition 1925).

Jourdain, Margaret, *English Interior Decoration 1500–1830*, Batsford, London, 1950.

Mercer, Eric, *English Vernacular Houses*, HMSO, London, 1975.

Parry, Linda, *William Morris and the Arts and Crafts Movement*, Studio Editions, London, 1989.

Pepys, Samuel, *The Diary*, George Newnes, London, 1902.

Quiney, Anthony, *House and Home*, BBC, London, 1986.

Reid, Richard, *The Georgian House and its Details*, Bishopsgate Press, London, 1989.

Rowlandson, Thomas and Pugin, A.C., *The Microcosm of London*, Ackermann, London, 1808–10.

*Steer, Francis, W., *Farm and Cottage Inventories of Mid-Essex 1635–1749*, Phillimore, Chichester, 1969.

Stow, John, *The Survey of London*, Dent, London, 1970 (first edition 1598).

Thornton, Peter, *Seventeenth-Century Interior Decoration in England, France and Holland*, Yale University Press, New Haven, 1978.

Thornton, Peter, *Authentic Decor: The Domestic Interior 1620–1920*, Weidenfeld & Nicolson, London, 1984.

Trevelyan, G.M., *Illustrated English Social History*, Penguin, London, 1966 (first edition 1949–52).

Wood, Margaret, *The English Mediaeval House*, Phoenix, London, 1965.

TIMBER AND CONSTRUCTION

Bennett, Michael, *Discovering and Restoring Antique Furniture*, Cassell, London, 1990.

Bramwell, Martyn (editor), *The International Book of Wood*, Mitchell Beazley, London, 1976.

Goodman, W.C., *The History of Woodworking Tools*, London, 1976 (first edition 1964).

Latham, Bryan, *Timber. A Historical Survey*, Harrap, London, 1957.

*Massingham, H.J., *Men of Earth* (Chapter VII: The Chair-Maker), Chapman & Hall, London, 1943.

Mills, John Fitzmaurice and Mansfield, John M., *The Genuine Article*, BBC, London, 1979.

PHOTOGRAPHIC ACKNOWLEDGEMENTS

Agecroft Hall, Richmond, Virginia, U.S.A.: 32.
Mrs E. Allan: 212, 258.
Anthemion, Grange-over-Sands, Cumbria: 335.
Mrs E. Barnsley: 202.
Mrs A. Bell: 265, 266.
Birmingham City Museums and Art Gallery: 88.
City of Birmingham Public Libraries: 17.
Bonham's: 148, 164, 191, 216, 242, 308, 313, 340.
The Bowes Museum, Barnard Castle, Co. Durham: 345.
Mrs G. Bradley: 277.
Brasenose College, Oxford: 20.
Mrs W. Carmichael: 15, 211, 228, 274, 311; X.
Paul Cater Antiques, Moreton-in-Marsh, Gloucestershire: 92, 260, 293.
Mark Chapman: 18, 141, 167, 218, 234, 259, 291.
Dean and Chapter of Chichester Cathedral: 21.
Victor Chinnery: 35 (property of the Victoria & Albert Museum).
Christie's, London: 37; VII.
Christie's South Kensington: 309.
Dr Bernard D. Cotton: 183, 185, 306.
Mr and Mrs J. Critchlow: 138, 208.
Garth Denham & Associates: 230.
The Dorset Natural History and Archaeological Society, Dorset County Museum: 102.
Hy. Duke & Son, Dorchester, Dorset: 114.
Brian Emerson: 203.
Vicki Emery, Antiquated, Petworth, Sussex: 153, 204, 214, 237, 270, 286, 295, 302, 329, 332.
Frith Antiques: 49.
Derek Green, Cedar Antiques, Hartley Wintney, Hampshire: 6, 12, 107, 174, 179, 352.
Grove House Antiques: 94, 254.
Mrs E. Hand: 8, 16, 137, 165, 302.
Heathcote Ball & Company, Leicester: 99.
Mrs P. Helman: 257.
Nick Herman: 165, 178, 217, 267.
Paul Hopwell Antiques, West Haddon, Northamptonshire: 42, 44, 55, 62, 79, 97, 103, 109, 115, 117, 118, 123,

146, 186, 187, 221, XV.
Mrs A. Howgill: 330.
Humphry Antiques, Petworth, Sussex: 129, 139, 206, 256.
Huntington Antiques Ltd., Stow-on-the-Wold, Gloucestershire: 342.
Ipswich Museums & Galleries: 67, 142.
Tobias Jellinek: 68.
H.W. Keil Ltd, Broadway, Worcestershire: 56, 58, 101, 113.
William Lait: 263.
Leeds Central Library: 353.
Leeds City Art Galleries: 100, 322; XIX.
Madison Gallery: 222.
David Martin-Taylor Antiques: 14.
The Mary Rose Trust: 22, 25, 26, 33, 34, 36.
David Morgan-Wynne: 285.
Mrs P. Murfin: 348.
Museum of English Rural Life, University of Reading: 7, 315, 323.
Old Maltings Antique Co.: 231.
Gabriel Olive: 39, 40, 102, 119, 125, 215, 224, 225, 307, 320.
Phillips, London: 105
Phillips, Chester: 130, 131, 161, 162, 197, 281.
Phillips, Sevenoaks: 43.
Mr and Mrs M. Pritchard: 140.
Mrs D. Rayment: 251, 296.
Rosebery's, London: 160.
Russell, Baldwin and Bright, Leominster, Herefordshire: 269, 273.
His Grace the Duke of Rutland, Haddon Hall, Derbyshire: 28, 30.
Ryedale Folk Museum, Hutton-le-Hole, Yorkshire: 322.
Miss S. Ryder: 8, 205, 208, 209, 235, 248, 249, 253, 278, 321, 327, 328, 334.
M. & D. Seligmann: 143a.
Oswald Simpson, Ipswich, Suffolk: 176, 298, 303, 304, 308.
Sotheby's, London: 9, 23, 31, 38, 46, 48, 59, 60, 69, 73, 77, 81, 86, 106, 155, 157, 171, 183, 185, 193, 349.

Sotheby's, Chester: 52, 64, 93, 108, 111, 116, 122, 126, 132, 134, 143, 156, 166, 170, 219, 236, 239, 282, 287, 303, 310, 312, 319, 336, 343, 350, 351.
Sotheby's, Sussex: 3, 10, 24, 41, 45, 53, 54, 61, 63, 65, 66, 70, 71, 72, 74, 80, 95, 98, 104, 112, 127, 132, 135, 136, 144, 145, 150, 151, 152, 177, 184, 188, 190, 220, 226, 238, 240, 280, 292, 341, 344, 346, 347; III, VI, VIII, XVII, XXII.
Spencer's, Nantwich: 84, 285, 297.
Spencer's, Retford: 4, 180.
Stewart Antiques: 252.
Mrs R. Stewart-Jones: 299.
Storey's Furnishings: 243, 250.
Tennant's, Leyburn, North Yorkshire: 121, 195.
Derek Thrower, William Hockley Antiques, Petworth, Sussex: 290, 294, 316.
Charles Toller, Datchet, Berkshire: 158.
C.J. Tutt Antiques: 90, 337.
Jeremy Uniacke: 300.
Up Country, Tunbridge Wells, Kent: 210, 223, 227, 229, 232, 241, 244, 314, 326.
Board of Trustees of the Victoria & Albert Museum: 2, 29, 50, 75, 76, 172.
Michael Wakelin and Helen Linfield, Petworth, West Sussex: 57, 110, 120, 124, 128, 149, 194, 245, 246, 247, 264, 275, 276, 317, 325; I, V, XX, XXIV, XXVI.
Weald & Downland Open Air Museum, Singleton, West Sussex: XII.
David Weston Ltd: 189.
Mrs E. Williams: 278, 324, 339.
Clare Wilson: 8, 13a, 201, 255, 271.
Rod Wilson, Griffin Antiques: 154, 163.
Christopher Wood Gallery, London SW1: 198.
Robert Young Antiques, London SW11: 181, 182, 262, 333; II, IV, IX, XI, XVI, XXIII, XXV, XXVII.
Plate XVIII is from The World of Mary Ellen Best by Caroline Davidson, published by Chatto & Windus Ltd.

INDEX

*Numerals in bold type refer to figure numbers
and to information contained in the captions.
Roman numerals refer to plate numbers.
References to notes are suffixed by the letter 'n'.*